MORMONS

in the

MAJOR LEAGUES

CAREER HISTORIES OF
44 LDS BASEBALL PLAYERS
OVER 60 PHOTOS

Containing the Following

Photographs
Baseball Biographies
Year-by-Year Statistics
Awards and Post-Season Records
Rookie Season and Team/Position Lists
Baseball Card Checklists (Over 1,200 Cards)
Trivia Questions and 200 Reading References

By James L. Ison

Dedication

This book is dedicated to my family. First to my mother who taught me how to swing a baseball bat while my father was serving in Korea. Also to my dad who bought a baseball game for my brother and me that we played with for hours at a time over a three-year period. Anyone who has written a book knows that family support is necessary from spouse and children. I appreciate the constant support of my wife, Kathy, who always gave her honest opinion in an encouraging manner. My son, Daniel, was helpful in pointing out confusing or boring areas and offering suggestions. He also helped in the photo selection and sketched the book cover. My daughters, Melinda, Amy, and Tamara, were always patient when I seemed chained to the computer or endlessly on the telephone instead of being with them. My son, Jon, was supportive while at school and now on a mission. My brother, Glenn, was an excellent source of baseball information that I relied upon frequently.

Copyright

Published by Action Sports
P.O. Box 54162, Cincinnati, OH 45254
Printed in the United States of America
by The C. J. Krehbiel Company, Cincinnati, OH
First Printing July 1991

Library of Congress Catalog Card Number 91-73265

ISBN 0-9630122-0-7

PREFACE

In 1923, Spencer Adams played second base and shortstop with the Pittsburgh Pirates becoming the first Mormon to make the big leagues. In 1990, Mike Fetters and Colby Ward won their first Major League games for the California Angels and Cleveland Indians, respectively. During the past 70 years, over 40 members of The Church of Jesus Christ of Latter-day Saints (the Mormons) have played in the Major Leagues. Baseball is the national pastime and playing in "The Show" is the ultimate accomplishment--only about five percent of the people who sign professional baseball contracts ever make it to the big leagues.

Only a few players in this book such as Vernon Law, Dale Murphy, Harmon Killebrew, and Wally Joyner are well-known. But all of the players have interesting career histories. Here are just a few snapshots to give you a flavor of what's ahead.

* * * * * * * * * *

Broken Windows

During the summer every window on the backside of the Charlie Iorg house was broken at least once. Charlie wasn't necessarily pleased, but he accepted it as part of the price to be paid. You see, he was raising his three boys to play in the big leagues. Charlie and Leona Iorg hold a unique record; their sons Dane and Garth are the only brothers to ever play against each other in a Major League Championship Series. Dane Iorg of the Kansas City Royals met Garth Iorg of the Toronto Blue Jays in the 1985 American League Championship. Garth said, "It's like a dream come true, Dane and I in a play-off series against each other." One son was certain to go to the World Series. It was Dane who became the hero of the sixth World Series game against the St. Louis Cardinals. Middle son, Lee, played center field for BYU and reached the Triple-A level in the New York Mets organization before leaving baseball.

* * * * * * * * * *

Agony and Ecstasy

Baseball can be devastating and it can be electrifying. Someone who knows both feelings is Jim Gott. *The Sporting News* printed an article on October 1, 1984, entitled, "Gott Experiment in Relief a Failure." How would you feel to have your difficulties highlighted for the entire world to read? Well, September 18, 1984, was a disaster for Jim. Pitching in relief for the Toronto Blue Jays, his first pitch was hit into the stands. He walked the next batter. Then Tony Armas and Mike Easler hit back-to-back home runs. Ten Pitches: three homers and four runs scored. How could it be any worse?

Nearly four years later, on September 22, 1988, Jim Gott etched his name into Pittsburgh Pirates history, breaking the record for most saves in a season and finishing the year with 34 saves, 6 victories, and 76 strikeouts in 77 innings. The Pirates 1988 season highlight video has a cover picture of Jim "charged up with emotion," saving another Pirate victory. He gained recognition as one of the best relief pitchers in the National League.

Success is sometimes sweeter when it occurs after failure. Oh yes, an article in the October 3, 1988 edition of *The Sporting News* is entitled, "Jim Gott Set Club Record for Saves."

* * * * * * * * * *

Baptism

The 1978 season was a turning point in the life of Luis Gomez, starting shortstop for the Toronto Blue Jays. On a plane trip, Luis noticed that teammate Garth Iorg was intently reading a book in the seat in front of him. Looking over the seat, he asked the first of many questions that would change his life. Garth soon gave Luis a copy of the book he had been reading, *The Book of Mormon.* Two other church members and teammates, Alan Ashby and Jerry Garvin, answered questions and shared their testimonies. Luis was quickly ready to join the Church, but his wife was upset with his decision. Luis decided to wait and rely on prayer and fasting.

Later his wife became ill and she received a blessing. Her attitude changed and Luis was baptized in December 1978. He was ordained to the Aaronic Priesthood by Alan Ashby. A few weeks later Luis baptized his wife. They were sealed in the Los Angles Temple a year later. Recently Luis said that his wife, Petra, is one of the strongest members in the Church and that joining the Church was the highlight of his Major League career.

* * * * * * * * * *

Predicting a No-Hitter

One of the famous moments in baseball history was when Babe Ruth pointed his bat to the outfield stands to indicate to everyone that he intended to hit a home run--and did. But have you ever heard of a professional baseball pitcher predicting before a game that he would pitch a no-hitter--and do it? Well it happened on June 8, 1988.

In a pre-game TV interview, Pam Nielsen revealed that her husband, Scott, had promised to pitch a no-hitter that night. It was a windy, rainy night, but Scott was on target. In a nine-inning game, he threw only 82 pitches, 56 for strikes. Columbus, the New York Yankee Triple-A team, beat Maine 3-0. It was a classic game--and to think, Scott was only kidding.

* * * * * * * * * *

All-American

*H*ow would you like to be good enough to be captain of your high school football, basketball, track, and baseball teams two years in a row? To run the 100-yard dash in 9.9 seconds? To sign a professional baseball contract with the St. Louis Cardinals, at age sixteen? To be the number one draft choice of the Los Angeles Rams as a running back? To play professional basketball? Sounds impossible, doesn't it? Well, enjoy reading about Jay Van Noy, because he did it!

* * * * * * * * * *

Only One Good Eye

*T*oday Jim Abbott pitches with only one arm. But in 1970, John Noriega pitched for the National League Champion Cincinnati Reds with only one good eye. His left eye had been paralyzed since birth. It would not move, so he could only see straight ahead with his left eye. Pretend to be a right-handed pitcher attempting to pick off a runner at first base and do it without moving your left eye. Pretty hard isn't it?

Now pretend that you are teased about your handicap. Maybe you would prefer to sit in the stands and avoid any chance of unkind comments. Not John, who created admirers along the way. John never won a Major League game, but he won a lot of respect. Big league reporter, Bucky Albers, wrote of John, "This conservative 26-year old Mormon is a refreshing athlete in these days of greed and it's a shame that he will never realize the success enjoyed by many others less deserving."

* * * * * * * * * *

A Role Model

*F*rom 1950 to 1967, Vernon Law was the only player regularly recognized as a Church member. Since his retirement in 1967, over 25 Church members have played at the Major League level. Vern created an excellent image for the Church within baseball. He won the Cy Young award in 1960 and led the Pittsburgh Pirates to a World Championship over the powerful New York Yankees. In the September 4, 1965 issue of *The Sporting News*, reporter Les Biederman told of Vern's values as a Church member and then recounted the following story.

> I've known Vern Law ever since he first reported to the Pirates in 1950 and he's become one of my all-time favorite players. And I've seen hundreds of them in Pirate uniforms in the past 28 years. In success and in adversity, Law always has had compassion for his fellow man. He doesn't change to any extent whether he wins or loses.
>
> The morning after he won his seventh straight game by beating the Giants 6-0 on four hits at Candlestick Park late in June, Law came out of the Sheraton Palace Hotel. As he approached the Pirate bus he noticed a legless man sitting on a stool selling pencils.
>
> Law automatically reached into his pocket for some change, dropped it into the cup of the legless man and stopped to chat with him until it was time for the bus to leave for the park. The man without legs recognized Law and congratulated him on his fine performance the night before and also for the season.
>
> Law almost blushed and tried to change the subject. Yet he took the time to stand there and talk to a stranger who had no legs while other players passed up the man and stepped into the bus. This incident is typical of Vernon Law. He has always had compassion for his fellow man: he never has belittled an opponent or embarrassed anybody.
>
> This is a man.

* * * * * * * * * *

*I*f you thought these snapshots were interesting and fun, then you will really enjoy the career histories in Section 1. You will learn which team a player rooted for when he was a youth and what he did in high school or college sports. You will learn about his climb through the minors and his highlights and disappointments. You will learn about his hobbies and occupation since baseball if he has retired. The biographies include season-by-season statistics for each year in the Major Leagues, at least one full-size photograph, and a baseball card image.

We revel in baseball statistics. Section 2 presents even more interesting insights. You can see the best performance of each hitter and pitcher as well as tell how they stand comparatively for a single season and lifetime.

Post season play is baseball's glory time, and Church members have played prominent roles in division championships and the World Series. Do you know which player earned four World Series rings? Section 3 contains post-season records.

Section 4 tells you about teams and positions. Do you know which team has had the most Mormon ball players? Do you know which teams have never had a Church member on their roster? Have you thought about putting together your own all-Mormon team? Do you know which position has been the most popular for LDS players? Well, turn to Section 4.

Section 5, the Awards Section, lists players who have achieved significant recognition. You may be surprised to learn that practically every award given in baseball has been earned by at least one Mormon ball player.

Beginning with 1923, Section 6 tells you year-by-year when players began their Major League careers. Rookie baseball cards are identified for each player. A current roster of Mormon Major League players is supplied. A birthday listing is also included.

There is a saying that you can't tell the players without a scorecard. It's also true that you don't really have a baseball card collection unless you have a checklist. Section 7 contains the checklists of all Mormon baseball players with Major League cards. Use the checklists for your own collection to keep track of what you have and what you want.

A large selection of trivia questions is listed in Section 8. You'll love stumping your friends and testing yourself. Just in case you don't know all the answers, an answer sheet is included.

If you enjoy reading and want to know where to find more about your favorite players, then turn to Section 9 and look out! Plenty of additional references are listed.

This book is fun for all ages. So settle back and treat yourself to page after page of interesting facts and a good time.

ACKNOWLEDGEMENTS

*I*n 1987, I began serving as master chauffeur for my two sons, Jon and Daniel, as they attended numerous baseball card shows and visited card stores. At first, I enjoyed driving them around because I vividly remembered buying Topps baseball cards way back in 1956--my favorite card was Ted Kluszewski. Like most of my generation I played with my cards, and not a single one exists today. After a while, I tired of these weekly excursions. Just as I attempted to curtail my boys' interest, my brother, Glenn, moved to Cincinnati. Glenn is a baseball fanatic! He organizes card shows, invests in rookie cards, collects star cards, and arranges for star players to sign autographs at card shows. When Glenn started giving tips to my sons, I could see I was doomed to more shows and stores.

As a defense against boredom at these shows, I decided to start my own card collection of Mormon baseball players. I enjoyed reading the backs of the cards. In 1988, I wrote a number of biographies solely from information on the cards and put together a first draft of this book. I received encouragement from everyone who read it. One of the suggestions I received was to expand the career histories by using other sources and including more insight from the player's perspective. This led me to research all of the reading references listed in Section 9 and to conduct multiple interviews with most of the players.

This book required more work than I ever imagined and it could not have been written without the help of many people. I wish to recognize the cooperation of Donruss and Topps for allowing me to reprint their cards. Nearly all of the Major League teams supplied photos. Photo credits are listed on pages x and xi. Steve Geitscher, archivist for *The Sporting News*, was always helpful in answering questions, sending me copies of articles, and allowing me access to their extensive photo collection.

Special thanks to Alan Ashby who was the first active player I interviewed; to Jim Gott for being so positive when he read the career history I wrote of him; to Dale Murphy for allowing my brother and my son to meet him during our interview and for his kind words of support; to Vernon Law for supporting my efforts; to Gary Pullins for his initial help in 1988 and hearty encouragement; to John Mooney, Glen Tuckett, and Dutch Belnap for helping to identify players; to Robert Glutz Photography; and to Sharon Obermeyer, Bob Lewis, Kevin Stoker, Mark Sessions, and Tim Eisenhardt for their assistance.

I wish to acknowledge the baseball players who perfected their talents and persevered sufficiently to reach the Major Leagues. I have personally talked with most of the players or relatives of players included in this book. Although I was a stranger to them, they were cooperative in supplying information about themselves. Just as members of the Church have different levels of activity, some ball players are very active; others are not active in the Church. I have honored the request of any player who told me he was uncomfortable with being included in the book.

I hope you enjoy this book. I wish each player success in and out of baseball. I wish each reader, whether 8 or 108, many more days of baseball fun.

TABLE OF CONTENTS

PHOTO CREDITS

The photos in this book were obtained from the following sources and are used with their permission.

Page	Player	Source
4	Spencer Adams	National Baseball Library, Cooperstown
8	Danny Ainge	The Sporting News
12	Alan Ashby	R & R Sports
16	Tommy Barrett	Tommy Barrett
20	Barry Bonnell	National Baseball Library, Cooperstown
22	Barry Bonnell	The Sporting News
26	Ron Brand	Montreal Expos
30	Dave Downs	Philadelphia Phillies
34	Kelly Downs	Photo File
38	Dennis Eckersley	The Sporting News
40	Dennis Eckersley	Oakland Athletics
44	Mike Fetters	California Angels
48	Jerry Garvin	The Sporting News
52	Luis Gomez	The Sporting News
56	Jim Gott	Pittsburgh Pirates
60	Doug Hansen	The Sporting News
64	Doug Howard	The Sporting News
68	Ken Hubbs	The Sporting News
72	Ken Hunt	Cincinnati Reds
76	Bruce Hurst	Boston Red Sox
78	Bruce Hurst	R & R Sports
82	Dane Iorg	Kansas City Royals
86	Garth Iorg	Toronto Blus Jays
90	Ray Jacobs	Glenn Jacobs
92	Ray Jacobs	Glenn Jacobs
96	Wally Joyner	The Sporting News
98	Wally Joyner	California Angels
102	Harmon Killebrew	The Sporting News
104	Killebrew, Mays, Mantle	Photo File
108	Newt Kimball	The Sporting News
112	Don Kirkwood	California Angels
116	Gary Kroll	New York Mets
120	Vance Law	R & R Sports
124	Vernon Law	The Sporting News
126	Vance & Vernon Law	Vernon Law
130	Jack Morris	Photo File
132	Jack Morris	Minnesota Twins

136	Dale Murphy	The Sporting News
138	Dale Murphy	The Sporting News
142	Scott Nielsen	The Sporting News
146	John Noriega	Cincinnati Reds
150	Jerry Nyman	National Baseball Library, Cooperstown
154	Monte Pearson	The Sporting News
156	Monte Pearson	New York Yankees
160	Red Peery	Dick Peery
164	Wally Ritchie	Philadelphia Phillies
168	Fred Sanford	New York Yankees
172	Elmer Singleton	Pittsburgh Pirates
174	Elmer Singleton	Chicago Cubs
178	Tommie Sisk	Tim Eisenhardt
182	Cory Snyder	Cleveland Indians
186	Bob Usher	The Sporting News
190	Jay Van Noy	National Baseball Library, Cooperstown
194	Colby Ward	Colby Ward
198	Jim Wessinger	Atlanta Braves
220	Harmon Killebrew	The Sporting News

COLOR PHOTOS

cover	Wally Joyner	Photo File
cover	Vernon Law	Photo File
cover	Dale Murphy	Photo File
insert	Kelly Downs	Mark Sessions
insert	Dennis Eckersley	Photo File
insert	Dennis Eckersley	Mark Sessions
insert	Jim Gott	Mark Sessions
insert	Bruce Hurst	Photo File
insert	Wally Joyner	Photo File
insert	Wally Joyner	Mark Sessions
insert	Harmon Killebrew	Photo File
insert	Harmon Killebrew	Photo File
insert	Vance Law	Photo File
insert	Vernon Law	Photo File
insert	Jack Morris	Photo File
insert	Jack Morris	Photo File
insert	Dale Murphy	Ponzini Photography
insert	Dale Murphy	Photo File
insert	Cory Snyder	Photo File

BASEBALL PLAYER BIOGRAPHIES

SECTION 1

BASEBALL CAREER HISTORIES

AND

YEAR-BY-YEAR STATISTICS

This section contains the baseball career history, and year-by-year statistics for each member of the Mormon church who played in the Major Leagues. The career histories are full of interesting information about each player. Biographical sources include , *The Sporting News, Sports Illustrated*, feature stories from other periodicals, baseball cards, newspaper articles, and interviews.

The year-by-year statistics are gathered from a number of sources including *The Baseball Encyclopedia, Who's Who in Baseball,* Elias Sports Service, *The Baseball Register,* baseball cards, and baseball magazines.

The baseball cards were reproduced with the permission of Donruss, Topps, and Upper Deck. Section 7 contains a checklist of all baseball cards for each Major League player.

The photographs are great for autographing. They were selected from many sources including nearly all of the Major League teams, The National Baseball Hall of Fame at Cooperstown, NY, *The Sporting News*, Photo File, and individual players. The photo credits page lists the source of all photos actually used in the book.

Don't feel like you have to read all the career histories in one sitting. This is fun, not a school or work assignment. If you want to read more about a player, refer to Section 9 for further reading references.

SPENCER ADAMS YEAR-BY-YEAR STATISTICS

Name: Spencer Dewey Adams

Born: June 21, 1897
Layton, UT

Hgt: 5′ 9″ Wgt: 158

Bats: Left Throws: Right

Died: November 25, 1970

Minor League: 1921-1924, 1928-1930

Year	Club	L	POS	G	AB	R	H	2	3	HR	RBI	SB	AVG
1923	Pittsburgh	NL	2,S	25	56	11	14	0	1	0	4	2	.250
1925	Washington	AL	2,S	39	55	11	15	4	1	0	4	1	.273
1926	New York	AL	2,3	28	25	7	3	1	0	0	1	1	.120
1927	St. Louis	AL	2,3	88	259	32	69	11	3	0	29	1	.266
	Lifetime			180	395	61	101	16	5	0	38	5	.256

SPENCER ADAMS

Spencer was the first Church member to play in the Major Leagues. In 1923, he played for the Pittsburgh Pirates--that's before most people reading this book were born! He is the only Church member born in the nineteenth century to be a Major League player. Spencer loved sports. He was a running back on his high school football team, a guard on the basketball team, and a member of the track team (he ran the 440). After high school, he volunteered to serve in the Army as World War I was in full swing. He served for six months and then attended classes at the University of Utah.

He played pro ball at Tremonton in the Northern Utah League in 1921 and 1922. The 1922 edition of *Spalding's Official Baseball Guide* commented on Spencer's baseball capabilities. It said,

> Spencer Adams, a Utah boy, was the sensation of the circuit in the hitting department. Batting against good pitching, Adams hit .432 for the season. He not only led the batters but also excelled in home runs, triples, and total bases. So great was his work of the season that scouts from both majors and minors were on his trail during most of the season.

Promoted to Seattle in the Pacific Coast League in 1923, he played shortstop and second base, hitting .256 in 123 games. He made the Pittsburgh Pirate roster at the end of the season and played in 25 games. He played for Oakland in the PCL during 1924 and part of 1925. Over a 200-game span, he batted .273 with 42 doubles, 7 triples, and 4 homers. He was noted for his aggressive play at second base. He was second in the league in assists and putouts.

Spencer went to spring training in 1925 with the world champion Washington Senators and made the team. It was a good year. He batted .273 and helped the Senators go to the World Series for the second year in a row. In the Series, he pinch-hit in the ninth inning of game five and went in at third base as a defensive replacement in the eighth inning of game six. They lost the Series, but it was a thrill for Spencer. He liked playing with Big Train Johnson of the Senators who remembered every pitch he threw.

Spencer was traded to the New York Yankees and played with them during the 1926 season. In an article written at the time of the trade, the sportswriter for the Washington Senators wrote:

> Spencer Adams is a real ball player, qualified to shine with any club that gets him. Some of his fielding last season was the most sensational seen at Clark Griffith's stadium and astonished the most jaded of the veteran fan regulars. His batting was streaky and sometimes gave the impression that he might develop into a .300 hitter.

Spencer was the first LDS player in the Major Leagues. He played in the World Series for the 1925 Washington Senators and the 1926 New York Yankees.

Spencer's son said, "A definite highlight for my father was rooming with Lou Gehrig." He also roomed with Tony Lazzeri who had occasional epileptic seizures that Spencer would help treat. He was a part of the 1926 Yankee World Series team and played in games six and seven as a pinch-runner. He is the only Church member to play in two consecutive World Series for different teams.

When Babe Ruth was on a trip in Utah, he was asked whether he knew Spencer Adams. Babe said, "Sure I do, he was the best poker player in the American League." This unexpected praise had its origin in a train car carrying the Yankees to a game. The Babe was engaged in a favorite pastime, playing poker. When he needed to leave the game temporarily, he said to Spencer, "Hey rookie, sit in for me." When Ruth returned, he was $300 richer!

Spencer played with the St. Louis Browns in 1927 and played in more games than his previous three Major League seasons combined. In one game, Spencer and Ty Cobb squared off against each other. Cobb regularly tried to intimidate infielders by sharpening his spikes in their view before the game and commenting on how sharp they were. He came into second base with spikes three to four feet off the ground, clearly intent to chase the second baseman out of the play, but Spencer held his ground to make the play and was spiked across the chest hard enough to carry the scars the rest of his life. As Cobb went off the field, Spencer threw the ball at him, missing his head by only inches. The benches emptied as Cobb wheeled around and yelled, "The base path is mine. If you're in the way, I'll kill you." Despite Cobb's outrageous behavior, it was Spencer who always regretted losing his temper.

For the next several seasons he played for minor league teams at Milwaukee, Kansas City, and Mobile. He was a tough player. For example, travelling from Milwaukee to Kansas City in a mid-season trade, he injured his leg and was advised by a doctor to stay off the leg for at least a week. The next day he was in the Kansas City lineup and hit a triple that won the game. With the depression, teams cut their player rosters, and Spencer saw his chances diminish for returning to the Majors.

He worked at the Hill Air Force base near Ogden, Utah as a millwright and fireman. He enjoyed hunting and fishing on occasion. He died in November 1970 at the age of 72.

DANNY AINGE YEAR-BY-YEAR STATISTICS

Name: Daniel Ray Ainge

Born: March 17, 1959
Eugene, OR

Hgt: 6′ 4″ **Wgt:** 175

Bats: Right **Throws:** Right

Home: Portland, OR

Minor League: 1978-1980

Year	Club	L	POS	G	AB	R	H	2	3	HR	RBI	SB	AVG
1979	Toronto	AL	2	87	308	26	73	7	1	2	19	1	.237
1980	Toronto	AL	O,3	38	111	11	27	6	1	0	4	3	.243
1981	Toronto	AL	3,S	86	246	20	46	6	2	0	14	8	.187
	Lifetime			211	665	57	146	19	4	2	37	12	.220

DANNY AINGE

*D*anny Ainge is well known for his competitiveness. It most likely began as he tried to keep up with his older brothers, Doug and Dave. Whether games of burnout (when you throw a baseball at each other as hard as you can), two-on-one football, or one-on-one basketball, Danny was always trying to outdo his brothers. Sometimes the games ended in outright combat. Danny became the only high school student in Oregon history to be named to three all-state teams in one year. His basketball team won two straight state titles. As a guard, he led his team in rebounds and was MVP of the state all-star tournament. He was included on many high school All-America rosters. *Parade* magazine named him to their All-America team in three sports. He quarterbacked his football team his senior year after catching 82 passes during the two previous years.

Danny decided to go to Brigham Young University on a basketball scholarship even though the coach said he would start out as the twelfth player on the team. It sounded like a great challenge. He received a query from the San Diego Padres to play baseball, but he said no thanks. To his great surprise, the Toronto Blue Jays picked him in the fifteenth round of the 1977 draft. He ignored their offers at first but amazingly the Blue Jays said he could attend BYU, play college basketball, and then play pro baseball from May through August, like a summer job. A great job too--starting at the Triple-A level with a good bonus. Danny went on a road trip against the Angels, A's, and Mariners as a non-roster player in uniform, taking batting and infield practice.

One of the most fantastic stories in sports history was set in motion--a college student becoming a Major League baseball player and the college basketball Player of the Year. Some people belittle Danny's baseball record, but taken in perspective, his accomplishment is a marvel. He made the BYU starting basketball team--in fact, he broke BYU's record for most points scored in a season. He made all-WAC and was the only WAC player to be honorable mention All-American by UPI. Then without any spring training or any previous pro baseball experience, it was off to the Syracuse Chiefs where the 1978 season had already begun. Not unexpectedly, he had a slow start, batting only .167 after a month. However, during the second half of the season he hit .280 and was named the Chiefs' August Player of the Month.

In November 1978, *Sports Illustrated* picked Danny as one of the ten best sophomores in the nation. He again made the all-WAC team. Danny had a better start at Syracuse in 1979. He was switched to second base and after 27 games he was hitting .248. The regular Blue Jays' second baseman was batting only .200 so the Blue Jays called Danny up on May 20. He had a super first game going 3-for-4. In June at a packed Yankee Stadium, he scored the game-tying run and then drove in the winning run off Tommy John. He hit .237 in over 300 at bats in his first Major League season at age twenty.

Danny played Major League baseball for the Toronto Blue Jays while also starring on the BYU basketball team. His senior year, he earned All-American honors.

Danny again led BYU and made the all-WAC team in his junior year. The Blue Jays acquired Damaso Garcia at second so Danny started the year at Syracuse batting .244. In August, he joined the Blue Jays to sub for Church member Barry Bonnell who was injured. He finished the year hitting .243. He made only one error in 38 games. After the 1980 season, he signed a three-year contract that prohibited him from playing pro basketball. Danny said in an interview at the time regarding his decision, "I feel like a load has been lifted off my back." Little did he realize how much difference a year would make.

In his senior year at BYU, he averaged 24.4 points per game, hitting 52 percent of his shots. In the NCAA tournament, he led BYU to a 78-55 win over Providence by scoring 37 points. In the Eastern Regionals with eight seconds left, he dribbled the length of the floor, eluded defenders, and scored the winning basket against Notre Dame. It was a play shown repeatedly on NCAA TV highlights. By vote of college coaches, Danny was named Eastman Kodak Basketball Player of the Year. Obviously pro-basketball teams were drooling for Danny, but he was off to Toronto.

The Blue Jays felt Danny could become a .280 hitter with fifteen homers a year. The Boston Celtics thought he could help them win an NBA championship and surprised everyone by selecting him as their third pick in the June 1981 draft. His senior year gave Danny a different view of his future. He asked the Blue Jays to let him sign with the Celtics. After a miserable season hitting only .187 in 86 games, he retired from baseball on September 14. The Blue Jays released him on November 27, 1981 when they allowed the Celtics to purchase his contract. He found a home in the NBA as a starting guard for the Celtics where he earned a reputation for tough, aggressive play and helped them win the NBA title.

Besides everything else, Danny is a good piano player so don't think that music lessons and athletics are incompatible!

ALAN ASHBY YEAR-BY-YEAR STATISTICS

Name: Alan Dean Ashby

Born: July 8, 1951
Long Beach, CA

Hgt: 6′ 2″ Wgt: 190

Bats: Both Throws: Right

Home: Sugarland, TX

Minor League: 1969-1974

Year	Club	L	POS	G	AB	R	H	2	3	HR	RBI	SB	AVG
1973	Cleveland	AL	C	11	29	4	5	1	0	1	3	0	.172
1974	Cleveland	AL	C	10	7	1	1	0	0	0	0	0	.143
1975	Cleveland	AL	C,1	90	254	32	57	10	1	5	32	3	.224
1976	Cleveland	AL	C,1	89	247	26	59	5	1	4	32	0	.239
1977	Toronto	AL	C	124	396	25	83	16	3	2	29	0	.210
1978	Toronto	AL	C	81	264	27	69	15	0	9	29	1	.261
1979	Houston	NL	C	108	336	25	68	15	2	2	35	0	.202
1980	Houston	NL	C	116	352	30	90	19	2	3	48	0	.256
1981	Houston	NL	C	83	255	20	69	13	0	4	33	0	.271
1982	Houston	NL	C	100	339	40	87	14	2	12	49	2	.257
1983	Houston	NL	C	87	275	31	63	18	1	8	34	0	.229
1984	Houston	NL	C	66	191	16	50	7	0	4	27	0	.262
1985	Houston	NL	C	65	189	20	53	8	0	8	25	0	.280
1986	Houston	NL	C	120	315	24	81	15	0	7	38	1	.257
1987	Houston	NL	C	125	386	53	111	16	0	14	63	0	.288
1988	Houston	NL	C	73	227	19	54	10	0	7	33	0	.238
1989	Houston	NL	C	22	61	4	10	1	1	0	3	0	.164
	Lifetime			1370	4123	397	1010	183	13	90	513	7	.245

ALAN ASHBY

As a youth, Alan regularly went to Dodger Stadium to watch his favorite players, Sandy Koufax and Tommy Davis. He saw Koufax pitch no-hitters twice, hardly realizing that someday he would catch Major League no-hitters. In fact, Alan didn't catch until his senior year in high school. He batted .350 his senior year and was selected for the All-Los Angeles first team. The Cleveland Indians picked him in the third round of the 1969 amateur draft. In 1971, he hit .293 with 18 homers and 60 RBIs in only 77 games, making the California League's All-Star team. He spent six years in the minors, getting short call-ups in 1973 and 1974. Alan felt that part of his difficulty in getting a solid Major League opportunity was a bias of some managers who felt that Mormons were not tough enough to be good ballplayers. Alan proved them wrong! He singled in his first Major League at bat on July 4, 1973, driving in his first run to begin a seventeen-year Major League career.

In 1975, he spent the whole season with the Indians. He led the team with sixteen sacrifices and smashed a grand-slam homer against the Red Sox. Manager Frank Robinson said, "Alan was one of our better hitters the last two months of the season." Alan's teammates awarded him the "Golden Tomahawk" for "making the greatest contribution to the total team effort in 1975." Alan said that he really liked his teammates and feels they admired him for his positive, uplifting lifestyle.

After the 1976 season, Alan was traded to the Toronto Blue Jays with Church member, Doug Howard. He was the regular catcher in 1977. In 1978, he was among leading American League catchers in assists and double plays. Always recognized for his strong arm, he threw out 53 percent of attempted basestealers. During the 1978 season, he was instrumental with Garth Iorg and Jerry Garvin in helping to bring the gospel to fellow player, Luis Gomez. When Luis's wife, Petra, was sick, Alan participated in her healing. He ordained Luis to the Aaronic Priesthood and later confirmed Luis's wife a member of the Church.

In November 1978, Alan was traded to the Houston Astros. He caught all of the 1979 season until August 29, when he shattered both joints of his index finger trying to catch an errant Joe Niekro knuckleball. It is probable that catching the knuckleball so much contributed to a shorter career. Manager Bill Virdon praised his catching saying, "He handles pitchers as well as anyone around." He had a good year at the plate in 1980, attaining career highs in hits, doubles, and RBIs. He separated a rib in a collision with Joe Ferguson in the one-game 1980 National League West Playoff against the Los Angeles Dodgers. Despite the pain, he played with the injury during the Championship series against the Philadelphia Phillies.

Alan was the regular catcher during the strike-shortened 1981 season. He batted .271, helping the Astros win first place for the second half of the season. He experienced two of his career highlights in a ten-day period. On September 26, he

On September 26, 1981, Alan caught Nolan Ryan's record-breaking fifth no-hitter. He called it a "mind-boggling experience." Alan also drove in two runs in the game.

caught Nolan Ryan's record-breaking fifth no-hitter, a 5-0 win over the Dodgers. On October 6, Alan smashed a two-run homer in the ninth inning to win the first game of the NL West playoff against the Dodgers. In 1982, he placed second on the team in homers while playing in only 100 games. On June 4, 1983, he hit two homers and drove in six runs against the Reds. Unfortunately he broke his hand in August 1985, ending his season as he went on the disabled list for the third season in a row.

On September 25, 1986, he caught Mike Scott's no-hitter against the San Francisco Giants. For Alan, it was the third no-hitter he had caught putting him in a class with only ten other catchers in Major League history who had three no-hitters to their name. Undoubtedly 1987 was Alan's finest year. He set season highs in homers, RBIs, and batting average and led all NL catchers in fielding percentage. In 1988, he suffered back problems that limited his play to 71 games. Two of those games were no-hitters through eight innings only to end up as one-hitters. You can imagine his disappointment.

After the 1988 season, Alan was a free agent and could have signed with any team. He elected to remain with the Astros. In May 1989, the Astros informed Alan that they intended to trade him to Pittsburgh. As a ten-year veteran with more than five years with the same team, he had the right to reject the trade which he did. He said in an interview at the time, "Why would I want to go elsewhere now when I didn't want to before?" The Astros responded by releasing him from the team.

During his tenure with the Astros, Alan caught for some of the best pitchers in the game including Nolan Ryan, J.R. Richard, Mike Scott, and Joe Niekro. Ryan and Richard were 100-mph pitchers. Scott was a Cy Young winner with a great split-fingered fastball. Niekro was the league's premier knuckleball pitcher. Richard was the NL's strikeout leader in 1979, Scott had the honor in 1986, and Ryan had it in 1987. It's safe to say that no catcher "caught more heat" in his career than Alan did. Richard represented the feeling of the pitchers toward Alan when he said, "I've got all the respect in the world for him."

Raised in the Church, Alan has served as a Sunday School and Primary teacher, Young Men's president, and as his ward's Communication Specialist. Alan enjoys playing golf. After his release, he entered a business venture that built the Old Orchard golf course in southwest Houston. He plays the guitar. Occasionally he would take his guitar on road trips for relaxation. He collected baseball cards as a youth and still has his collection. His favorite card of himself is his Topps rookie card. He played in the 1990 Senior League and later that year, he became the Sports director and Sports anchor on the 7 and 11 p.m. News for Channel 39 in Houston.

The following statement made only weeks before his release by the Astros sums up Alan's approach to life and baseball. He said, "I'm a competitive ballplayer and baseball is very important to me, but nothing is more important than my family and my relationship with Jesus Christ."

TOMMY BARRETT YEAR-BY-YEAR STATISTICS

Name: Thomas Loren Barrett

Born: April 2, 1960
San Fernando, CA

Hgt: 5′ 10″ Wgt: 170

Bats: Both Throws: Right

Home: Tucson, AR

Minor League: 1982-1989, 1991

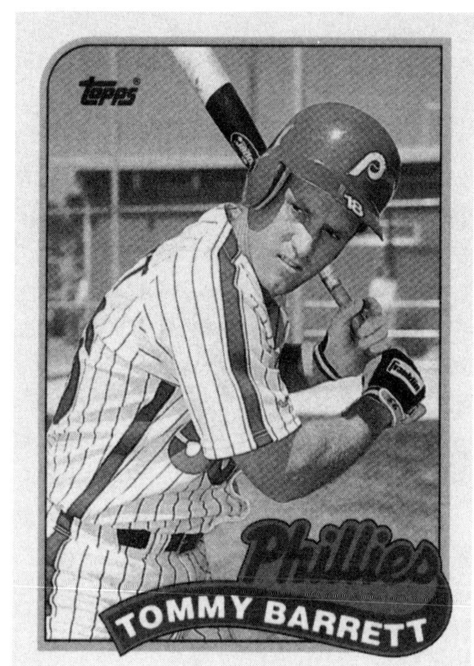

Year	Club	L	POS	G	AB	R	H	2	3	HR	RBI	SB	AVG
1988	Philadelphia	NL	2	36	54	5	11	1	0	0	3	0	.204
1989	Philadelphia	NL	2	14	27	3	6	0	0	0	1	0	.222
1990	Disabled List												
	Lifetime			50	81	8	17	1	0	0	4	0	.210

TOMMY BARRETT

*A*pproaching spring training with the Philadelphia Phillies in 1990, Tommy had big hopes after toiling in the minor leagues for eight years. He had some great minor league seasons and appeared in 50 Major League games in 1988-1989. He was planning for 1990 to be the year he made it big like his brother, Marty, had with the Boston Red Sox. It was not to be. During the first week of spring training, his knees gave way, worn out by years of pounding from stealing bases and diving for balls, usually on Astroturf. As his teammates began the season, Tommy underwent surgery on his right knee and two months later his left knee was under the knife. He missed the entire season and was released outright by the Phillies. He is attempting a comeback because he loves baseball so much. It's still a game to him and he definitely wants to stay part of it.

Tommy's favorite player as a kid was Brooks Robinson, and his favorite team was the Baltimore Orioles. He had plenty of baseball cards but they were used in games instead of being kept in mint condition on a shelf. With his five brothers and his friends, his life centered around sports, especially baseball. And when he wasn't on the field, he was engaged in a baseball board game, Strat-o-matic--a game that everyone treated with utmost seriousness. It included double steals, hit and run plays, and keen strategy on when to bring in relief pitchers. Tommy loved it.

When Tommy was thirteen, his brother, Charlie, was drafted out of high school by the Los Angeles Dodgers. Everyone in his family was excited, and Tommy knew he wanted to be a Major League player. He played on his high school team in Las Vegas, was named to the all-state team his junior year, and helped his team play in the 1977 state championship game. He played three years of American Legion ball and went to the state finals one year. His brother Marty was a teammate one year and other teammates included future Major League players Mike Morgan and Mike Maddox.

Tommy was a well-rounded athlete. Beside baseball in high school, he played soccer and tennis. He was the number one player on the tennis team and compiled a 117-15 record over three years. Upon graduating from high school, he spent the summer with Charlie who was playing A level baseball. This experience further motivated Tommy to become a Major Leaguer although no team had shown any interest in him. He attended Mesa Community college in 1979 and 1980, batting .360 and .393, respectively. He had 43 stolen bases in 1980 and helped to lead Mesa to the national tournament. Still no pro offers. He played for the University of Arizona in 1981 and 1982, hitting .353 and .341. Finally, he was drafted in the 26th round in June 1982 by the New York Yankees.

As a late draft choice, Tommy knew he had to make a good impression right away, and he did by batting .364. Only Kirby Puckett had a higher average that year in the rookie league. In 1983, Tommy won the batting title with a .327 average. He missed a

Tommy is a fine fielder and had big hopes of being the regular second baseman for the Phillies before undergoing operations on both knees in 1990.

month of 1983 sitting out an injury caused by a three-way collision with himself, the right fielder, and the center fielder. He performed well in 1984 at the Double A level batting .308. He started the 1985 season at the Yankees' Triple A club in Columbus. After 55 games, he was hitting .260, had 11 doubles, a triple, and even his first homer in pro ball. He was extremely discouraged when the Yankees sent him back to the Double A level. He said, "It was a slap in the face, but what could I do other than to accept it." Then his season ended in August when he incurred a severe rug burn to his hand from a diving catch on Astroturf.

Tommy returned to the University of Arizona each off-season to continue his education. After the 1984 season, he met a coed who was a Church member and was introduced to the Church through her. In high school, Tommy had many friends who were Church members. Now, as he learned about the gospel, their example became important to him. He had also met Scott Nielsen at Columbus in 1984 and felt that Scott was a strong example. Tommy joined the Church in the summer of 1985. And yes, he married the member missionary.

After another season at Double A ball, the Yankees traded Tommy to the Philadelphia Phillies. In 1987, he led Eastern League second basemen in putouts, assists, double plays, and fielding percentage. He had nine triples, a .334 average, and he led the league with 95 walks. He was promoted to the Triple A level in 1988, hitting .285 at Maine and leading the International League in putouts and assists. He joined the Phillies in mid-season and singled in his first at-bat. Reliving the moment, he said, "It was great! A dream come true." Unfortunately, he went 0-for-20 in his next four games. He became their regular pinch-hitter going 8-for-21 and walking four times. One of his pinch hits was a game-winning single off Roger McDowell in the bottom of the ninth inning to beat the New York Mets.

He began the 1989 season at Scranton where he was a teammate of Wally Ritchie. He led the league with 44 stolen bases and tied for the league lead with 10 sacrifice hits. He led second basemen with a .985 fielding percentage. He was called up at the end of the season by the Phillies. He had worked extremely hard to make the Majors and was hoping that 1990 would be his big year. Instead of hitting doubles off the wall at Veteran Stadium, he underwent double knee surgery.

With the determination that he has always demonstrated, Tommy embarked on an aggressive rehabilitation program to strengthen his knees. In February 1991, he signed a Triple-A contract with the Boston Red Sox organization. He said, "I'll be playing with pain but I want to prove I can still play." A good omen is he was assigned to Pawtucket where he hit his first pro home run.

If he is unable to return to the Majors, he is seriously considering a role as a manager. Maybe Strat-o-matic is still in his blood. Tommy enjoys playing tennis and golf. He has served in Church callings, recently as a Valiant A teacher in Primary.

BARRY BONNELL YEAR-BY-YEAR STATISTICS

Name: Robert Barry Bonnell

Born: October 27, 1953
Cincinnati, OH

Hgt: 6′ 3″ **Wgt:** 200

Bats: Right **Throws:** Right

Home: Redmond, WA

Minor League: 1975-1977

Year	Club	L	POS	G	AB	R	H	2	3	HR	RBI	SB	AVG
1977	Atlanta	NL	O,3	100	360	41	108	11	0	1	45	7	.300
1978	Atlanta	NL	O,3	117	304	36	73	11	3	1	16	12	.240
1979	Atlanta	NL	O,3	127	375	47	97	20	3	12	45	8	.259
1980	Toronto	AL	O	130	463	55	124	22	4	13	56	3	.268
1981	Toronto	AL	O	66	227	21	50	7	4	4	28	4	.220
1982	Toronto	AL	O,3	140	437	59	128	26	3	6	49	14	.293
1983	Toronto	AL	O,3	121	377	49	120	21	3	10	54	9	.318
1984	Seattle	AL	O,3	110	363	42	96	15	4	8	48	5	.264
1985	Seattle	AL	O	48	111	9	27	8	0	1	10	1	.243
	Lifetime			959	3017	359	823	141	24	56	351	63	.273

BARRY BONNELL

*E*ver since Barry can remember he has had two goals in life: to play Major League baseball and to fly airplanes. Ball playing started first. He played nearly everywhere on his high school team--first, second, outfield, and pitcher. In one game, he struck out 19 batters in a seven-inning game. His team won their league and he was on the league all-star team. He played summer ball and his team placed second in the Connie Mack nationals. His favorite ball players were Brooks Robinson and Carl Yastrzemski, and his favorite team was the hometown Cincinnati Reds.

Barry was drafted by the Chicago White Sox in 1971, but he was disappointed in their offer and decided to play basketball and baseball at Ohio State instead. He averaged ten points a game on the freshman basketball team. In his junior year on the baseball team, he won the Potter Run Maker award as the 'Offensive Star' of the Ohio State team, and he also performed well on summer teams. In January 1975, he was the first draft pick in the nation being selected by the Philadelphia Phillies. He used some of his bonus money to begin flying lessons.

In the summer of 1973, Barry was the recipient of a "Golden Question." He was playing for a summer league team located in Grand Junction, Colorado. His team played some games in Alaska and on the flight back, a Church member sat next to him and told him about the restored gospel. A member referral brought missionaries to his door in Grand Junction. He was baptized in August before the season was over. He hadn't known many Church members but those he knew from high school had set a good example that Barry said was important when he learned about the Church.

After only 23 games in the minors, the Phillies traded Barry to the Atlanta Braves. Undaunted, Barry led the Western Carolina league in 1975 with a .324 average and was selected to the All-Star team. He had decided to use his extra time to completely read *The Book of Mormon*. During the night on bus trips, he would use a flashlight to read. Several players would ask him what he was reading and he would explain. One player, Dale Murphy, wanted to learn more. The day after the 1975 season ended, Barry baptized Dale.

During the 1976 season, Barry joined the Triple-A Richmond team in mid-year and batted .282. He was hitting .380 for Richmond early in 1977 when he was called up by the Braves to sub for an injured player. Barry used the opportunity to stay in the Majors. He started off hot, going 5-for-5 on May 27 against the Giants. He hit a grand slam homer on June 5, and had a 14-game hitting streak. Playing third base and outfield, he committed only one error in 100 games. His .300 batting average was the highest for any rookie in the National League. He was injured for a month which probably cost him Rookie of the Year honors.

Barry's .300 batting average was the highest of any rookie in the NL in 1977. He led all Blue Jays' hitters in 1983 with a .318 batting average.

In 1978, Barry and Dale both played in more than 115 games for the Braves sometimes in the same infield and sometimes in the outfield together. The highlight of 1978 was going 5-for-5 against the Reds. Barry helped run a Sunday Service for players who couldn't get to church on Sunday. Normal attendance was eighteen. He was also active in Athletes in Action, sometimes sponsoring *Bible* study during the week. During a newspaper interview Barry said, "We believe in taking care of our bodies. Our purpose in life is to control our bodies and our minds."

An experience occurred during the 1978 season that Barry described as "life-changing." He was struggling terribly, batting about .200. Because of his poor performance, he was down on himself and felt miserable. He really didn't want to go when Dale Murphy asked him to come along to the hospital, but he went anyway. There he met Ricky Little, a stalwart Braves' supporter, but a youngster afflicted with leukemia. It was readily apparent that Ricky was near death. Barry felt a deep desire to think of something comforting to say but nothing seemed adequate. Finally, he asked if there was anything they could do. The youngster hesitated, and then asked if they would each hit a home run for him during the next game. Barry said, "That request wasn't such a hard thing for Dale, who in fact hit two homers that night, but I was struggling at the plate and hadn't hit a homer all year. Then I felt a warm feeling come over me and I told Ricky to count on it." Barry hit his only home run of the season that night. The experience with Ricky magnified for Barry how fortunate he was even if he was only batting .200 and that feeling sorry for himself and making life miserable was inappropriate when there were people like Ricky who endured real suffering while keeping a positive attitude.

Barry was super hot at the beginning of the 1979 season, leading the National League with five homers and a .343 average in April. He was very disappointed when manager Bobby Cox benched him against right handers as soon as he went hitless in a game. Barry felt he deserved to be a full-time player. He also felt that women reporters should not conduct interviews at player's lockers. He believed in access to players, just not at their lockers. Preceding Sam Wyche of the Cincinnati Bengals by more than ten years, Barry organized an "interviewing room" and arranged for players to do their interviews there.

He became a Toronto Blue Jay in a trade that sent Luis Gomez to the Braves in December 1979. He set a Blue Jay record in his first month by slashing three doubles in three successive at bats in a game against the Indians. His 1980 season was cut short in August when he was hit in the face by a pitch, and he played in only 62 games in 1981 because of torn tendons in his knee.

He rebounded in 1982 hitting nearly .400 for much of the first half of the year. He was interviewed by Howard Cosell as a star of the Blue Jays during a Monday night ABC telecast. He went 5-for-5 on April 10, getting the game winning RBI. Nine days later, he won another game with a home run. Barry ended the season with career highs in hits, doubles, and stolen bases. He batted .335 on the road, second-best in the

Barry's biggest hit of 1983 was a game-winning grand slam homer. He had eleven, three-hit games with the Mariners in 1984. A lifetime highlight was baptizing Dale Murphy in 1975.

American League. An article about Barry written in 1982 stated that he was from the Norman Rockwell era "before heros began to disappoint us all. He's almost too good to be true."

1983 was one of Barry's best years. He batted .318 and had a .469 slugging average-both career highs. On May 1, he hit a game-winning grand slam homer. The next month, he hit two triples in a game, one with bases loaded. He capped the year off with his first inside-the-park homer. In December 1983, Barry was traded to the Seattle Mariners. He singled in his first at bat as a Mariner and had eleven, three-hit games in 1984. He suffered through a series of injuries during August and September that limited his playing time. He worked hard in the off-season. Trainer Rick Griffen said, "In overall conditioning, nobody on this club may have improved more than Barry." Unfortunately, manager Dick Williams seemed to forget that he was on the team in 1985. Then to complicate matters, he was disabled for a month. Barry said, "Instead of being an utility player for several years, I decided to retire and do something else I love-flying."

Barry never did fly for the Mariners as is sometimes reported. However, he did fly business travelers in a Cesna 310 including Toronto teammate and fellow Church member, Jerry Garvin. In 1989, Barry became a pilot for Northwest Airlink. While he enjoyed flying, he didn't like being away from home so much. Realizing that it would take several more years to become a captain in a major airline, Barry decided to give up flying as a profession. He joined a medical equipment firm and serves as one of their program managers.

Many ball players mentioned the support of their wife as a key factor in their success. Barry is no exception. He credits his wife with "putting up" with a lot with all the moving, and being left alone so much with the children. Since retiring from baseball, he has served as Teachers Quorum advisor and Bishop.

RON BRAND YEAR-BY-YEAR STATISTICS

Name: Ronald George Brand

Born: January 13, 1940
Los Angeles, CA

Hgt: 5′ 7″ Wgt: 170

Bats: Right Throws: Right

Home: Roseville, CA

Minor League: 1958-1964

Year	Club	L	POS	G	AB	R	H	2	3	HR	RBI	SB	AVG
1963	Pittsburgh	NL	C,3	46	66	8	19	2	0	1	7	0	.288
1965	Houston	NL	C,3	117	391	27	92	6	3	2	37	10	.235
1966	Houston	NL	C,2	56	123	12	30	2	0	0	10	0	.244
1967	Houston	NL	C	84	215	22	52	8	1	0	18	4	.242
1968	Houston	NL	C	43	81	7	13	2	0	0	4	1	.160
1969	Montreal	NL	C,O	103	287	19	74	12	0	0	20	2	.258
1970	Montreal	NL	S,3	72	126	10	30	2	3	0	9	2	.238
1971	Montreal	NL	S,O	47	56	3	12	0	0	0	1	1	.214
	Lifetime			568	1345	108	322	34	7	3	106	20	.239

RON BRAND

*R*on grew up loving baseball. His favorite team was the Brooklyn Dodgers. His neighbor, George Genovese, played in the Pittsburgh Pirate system. When Ron was as young as eight, George would play catch with him. Later, George informed Pirate scouts that Ron was a good player. Ron's father worked with Don Drysdale's dad so Ron watched Don, who was four year's older, become a star in high school. Ron would later bat against Don in the Major Leagues. Ron performed well in high school, starring in two sports. He was the Los Angeles All-City shortstop batting .390 and led his team to the city championship. He was also a superb running back in football and was named as his league's Most Valuable Back. Ron was selected to play in the 1957 Hearst All-Star Baseball Tournament in New York City. He was excited to shake hands with Willie Mays, Mickey Mantle, and Joe DiMaggio.

At eighteen, Ron played his first pro game as a shortstop in 1958, having signed with the Pittsburgh Pirates. He had a good season in 1959 batting .317, but his average fell to .240 in 1960. In January 1961, he met a stranger who was working out at the same field as Ron. The stranger volunteered to pitch batting practice. After Ron had taken five swings, the stranger said, "You could be a good hitter if you learned to hit line drives to all fields." Ron was insulted. Who was this guy telling him, a professional baseball player, how to hit? But deep down, Ron knew his career wasn't going anywhere, so he swallowed his pride and listened. Every day for six weeks, Ron did everything the stranger told him. This included a completely new diet, a rigorous exercise program, and hours of hitting practice. The stranger also taught Ron how to judge himself by the quality of his effort instead of merely by the end result. In baseball, dealing with failure is critical and Ron had been much too quick to heap abuse on himself for his failings. On the first day of spring training, Ron was clocked in the 60-yard dash .4 of a second faster than his previous best and his coaches commented on his improved hitting. Ron said, "I appreciated what had been done for me, but I still didn't realize how selfless this person was. A few years later, when Ron had made the Majors and was at Dodger stadium, he heard someone yelling to him. He looked up into the stands, and there he was, the stranger, pumping his fist up and down to signify, "Good job, Ron, I knew you could do it." When Ron tells this story to youth, he relates it to the selfless concern of the Savior who is rooting for us and helping us, but we need to be obedient and follow His directions.

Ron switched to catcher in 1961 when he subbed for his team's injured catcher. He did so well the Pirates asked him to make a permanent switch to catcher. He caught a no-hitter that year, one of his top thrills in pro ball. He batted .316 in 1961 and .318 in 1962 and was selected to his league's all-star team both years. Upon becoming a catcher, his dream was to catch for the Pirates ace pitcher and fellow Church member, Vernon Law. Vernon was experiencing sore arm problems in 1963, but Ron was able to

On April 9, 1965, Ron became the first Astro player to get a hit in the Astrodome.

catch a few innings of an exhibition game against Cleveland when Vernon was pitching. Ron and Vernon became life-long friends. Ron said, "Vernon took me under his wing when I first came up." Ron played his first Major League game in 1963. He batted .288 in 49 games and played nearly every fielding position.

Ron was selected to the International League All-Star team in 1964. He led his league with 87 assists. He was acquired by the Houston Astros and was their regular catcher in 1965, playing in 117 games. One of Ron's highlights occurred on April 9, 1965, when he became the first Astro player to get a hit in the Astrodome. Ron exclaimed, "The roar of the 55,000 fans was deafening." To make it even better, the hit was a triple and Ron's parents were in the stands. Ron was the "Star of the Game" on June 4, 1965, hitting a ninth inning homer off of Hall of Fame pitcher, Bob Gibson, to break a 2-2 tie and win the game 4-2. He had a number of clutch hits that year driving in 37 runs. In 1966, Ron and fellow-Mormon Gary Kroll were roommates.

He became an original member of the new National League team, the Montreal Expos, in 1969. He played in the first official NL game ever held outside the United States. He was the starting catcher for the Expos playing in 103 games and batting .258. He played in 119 games over the 1970 and 1971 seasons. He was asked to be his team's representative to the Player's Union in 1972. As always Ron did his best in what he was asked to do, but baseball management did not appreciate the new union. Montreal would not trade him or play him and no team would make offers for player reps. Ron believes his career ended four or five years early because of his legitimate efforts to represent his teammates.

Ron's approach to the game during his career is best summarized by former Astros manager, Grady Hatton, who said, "Brand is the last of the hungry ball players. It doesn't make any difference what you ask of him. He doesn't question it, he just gives you 100 percent." His love of the game led him to managing in the minors for the 1974-1976 seasons. In 1976, his team won the pennant and he was picked as the Manager of the Year. Of the 85 players he managed in the minors, 17 became Major League players which Ron feels is a pretty good ratio given that he never managed higher than the Class A level. Also during the 1976 season, he attended the baptism of Glenn Bonnell, Barry Bonnell's brother. Ron enjoyed managing but with six children, he felt he needed a better paying job.

Ron has worked as a General Contractor building townhouses and custom homes. He is still active in baseball, playing in a Men's Senior League. His team won their World Series two years in a row. Ron is contemplating a move to Phoenix, Arizona to open a baseball hitting and fielding complex. He has served as Ward Mission Leader, High Councilor, and Young Men's President in the Church. He receives several letters a month asking him to autograph cards. His favorite card of himself is the 1972 Topps card number 733.

DAVE DOWNS YEAR BY YEAR STATISTICS

Name: David Ralph Downs

Born: June 21, 1952
Logan, UT

Hgt: 6′ 5″ Wgt: 220

Bats: Right Throws: Right

Home: Centerville, UT

Minor League: 1970-1976

Year	Club	L	POS	G	IP	W	L	SO	BB	H	ERA	SV	SHO
1972	Philadelphia	NL	P	4	23	1	1	5	3	25	2.74	0	1
	Lifetime			4	23	1	1	5	3	25	2.74	0	1

DAVE DOWNS

*I*n high school, Dave's teams played in the state basketball and baseball tournaments. During his junior year, his baseball team won the state championship and in his senior year he was selected to the all-state baseball team as a pitcher. He was followed by a lot of baseball scouts and was drafted by the Philadelphia Phillies in June 1970.

He was assigned to Walla Walla in the rookie league and posted a 5-7 record and 5.63 ERA in 14 games. In 1971, he played in the Class A league at Spartanburg, South Carolina, winning 5 and losing 4 while lowering his ERA to 4.43. He blossomed the following year at Reading in Double A ball, surprising everyone with a 15-7 record and a superb 2.41 ERA. Dave's accomplishments were noted in the September 2, 1972 issue of *The Sporting News*. An article read, "When it comes to finishing what he begins, Dave Downs could boast of five straight complete games and 10 in his last 11 starts after he defeated Sherbrooke 3-0 on August 12." Dave revealed his success formula in the article. He said, "The secret is good conditioning, concentration, and staying ahead of the hitters." Two weeks later, Dave was noted again in *The Sporting News*--this time for pitching his third consecutive shutout when he beat Pawtucket 1-0. He scored the only run of the game in the ninth inning when he led off with a single.

Dave was the only pitcher the Phillies called up at the end of the season. He made his Major League debut on September 2, 1972 against the Atlanta Braves. He said, "I will never forget it. It was another world." The score was 1-0 going into the ninth inning with the Phillies ahead. In the top of the ninth, Dave helped his own cause by getting a single and driving in one of two runs scored by the Phillies. With a 3-0 lead, he pitched another scoreless inning to win a complete game shutout. Wow! As a twenty-year old, he was on top of the baseball world with bright prospects as the young hurler the Phils needed to join the pitching rotation with Steve Carlton.

He started against the Chicago Cubs and future Hall of Fame pitcher, Ferguson Jenkins, on September 8. Dave left the game after seven innings with the score tied 3-3. He pitched well, giving up only five hits, but one was a two-run homer to Billy Williams. In reporting the game, the *Philadelphia Inquirer* made the observation that Dave may be the Phillies' best-looking prospect since Ferguson Jenkins in 1965. He had less fortune on September 13 when he lost to the New York Mets, giving up three runs in three innings. He did earn his first RBI, but it was of little satisfaction. On September 19, he was engaged in a pitcher's duel with future Hall of Famer, Bob Gibson of the St. Louis Cardinals. Dave pitched four innings of one-run baseball when he experienced pain in his pitching shoulder. He sat out the last two weeks of the season.

He didn't know it, but his Major League career was over. An operation, a lot of rehabilitation, and trying to regain his form to make it back to the Majors was still ahead. In 1974, he had a 2-1 record at Rocky Mount but also a 5.10 ERA. He said, "I

Dave's first Major League game was a complete game shutout over the Atlanta Braves on September 2, 1972. He had a hit and RBI in the game to help the Phillies win 3-0.

kept going down in the organization instead of up." In 1976, at Spartanburg, he was pounded. He felt he gave it his best but that it just wasn't going to happen for him. He retired in 1976. When asked about his disappointment and what might have been, he replied, "I don't look back. The Phillies were good to me. Yesterday is gone and today is today."

Leaving baseball unexpectedly left him unprepared for making a living. Since he didn't have other work experience, he went into construction as a laborer. He said those first years were tough. Later, he went into the boat business in Spokane, Washington. Recently he started a marine parts and boat distributorship in Utah so he could be closer to his parents and family.

He coached American Legion ball and one of his players was his brother, Kelly. He feels that sharing his pro experiences was helpful to Kelly, especially the mental aspect of the game in knowing how to set hitters up and how to keep your confidence after a hitter knocks one out of the park. Just as Kelly's favorite player was Dave, it is obvious that Dave has a lot of satisfaction in the accomplishments of his brother.

KELLY DOWNS YEAR-BY-YEAR STATISTICS

Name: Kelly Robert Downs

Born: October 25, 1960
Ogden, UT

Hgt: 6′ 4″ Wgt: 200

Bats: Right Throws: Right

Home: Centerville, UT

Minor League: 1980-1986

Year	Club	L	POS	G	IP	W	L	SO	BB	H	ERA	SV	SHO
1986	San Francisco	NL	P	14	88	4	4	64	30	78	2.75	0	0
1987	San Francisco	NL	P	41	186	12	9	137	67	185	3.63	1	3
1988	San Francisco	NL	P	27	168	13	9	118	47	140	3.32	0	3
1989	San Francisco	NL	P	18	83	4	8	49	26	82	4.79	0	0
1990	San Francisco	NL	P	13	63	3	2	31	20	56	3.43	0	0
	Lifetime			113	588	36	32	399	190	541	3.55	1	6

KELLY DOWNS

When Kelly was nine years old his brother, Dave, signed a contract with the Philadelphia Phillies as a pitcher. When Kelly was asked who his favorite player and team were as a youth, his answer was immediate, "My brother, Dave, and the Phillies." Few people would have guessed that ten years later Kelly would follow in his brother's footsteps by signing a contract with the Phillies as a pitcher.

In high school, Kelly played basketball, but baseball was his primary sport. He pitched and played shortstop, and his team finished second in the state twice. He played American Legion ball and won two games in the state tournament. In his junior year in high school, he hurt his back playing basketball. He reinjured his back during the baseball season, so he didn't get a lot of publicity. He had intended to go to Brigham Young University but when the Phillies drafted him, he decided to sign.

He started off well his first two years with ERAs of 2.60 and 2.98 in 1980 and 1981, respectively. The next three seasons were very difficult. During 1982-1984, he had a combined record of 18 victories and 30 defeats, and two years his ERA was over 5. He had to fight hard to overcome discouragement--a ballplayer's worst enemy. He said, "I always knew I had the ability to play in the Majors, I was just too inconsistent." The Phillies traded Kelly to the San Francisco Giants at the end of the 1984 season.

In the Giant organization, Kelly learned to throw the split-finger fastball and it made a big difference. He lowered his ERA in 1985 to 4.01 and in 1986 to 3.42 while pitching at the Triple A level. He was 8-5 at Phoenix on July 27, 1986, when his good friend, Jim Gott, who was on the Giants, called to give him the news that he was being brought up by the Giants. Good news also occurred at the hospital that day when his wife gave birth to their first child.

In his first seven starts, the Giants scored only nine runs making it pretty tough on Kelly. He was 0-4 after his first month; nevertheless, he managed a 4-4 record to go along with a splendid 2.75 ERA. Manager Roger Craig said, "I really can't say enough about Kelly's pitching. He has a good, live fastball, a good slider, and two different split-finger fastballs. I'll go out on a limb and say he can be a 20-game winner."

In 1987, Kelly helped the Giants win the National League West. His 12 victories were second highest on the team. He pitched his first Major League shutout on April 15. He tied for third in the NL for shutouts with three. After being a starting pitcher nearly all season, Kelly unselfishly moved to the bullpen to strengthen the relief pitching. He earned his first save on September 5. His 137 strikeouts were second on the team.

Kelly achieved a career high 13 victories in 1988 and led the team in shutouts for the second straight year. In June he pitched shutouts against Houston and Atlanta. During

Normally a starter, Kelly pitched in relief in games two and four of the 1989 NL Championship series against the Chicago Cubs, winning game four.

the season he had an exceptional stretch where he faced 33 left-handers before one got a hit off him. In fact, left-handers batted only .184 against him all season. His season ended after 27 starts because of an inflamed shoulder that required surgery.

A number of baseball sources picked Kelly as their pre-season favorite to win the Cy Young award in 1989. Unfortunately, he spent much of the year tending a sore shoulder. His frustration in 1989 was tempered somewhat by returning to the starting rotation at the end of the year to help the team capture the NL championship. He was the winning pitcher in one of the play-off games against the Chicago Cubs. Of course, the 1989 World Series will be forever memorable because of the shocking intrusion of "Mother Earth." Kelly's whole family was at Candlestick Park when the earthquake struck. He made sure his family was okay. To his surprise, he was pictured on the cover of *Sports Illustrated*, helping his nephew leave the stadium. Kelly said, "The earthquake was a reminder that we are not really in control as much as we think we are."

The 1990 season was another tough year as he didn't pitch for the Giants until August because of a shoulder injury. In his first appearance back, Eric Davis of the Reds crushed a long home run; however, Kelly finished the season strong--ready for next year.

Kelly enjoys hunting, snowmobiling, and flyfishing. He said, "I'd rather be in a river fishing than almost anything." He has participated in several Church firesides. Kelly credits his father with being "my number one fan and greatest supporter."

DENNIS ECKERSLEY YEAR-BY-YEAR STATISTICS

Name: Dennis Lee Eckersley

Born: October 3, 1954
Oakland, CA

Hgt: 6′ 2″ **Wgt:** 195

Bats: Right **Throws:** Right

Home: Sudbury, MA

Minor League: 1972-1974

Year	Club	L	POS	G	IP	W	L	SO	BB	H	ERA	SV	SHO
1975	Cleveland	AL	P	34	187	13	7	152	90	147	2.60	2	2
1976	Cleveland	AL	P	36	189	13	12	200	78	155	3.44	1	3
1977	Cleveland	AL	P	33	247	14	13	191	54	214	3.53	0	3
1978	Boston	AL	P	35	268	20	8	162	71	258	2.99	0	3
1979	Boston	AL	P	33	247	17	10	150	59	234	2.99	0	2
1980	Boston	AL	P	30	198	12	14	121	44	188	4.27	0	0
1981	Boston	AL	P	23	154	9	8	79	35	160	4.27	0	2
1982	Boston	AL	P	33	224	13	13	127	43	228	3.73	0	3
1983	Boston	AL	P	28	176	9	13	77	39	223	5.61	0	0
1984	Bost-Chicago	NL	P	33	225	14	12	114	49	223	3.60	0	0
1985	Chicago	NL	P	25	169	11	7	117	19	145	3.08	0	0
1986	Chicago	NL	P	33	201	6	11	137	43	226	4.57	0	0
1987	Oakland	AL	P	54	116	6	8	113	17	99	3.03	16	0
1988	Oakland	AL	P	60	73	4	2	70	11	52	2.35	45	0
1989	Oakland	AL	P	51	58	4	0	55	3	32	1.56	33	0
1990	Oakland	AL	P	63	73	4	2	73	4	41	0.61	48	0
	Lifetime			604	2815	169	140	1938	659	2625	3.49	145	18

DENNIS ECKERSLEY

Dennis grew up rooting for the San Francisco Giants and the Oakland Athletics since both teams were within an hour's drive of his house. He played quarterback in high school until his senior year when he made a tough decision not to play football for concern over injuring his arm and ruining his baseball chances. In basketball, he described himself as "scrappy," definitely not the leading scorer. In baseball, however, he was awesome as a pitcher, notching several no-hitters and regularly making the local and regional all-star teams. He also played shortstop but he acknowledged that he wasn't a particularly good hitter. While he definitely planned to be a Major League baseball player, it is doubtful that he ever dreamed he would pitch in three consecutive World Series for the Oakland A's with one series, 1989, being played against the Giants.

In June 1972, he was drafted in the third round by the Cleveland Indians. He reportedly said, "Oh no, not the Indians," as he had hoped to be picked by the Giants and follow in the footsteps of his favorite player, Giants pitcher Juan Marichal. Dennis began his pro career by pitching a shutout in his first start and compiled a 5-5 record at Reno in 1972. Again at Reno in 1973, he mowed down the opposition registering 218 strikeouts in 202 innings. In 1974, he was promoted to Double A ball and really showed his stuff with a 14-3 record. He was picked as the right handed Pitcher of the Year for the Texas League and led all pitchers in strikeouts with 163 in only 167 innings. He would have done even better if it had not been for an ankle injury that ended his season in August.

Going to spring training with the Indians in 1975, Dennis was looking forward to a promotion to Triple A ball; instead, he landed a spot on the Major League roster as a member of the Indians relief pitching corps. He was in ten relief games without allowing an earned run. On May 25, he started his first Major League game and pitched a three-hit shutout against the Oakland A's. Unbelievably, his ERA after 28 big league innings was 0.00. On August 25, he had a no-hitter going into the seventh inning against the Chicago White Sox. He ended up winning with a three-hitter. After the game Dennis displayed his competitive attitude and ability to predict the future when he said, "Sure I was thinking no-hitter . . . and one of these times I'm going to get one." He finished the year with a 13-7 record and 2.60 ERA, third-lowest in the American League. He was an easy choice for the AL Rookie Pitcher of the Year award. In 1976, he struck out 200 batters in 199 innings en route to a 13-12 record.

Dennis had some really exciting moments in 1977. From May 25 through June 3, he rivaled the best pitching ever witnessed in baseball as he faced 71 batters in 22 1/3 consecutive innings without giving up a hit! He pitched no-hit ball during the last seven innings against the Seattle Mariners on May 25. On May 30, he gave 13,400 Cleveland fans a Memorial Day treat by making good on his promise by pitching a no-hitter against the California Angels. Pitching coach Harvey Haddix, who had pitched a thirteen-inning no hitter and lost his game, said of Dennis, "He was super . . . he was

On May 30, 1977, Dennis jumped in celebration, striking out the last batter of his no-hitter against the California Angels. In his next game, he came within two outs of breaking Cy Young's 1904 record of 23 consecutive hitless innings

outstanding . . . you pick the superlatives and Eckersley was all of them." The no-hitter extended his hitless streak to 16 innings. In his next start on June 2, Dennis had the legendary Cy Young "turning in his grave" as he came within two outs of breaking the record Young set in 1904 of pitching 23 consecutive hitless innings. Dennis described the streak as a great thrill, especially the no-hitter and then reported that his next goal was to win 20 games in a season. As you might expect, Dennis was selected to the AL All-Star team.

As the 1978 spring training came to a close, Dennis found himself wearing a Boston Red Sox uniform as he was traded on March 30. It was a great move by the Red Sox as he attained his 20-victory goal, with a stunning 11-1 record at Fenway Park, the best record at home by a Red Sox pitcher in over 30 years. He had another good year in 1979, recording his second straight year with an ERA under 3.00. He pitched seven straight complete game victories and was second in the AL with 17 complete games. His attempt for a second straight 20-game year was ruined when he came up with sore arm and won only one game after August 14. The start of the 1980 season was a nightmare as he had a 1-6 record and 7.16 ERA before going on the disabled list for a month with a back injury. He finished the year strong and led the Red Sox in wins, strikeouts, and complete games.

In Boston, Dennis and Bruce Hurst became close friends. Dennis had been baptized in the Church as a youngster but had virtually no contact with the Church after he was thirteen. Bruce was attracted to Dennis's pitching style and the way he handled pressure on and off the mound. In a 1988 *Sports Illustrated* article about Dennis by Peter Gammons, Bruce recounted, "The other day I found my '81 baseball card and I saw that I had grown a mustache to look like the Eck . . . He was always there to help me through some rough times. When you got to know him, you found out that Dennis was a really decent man."

In 1981, for the first time in his Major League career, Dennis failed to win at least ten games. He rebounded in 1982, being selected to the AL All-Star team and winning the game. He suffered a strained bicep in August and wound up with a 13-13 record. His 1983 season, 9-13 and 5.61 ERA was a miserable experience because of shoulder problems and a drinking problem. In the *Sports Illustrated* article, he said, "I hit bottom professionally. I wore it out, partying hard. I never pitched with a hangover, and I gave it everything I had out there. But I had no arm speed. It was humiliating." On May 25, 1984, he was traded to the Chicago Cubs and his pitching helped them win the National League East title. In 1985, he led all Cubs starters with a 3.08 ERA and had pitched 19 straight shutout innings.

During 1986, Dennis won his 150th game, but his career was in jeopardy because of his drinking. He recounted to Gammons, "All the day games in Chicago helped do me in. I was drinking a lot . . . I knew I had a problem . . . I was losing all my self-esteem in self-destruction, yet I couldn't do anything about it." In January 1987, he entered an around-the-clock treatment program for six weeks to rid himself of his alcoholism. It

Dennis was the best relief pitcher in baseball during 1988-1990, saving 126 games and appearing in three consecutive World Series. His 0.61 ERA in 1990 was the lowest ever for a pitcher with over 50 innings.

was a very hard and painful experience but it was a success. Again from the *Sports Illustrated* article, Dennis explained, "I'd always been afraid of not drinking. I was afraid of life being dull. By spring training I realized I was really looking forward to living. I was so excited I wanted to tell the world I was sober but I wasn't ready to take the heat."

This turning-point experience in his life was quickly followed by a turning-point change in his career that combined to bring Dennis back to the forefront as one of the most dominating pitchers in baseball history. The Oakland A's suffered injuries to three of their pitchers during the 1987 spring training so they arranged a trade with the Cubs on April 3 that brought Dennis back to his "hometown." It was a major surprise and disappointment when he learned he was being assigned to the bullpen. After 13 relief appearances and 36 innings, he had a 2.25 ERA. By June he said, "I'm starting to adapt to it. I can get warm quicker." He finished the year as the A's stopper and registered 16 saves. He said, "A year earlier I don't think it would have worked. I couldn't have been an everyday pitcher when I was drinking. But at Oakland I changed jobs at precisely the right time."

He started the 1988 season in amazing fashion compiling eight saves in his first eight appearances. The life of a relief pitcher can be the "best of times and the worst of times." May 11 was one of those "worst of times" as he gave up five runs on five hits, a walk, and a balk in only 1 1/3 innings. The five hits matched the total he had given up in his 12 previous appearances. Dennis said, " I remember everyone of these games" but he showed they don't slow him down as he led the Major Leagues with 45 saves. He was picked for the All-Star team, and he set a Major League record by saving each of the A's four victories over the Red Sox in the AL play-offs, allowing only one hit in six innings. He was the "hands down" MVP winner of the AL play-offs. Despite a marvelous season, the pitch he remembers most was the one Kirk Gibson tagged over the fence in the first game of the World Series against the Los Angeles Dodgers. He earned the Fireman of the Year award from *The Sporting News* for being baseball's best relief pitcher.

The 1989 season started well with Dennis saving 14 games by May 27, when he strained a muscle in his rotator cuff and was out for 40 games. Dennis picked up where he had left off, saving a total of 33 games with a super low ERA of 1.56. He earned every player's dream, a World Series ring, as the A's beat the Giants. Dennis said that pitching the last out to win the World Series was his greatest moment in baseball. He was in even better form in 1990, saving 48 games, striking out 73 batters in 73 innings, posting an incredibly low 0.61 ERA, and again making the AL All-Star team. In the past three seasons, he has saved 126 games and played in three consecutive World Series. In October 1990, he was on the cover of *Sports Illustrated.* His accomplishments on the field and his "new life" off the field are admired by all who know him. In 1991, he became the only pitcher in baseball to have won over 150 games as a starter and to have saved over 150 games.

MIKE FETTERS YEAR-BY-YEAR STATISTICS

Name: Michael Lee Fetters

Born: December 19, 1964
Van Nuys, CA

Hgt: 6′ 4″ Wgt: 200

Bats: Right Throws: Right

Home: EwaBeach, HI

Minor League: 1986-1991

Year	Club	L	POS	G	IP	W	L	SO	BB	H	ERA	SV	SHO
1989	California	AL	P	1	3	0	0	4	1	5	8.10	0	0
1990	California	AL	P	26	68	1	1	35	20	77	4.12	1	0
	Lifetime			27	71	1	1	39	21	82	4.31	1	0

MIKE FETTERS

Mike has the double distinction of playing on two state championship teams in his senior year in high school. He was an All-Hawaii performer in basketball and baseball. He played guard, forward, and center on his basketball team, but at baseball he was strictly a one-position player--pitcher. By the way, on the football team he played wide receiver on offense and safety on defense, and he ran the two-mile race in track.

He was selected by the Los Angeles Dodgers in the June 1983 draft. Instead, he accepted a full athletic scholarship from Pepperdine University to pitch on their baseball team. He didn't disappoint them, compiling a 33-13 record with seven saves over the 1984-86 seasons. He earned the nickname, "PAC MAN" his freshman year for wins over USC, UCLA, and Arizona State, all of the Pacific 10 League. He was selected by *Baseball America* to the "All-Freshman Team."

In his sophomore year, he defeated Stanford 5-1 in an NCAA Regional play-off game. He toured Canada and the Far East with a College All-Star team in 1985 and posted a 2-1 mark with two saves. In 1986, he had 158 strikeouts in 147 innings to go with 13 wins. He was the conference Pitcher of the Year and was chosen to the All-American team. After three years at Pepperdine, he had set school records for most wins, strikeouts, innings pitched, and appearances.

The California Angels selected Mike during the first round of the 1986 draft. He was 4-2 at Salem in 1986 and notched 72 strikeouts in 72 innings. He had a good year in 1987 with a 9-7 record and 3.57 ERA. In the 1988 season his ERA ballooned to 5.92 but he was promoted to the Triple-A level at Edmonton and responded with a 2-0 record and 1.93 ERA. He went to winter ball to further improve his pitching mechanics.

He played the 1989 season at Edmonton and pitched well with a 12-8 record. He led the Pacific Coast League with 144 strikeouts. He had a five-game winning streak from mid-July to August 19, when he struck out 43 hitters in 47 innings. The Angels called him up in late August and he pitched in one game. On September 1, he pitched against the New York Yankees in Yankee Stadium where he struck out four batters in three innings, but three runners scored. It gave him an 8.10 ERA, but he knew he could pitch in the Major Leagues. Besides, the two previous Angels' pitchers gave up seven runs to the Yankees in one and one-third innings for a combined 49.00 ERA, so Mike's performance looked pretty good in comparison.

He started the 1990 season at Edmonton but rejoined the Angels in mid-May. On May 19, he started against the Toronto Blue Jays and left the game in the fourth inning with the score tied, four apiece. As an aside, fellow Church member and teammate, Wally Joyner, hit a home run in each of Mike's first two games. Although

Mike was an All-American in 1986 on the Pepperdine University baseball team. In 1990, he filled a relief pitching role on the California Angels, appearing in 26 games.

Mike had been a starter all his career, the Angels used him as a middle relief pitcher the rest of the year. On May 24, he held the Blue Jays to no runs in two innings. The Texas Rangers had his number on June 8, as he suffered his first loss, giving up four runs in one inning. He had four successive scoreless appearances on June 19, July 1, July 5, and July 7. He was credited with his first victory in the July 7 game. He entered the game in the tenth inning against the Milwaukee Brewers with the score tied 3-3. He pitched a scoreless tenth inning. The Angels rallied for a run in the top of the eleventh, and Mike held the Brewers scoreless to secure the victory. It was a short-lived celebration because in the next game, the Brewers scored thirteen runs off the Angels in one inning, and Mike took the rap for five of them. He rebounded on July 12, holding the Blue Jays to only one run in nearly five innings.

He went to spring training in 1991 determined to make the team but was sent down to Edmonton on the last weekend of spring training. He was assigned to the starting rotation. Although he had one of the better ERAs on the team, his won-lost record was a dismal 2-7. When Fernando Valenzuela went on the disabled list, however, the Angels called up Mike on June 15. He pitched four innings of relief against the Milwaukee Brewers on June 18.

Mike enjoys a variety of music, including soul and jazz. He loves to play basketball.

JERRY GARVIN YEAR-BY-YEAR STATISTICS

Name: Theodore Jared Garvin

Born: October 21, 1955
Oakland, CA

Hgt: 6′ 3″ **Wgt:** 195

Bats: Left **Throws:** Left

Home: Morro Bay, CA

Minor League: 1974-1976

Year	Club	L	POS	G	IP	W	L	SO	BB	H	ERA	SV	SHO
1977	Toronto	AL	P	34	245	10	18	127	85	247	4.19	0	1
1978	Toronto	AL	P	26	145	4	12	67	48	189	5.54	0	0
1979	Toronto	AL	P	8	23	0	1	14	10	15	2.74	0	0
1980	Toronto	AL	P	61	83	4	7	52	27	70	2.28	8	0
1981	Toronto	AL	P	35	53	1	2	25	23	46	3.40	0	0
1982	Toronto	AL	P	32	58	1	1	35	26	81	7.25	0	0
	Lifetime			196	607	20	41	320	219	648	4.42	8	1

JERRY GARVIN

Growing up in the Bay area of California, it was only natural that Jerry followed the San Francisco Giants, particularly Willie Mays, Willie McCovey, Juan Marichal, and Gaylord Perry. Jerry played basketball and baseball in high school. In his senior year, he led his baseball team to second place in the North Central California Region with a 11-1 record. He mowed down the opposition, averaging two strikeouts per inning pitched.

He was selected in the June 1973 draft by the Baltimore Orioles, but he couldn't decide whether to go on a Church mission. He enrolled at Merced College instead. After much prayer and fasting, Jerry accepted an offer from the Minnesota Twins in January 1974. He had a combined 31-12 record for his first two minor league seasons, but he felt guilty about not serving a mission. Jerry sought the advice of Paul Dunn, a general authority of the church and a former minor league player. Elder Dunn told him to prayerfully consider his decision and whatever he did to stay close to the Lord. Jerry decided that the Lord needed worthy baseball players who would be a good influence and role model for others. He was right. Later, he would play an important role in the conversion of a teammate on the Toronto Blue Jays.

In 1976, Jerry was promoted to the Triple-A level at Tacoma in mid-season. He pitched well especially in three games against Hawaii, whose manager became part of the new Toronto Blue Jays and was influential in selecting Jerry on the second pick for the Blue Jays in the November 1976 expansion draft. He pitched well in spring training and made the team. Jerry and Alan Ashby became the first Mormon pitcher-catcher combination to play together on a regular basis.

Jerry won his first three games beating the White Sox, Tigers, and Yankees. He had a 6-2 record in June and could have become the Rookie-of the-Year except for the extremely weak offense of the Blue Jays. He went 75 days without a win even though he gave up only three runs or less in 9 of his 13 starts during his ten-game personal losing streak. Teammate Rick Cerone said, "That kid has more guts than any pitcher I've seen." Despite a 10-18 record, Jerry was selected by Topps to its all-rookie team. He led the Blue Jays with 12 complete games and 127 strikeouts.

The scriptures say you shouldn't steal and Jerry did his part to enforce the rule. In 1977, he amazed everyone by picking off 22 would-be baserunners. In one game he picked off Reggie Jackson twice and he once picked off three runners in one inning--that's keeping them honest. In comparison, most pitchers are fortunate if they pick off three or four baserunners during a season.

During the 1978 season, Jerry was able to participate with Alan Ashby and Garth Iorg to help Luis Gomez and his wife learn about the Church. Jerry recalls Luis saying that he had prayed when he left the Twins that he would find a team that would be best

Jerry led the Toronto Blue Jays in strikeouts and complete games in 1977. He was selected to the Topps Rookie All-Star team.

for his family. It was a thrill for Jerry to see Luis join the Church. Jerry also had the unique situation of having a fellow Mormon for an on-the-road roommate for his entire six years in the Majors.

Jerry hurt his elbow early in the 1979 season and wondered if he would ever pitch again. When he came back, it was as a short relief pitcher late in the year. He led the team with 61 appearances and a 2.28 ERA in 1980. Jerry said, "As a starter I never liked relief pitchers." Now he was one and was enjoying the game even more since he was part of so many games. He expressed his gratitude that he was able to pitch effectively again. In 1981, he pitched in 35 games with a respectable 3.40 ERA, but 1982 was a very long year with a 7.25 ERA in 32 appearances. It was his last season.

Jerry went into the construction field. He is currently developing residential subdivisions with his brother-in-law. He has served as Elders Quorum President and taught YM and Sunday School classes. He enjoys fishing for lake bass as well as open sea fishing.

His advice to would-be Major League players is "Really want to play and realize there will be obstacles that will test your determination. Stay in tip-top shape and learn to handle the mental pressure of the game, like bases loaded and none out. Keep your nose clean and be ready to take advantage of any breaks that come to you." Jerry said that the Church was a definite stabilizing factor during the ups and downs of his baseball career.

LUIS GOMEZ YEAR-BY-YEAR STATISTICS

Name: Jose Luis Gomez

Born: August 19, 1951
Guadalajara, Mexico

Hgt: 5′ 9″ Wgt: 150

Bats: Right Throws: Right

Home: Lawrenceville, GA

Minor League: 1973-74, 1976-77

Year	Club	L	POS	G	AB	R	H	2	3	HR	RBI	SB	AVG
1974	Minnesota	AL	S,2	82	168	18	35	1	0	0	3	2	.208
1975	Minnesota	AL	S,2	89	72	7	10	0	0	0	5	0	.139
1976	Minnesota	AL	S,2	38	57	5	11	1	0	0	3	1	.193
1977	Minnesota	AL	2,S	32	65	6	16	4	2	0	11	0	.246
1978	Toronto	AL	S	153	413	39	92	7	3	0	32	2	.223
1979	Toronto	AL	3,2	59	163	11	39	7	0	0	11	1	.239
1980	Atlanta	NL	S	121	278	18	53	6	0	0	24	0	.191
1981	Atlanta	NL	S,3	35	35	4	7	0	0	0	1	0	.200
	Lifetime			609	1251	108	263	26	5	0	90	6	.210

LUIS GOMEZ

*L*uis moved from Mexico to the United States in 1959--one year after the Dodgers moved from Brooklyn to Los Angeles. Luis lived within three blocks of Chavez Ravine where the stadium was, so you are right if you guessed that the Dodgers were his favorite team.

Most people thought Luis had lost his marbles when he announced as a 5′ 4,″ 120-pound sophomore that he was going to try out for the high school football team. In his junior year, he not only became the starting quarterback but he was named to the all league team. As a senior, he led the entire city of Los Angeles with over 2,800 yards of total offense. He was selected as his league's Player of the Year and his football jersey was retired. Luis also performed pretty well in baseball, hitting .559 his senior year and fielding superbly at shortstop.

Luis decided he wasn't big enough to play football at UCLA where he enrolled, so at 5′ 9″ he decided to try out for basketball! He almost made the team but on the last round he was cut by the legendary coach, John Wooden. He did make the baseball team at shortstop. His junior year he hit .301 and was drafted by the Minnesota Twins in the seventh round in June 1973.

Luis reached the Majors faster than practically anyone. He played at Orlando for 76 games in 1973. The next year after only twelve games at Tacoma, the Twins called him up, and he played 82 games at shortstop and second base. Luis became saddled with a "slick fielder, poor hitter" label that limited his role in 1975 and 1976 to being a late inning substitute for defensive purposes. Luis stated that getting to the Majors so quickly may have been a disadvantage since he didn't have a chance to prove that he could be a good hitter.

In 1977, Luis decided he would become a free agent after the season unless the Twins would play him regularly. Instead the Twins sent him to Tacoma where he batted .285 in 214 at bats. Upon his return to the Twins, he hit four doubles and two triples in his first twelve games compared to only two doubles in his previous three years. Luis said that his improved hitting was directly related to his playing more often.

After the 1977 season, Luis was granted his free agency and signed with the Toronto Blue Jays on November 11, 1977. He was the regular shortstop in 1978, playing in 153 games, second-most among American League shortstops and exceeding his total at bats with the Twins in the four previous seasons. With the extra playing time, Luis placed third in the AL for the number of sacrifice hits with 19, attesting to his bunting ability, speed, and team play.

When he knew he was leaving the Twins, Luis had prayed that he might go to a team that would be good for his family. During his first season at Toronto, he learned about

Luis joined the Church in December 1978 through the efforts of Toronto Blue Jay teammates Alan Ashby, Jerry Garvin, and Garth Iorg. Later, he was a teammate of Dale Murphy at Atlanta.

the Church from Blue Jay teammates, Garth Iorg, Alan Ashby, and Jerry Garvin. Luis said in jest, "They ganged up on me." On an airplane trip, Luis looked over the seat and asked Garth what he was reading and Garth said, "I'm reading about your people." He gave Luis a copy of *The Book of Mormon,* and Luis asked his Mormon teammates countless questions. Luis said, "The Lord had prepared my heart." He wanted to join the Church but his wife was against it so he decided to exercise his faith through prayer. Later his wife received a blessing when she was ill and softened her feelings toward the Church. He was baptized in December 1978, and Alan Ashby ordained him to the Aaronic Priesthood. Luis baptized his wife several weeks later. Speaking individually with Luis, Alan, Garth, and Jerry twelve years later, you can still sense the special memories they each have about this missionary experience.

After the 1979 season, Luis was traded to the Atlanta Braves in exchange for Barry Bonnell who is also a Church member. Luis considers the trade to have been an important event in his life. He said, "The Lord had a hand in my going to the Braves." He explained, "During the two years I was with the Braves, Dale (Murphy) helped me to become much stronger in the gospel." Luis and Dale attended the same ward. He said that Dale lived the gospel so well that he was spiritually fed by being around him.

He began the 1980 season as the regular shortstop. He was described as "a lifesaver for Atlanta pitching" because of his great fielding. He went 42 games without an error but lost his starting job to Rafael Ramirez in August and played sparingly in 1981. He was released by the Braves on March 29, 1982, practically the last day of spring training. Luis said, "It hurt, especially the way I was released and so late." The Texas Rangers offered him a Triple-A contract, but he turned it down--a decision that he regrets.

Since 1982, Luis has been a substitute teacher, fitness instructor, Atlanta Braves bullpen catcher in 1984 and 1985, and scout for the San Francisco Giants. He has worked on his undergraduate degree and still plans to get his degree. Luis played in the 1990 Senior League, hitting .293, and he was hitting .340 in 1991 when the league folded. He enjoys reading Church books and has served as a Sunday School teacher and stake missionary.

JIM GOTT YEAR-BY-YEAR STATISTICS

Name: James William Gott

Born: August 3, 1959
Hollywood, CA

Hgt: 6′ 3″ Wgt: 215

Bats: Right Throws: Right

Home: Los Angeles, CA

Minor League: 1977-1981

Year	Club	L	POS	G	IP	W	L	SO	BB	H	ERA	SV	SHO
1982	Toronto	AL	P	30	136	5	10	82	66	134	4.43	0	1
1983	Toronto	AL	P	34	177	9	14	121	68	195	4.74	0	1
1984	Toronto	AL	P	35	110	7	6	73	49	93	4.02	2	1
1985	San Francisco	NL	P	26	148	7	10	78	51	144	3.88	0	0
1986	San Francisco	NL	P	9	13	0	0	9	13	16	7.62	1	0
1987	SF-Pittsburgh	NL	P	55	87	1	2	90	40	81	3.41	13	0
1988	Pittsburgh	NL	P	67	77	6	6	76	22	68	3.49	34	0
1989	Pittsburgh	NL	P	1	1	0	0	1	1	1	0.00	0	0
1990	Los Angeles	NL	P	50	62	3	5	44	34	59	2.90	3	0
	Lifetime			307	811	38	53	574	344	791	4.07	53	3

JIM GOTT

*F*rom the time he was ten years old, Jim Gott's favorite number was "8," and he wore it every chance he had. Why? Because it was Carl Yastremski's number. Carl was Jim's idol and the Boston Red Sox was his favorite team. Jim's dad had played minor league ball in the White Sox organization, and he encouraged Jim in sports, especially baseball. In his senior year in high school, Jim was the division player of the year, hitting around .480. His pitching record was 9-0. He had a 95 mph fastball!

Before his junior year, some people said that Jim didn't have enough guts to play football. How wrong they were. He made all-conference two years as defensive end and middle linebacker. They probably didn't know that Jim had been active in karate since eighth grade. His brother Erich was on golf scholarship at Brigham Young University, so Jim looked into BYU and liked what he saw. Even though he was not a member of the Church, he was ready to attend when he learned he had been drafted by the St. Louis Cardinals. Instead, he signed with the Cardinals.

As a seventeen-year old pitcher with Calgary in 1977, Jim was wild. He struck out 60 batters in 60 innings, but he walked 83 and his ERA was over 9. His lifestyle was also on the wild side: partying and pitching, sometimes in that order. His 1978 season was an improvement, but he was still restless. During the off season, he lived with Erich who was still at BYU. Erich had joined the Church. Soon Jim was taking the missionary lessons. He was baptized on January 19, 1979.

In 1979 at Gastonia, Jim stuck out 102 batters in only 79 innings, but he also gave up more than a walk per inning. Discouraged, he almost gave up baseball but decided to give it one more try by playing winter ball. It worked. He was selected by the Toronto Blue Jays in December 1981 and made the team. Jim said, "My second start was against the Boston Red Sox and the third batter was Yaz." What do you do when you pitch to your hero? Jim struck Yaz out on a 2-2 curveball. He notched his first Major League victory on May 30, 1982 and hurled his first shutout on July 31. In 1983, he was second on the club in strikeouts with 121, and he had a career high nine victories. In 1984, he had a string of 21 consecutive scoreless innings, the best on the team.

In 1985, he was traded to the San Francisco Giants. On May 12, Jim surprised everyone except himself by hitting two home runs in the same game. Jim said, "In high school I regularly hit home runs." During the 1986 season, Jim learned that his good friend, Kelly Downs, was being called up to the Giants. He called Kelly and told him before the official call came. However 1986 was a tough year. Jim suffered tendinitis and then a career-threatening rotator cuff injury. He worked hard to recover and felt good, but the Giants thought otherwise, using him infrequently in 1987.

The Giants traded Jim to the lowly Pittsburgh Pirates on July 31, 1987. Jim quickly became their "stopper." He saved 13 games and was an inspirational factor for the

On September 22, 1988, Jim Gott etched his name into Pittsburgh Pirate history by setting a new save record. He finished the year with 34 saves, 6 victories, and 76 strikeouts in 77 innings.

Pirates, challenging his teammates to win 25 of their last 35 games. They won 27. Jim explained his turnaround. "The recovery from my injury made me realize how fortunate I am to be a Major League player. I developed a real desire to win, to go all out."

In 1988, Jim continued to be a major factor in the resurgence of the Pirates. He was credited with 34 saves, a Pirate record, and six victories while appearing in a career high 67 games. He fanned 76 batters in 77 innings. During the season, he arranged for a sponsor to donate $200 per save to the St. Francis Drug and Alcohol Rehabilitation Center to help people who could not afford treatment. Jim said, "I've learned that service to other people is the most important part of life." He credits Dale Murphy as setting an example of service that he wants to follow.

Jim was highlighted in George Will's book, *Men at Work*, as an intense relief pitcher. Unfortunately for Jim, he only worked one inning in 1989 because of an elbow injury that required surgery on May 12. He used his recovery time to become a certified trainer at St. Francis. He signed with the Los Angeles Dodgers for the 1990 season. He wasn't ready to pitch until after the All-Star break. When he did get into the lineup, he was really rusty. He said, "The batters really handed me my lunch." Despite several rocky relief appearances, Jim kept at it. Pitching as the setup man instead of his usual closer role, he regained his form, ending the season with an enviable 2.90 ERA and appearing in 50 games. He began the 1991 in strong style, helping the Dodgers gain first place in the NL West. He pitched two scoreless innings on the nationally televised game of the week against the Cincinnati Reds on May 25 to pick up a save.

Jim has owned a Championship Martial Arts center. He has a black belt in hapkido and enjoys opera. He has taught a Primary class.

DOUG HANSEN YEAR-BY-YEAR STATISTICS

Name: Douglas William Hansen

Born: December 16, 1928
Los Angeles, CA

Hgt: 6′ Wgt: 175

Bats: Right Throws: Right

Home: Orem, UT

Minor League: 1947-50; 1953-54; 1956

Year	Club	L	POS	G	AB	R	H	2	3	HR	RBI	SB	AVG
1951	Cleveland	AL	2	3	0	2	0	0	0	0	0	0	.000
	Lifetime			3	0	2	0	0	0	0	0	0	.000

DOUG HANSEN

Doug's family moved to Los Angeles from Utah only a few years before he was born. He attended the same elementary school, junior high school, and high school as Bobby Doerr, one of baseball's best second basemen. Doug played basketball in high school as something to do for the three months of the year that he wasn't consumed playing baseball. When he was thirteen, he decided that he would become a Major League baseball second baseman. In 1946, he helped his high school team win the Los Angeles city baseball championship. He finished high school in January 1947 and signed with the Los Angeles Angels, which was then part of the Chicago Cubs.

He had a good first year, batting .275 in 334 at bats. He possessed good speed as evidenced by scoring 125 runs and hitting 10 triples to go with a .280 average in 1948 at El Paso. Doug said, "Base stealing wasn't emphasized, but I was clocked circling all the bases in 13.6 seconds and the record was only 13.3 seconds." After the 1948 season, the Cubs left him unprotected, and the Cleveland Indians signed him. That was great with Doug because he had always liked the Indians.

In 1949, he played at Harrisburg and led second basemen with 124 double plays. He further developed in 1950 at Wilkes-Barre as he hit 17 homers: second in the league among right handers. He helped his team win the league pennant by leading the team with 84 RBIs and leading the Eastern League in fielding double plays. He was selected to the all-star team. His manager, Bill Norman, said of Doug, "You don't see many like him nowadays. He lives to play ball . . . There's no choke. No quit. He came to play ball and played it to the hilt. He talks baseball all the time."

Before the 1951 season started, Doug was drafted into the Army and his father died. Doug received an emergency hardship discharge to support his mother and two brothers. He reported back to the Indians and they placed him on their Major League roster. He appeared in three games during the first week, all as a pinch-runner, and scored twice. He learned that his mother was seriously ill and received permission to return home. While there, his brother, Howard, was hurt in a car accident while traveling to play football in a Canadian league. One of Howard's children died in the crash and two other children were injured. Howard's wife had died a couple years earlier. Doug said, "I forgot all about the Indians" as he hurried to help his brother's family. The Indians decided Doug was really still in the Army and had been on a week's leave.

Howard recovered to star in the Canadian league and the Army redrafted Doug since his brother could support his mother. In April 1952, tragedy struck again as Howard fell to his death in the Wasatch mountains near Provo. Doug and his brother had been very close and nearly 40 years later, Doug stated that Howard's death "took something out of him." Despite his grief, Doug shared his feelings of hope and faith in a 1953 newspaper article. Doug said, "My brother is just as much alive now as he was before. I believe that life is eternal."

Ron was in the Army during most of 1951 and all of 1952. Here he is taking batting practice on a grenade. One of his managers said of Doug, "He lives to play baseball."

He spent the entire 1952 season in the Army and got his whereabouts straightened out with the Indians. He attended spring training in 1953 and performed well. Reporter Hal Lebovitz wrote, "Without doubt, the most conscientious, hardest working player at Indiansville is Hansen." Doug hit a grand-slam homer in an intra-squad game and started 28 of the 35 exhibition games at second base. Lebovitz wrote, "Hansen, in ability is a Major League fielder right now . . . his get away on the double play can match the Major's best in speed and accuracy. The Californian doesn't allow a moment of practice time to be wasted." He made the team and travelled from spring training in Arizona to Cleveland playing in games along the way. In Denver, six inches of snow had fallen but they shoveled it off and put down sawdust and straw because the game had been sold out. He said, "It's the only time I saw a ground rule double because the ball was hit into a snow bank in centerfield." Doug avoided that problem by hitting a home run.

The regular second baseman, Bobby Avila, an American League batting champion, had recovered from an injury so the Indians sent Doug to Indianapolis soon after the season started so he could be an everyday player. In 1954, he hit five homers in one week and won three games in the ninth inning, but the season wasn't very satisfying so he retired. In 1956, he attempted a comeback and played at San Diego where Bob Usher was a teammate. Soon after the season began, he was reassigned to Richmond in the International League. He decided to retire for good instead of reporting.

Despite a shortened career because of Army service and family tragedy, Doug has no regrets or bitterness. He said that it was simply super to be on the same field with Ted Williams, Joe DiMaggio, and Bobby Doerr. He recalled proudly that he associated with five future Hall of Famers with the Indians: Early Wynn, Bob Feller, Bob Lemon, Al Lopez, and Red Ruffing. Doug didn't smoke or drink at a time when both were expected. He remembers being occasionally coaxed by veteran players to "live it up while you can." Attempts were made to spike his beverage, but he stood his ground and felt respected for it.

He attended Brigham Young University for three years and worked for eighteen years for U. S. Steel and Kaiser Steel as a supervisor and middle manager. He enjoys fishing, hunting, and golfing. He has served as a high priest group leader and stake mission president.

DOUG HOWARD YEAR-BY-YEAR STATISTICS

Name: Douglas Lyn Howard

Born: February 6, 1948
Salt Lake City, UT

Hgt: 6′ 3″ Wgt: 185

Bats: Right Throws: Right

Home: Sandy, UT

Minor League: 1970-1976

Year	Club	L	POS	G	AB	R	H	2	3	HR	RBI	SB	AVG
1972	California	AL	O,3	11	38	4	10	1	0	0	2	0	.263
1973	California	AL	O,3	8	21	2	2	0	0	0	1	0	.095
1974	California	AL	O,1	22	39	5	9	0	1	0	5	1	.231
1975	St. Louis	NL	1	17	29	1	6	0	0	1	1	0	.207
1976	Cleveland	AL	1,O	39	90	7	19	4	0	0	13	1	.211
	Lifetime			97	217	19	46	5	1	1	22	2	.212

DOUG HOWARD

*Y*oung Doug Howard was a Pittsburgh Pirates fan since the Pirates had a minor league team in Salt Lake City. He was particularly excited when the Pirates went to the World Series in 1960. His favorite player was Roberto Clemente. Doug used to spread his baseball cards in front of the television while watching the Game-of-the-Week. He always envisioned himself as a Major League player. He spent endless hours with friends playing "home run derby" with a broom and a golf ball.

Doug led his high school basketball team to the state championship his junior and senior year. *Scholastic* magazine named Doug to their All-American basketball team. He also helped his baseball team win the state title his senior year. He received a scholarship from Brigham Young University to play both sports and he excelled in both. As a 6′ 3″ guard, he led the BYU basketball team in scoring with 15.7 and 18.9 point averages his junior and senior year. He was drafted by the Chicago Bulls basketball team in 1970. Doug was having even better success on the baseball diamond. As a sophomore, he helped BYU go to the College World Series. BYU was beaten 3-1 by Burt Hooton of Texas. Seven years later, Doug would hit his only Major League home run off Hooton. In 1969, he batted .396, earning NCAA All-American selection and in 1970 he batted .427 and achieved first-team All-American honors.

The California Angels were impressed with Doug's play in the NCAA World Series and he signed with them. He batted .294 at Quad Cities in 1970 and .271 at Shreveport in 1971. In 1972, he was assigned to the Triple-A level and played at home in Salt Lake City. This meant some extra pressure since friends would be at every home game as would his father, a former minor league player. Doug said in a 1972 interview, "My dad attends each game and I can hear him all the time. If I make a mistake at bat, I can hear him yell at me to wait for my pitch." Doug responded with a great year, batting .301, hitting 24 homers, and driving in 109 runs. The Angels rewarded his performance by bringing him up at the end of the year. His first hit was off future Hall-of-Famer, Gaylord Perry.

He spent most of the 1973 and 1974 seasons at Salt Lake batting .297 and .271. He got short call ups to the Angels both years, getting in eight games and 22 games, respectively. One spring training game against the Oakland A's, the pitchers used a bright optic yellow baseball as an experiment of A's owner, Chuck Finley. Doug liked the experiment a lot since he went 3-for-4, the best of anyone on either team. The Angels were well-stocked with first basemen so he was traded on July 31, 1974 to the St. Louis Cardinals. He played with Tacoma and the Cardinals in 1975.

The Cardinals traded Doug to the Cleveland Indians in September 1975. He played first base and the outfield on the Indians with fellow Mormon, Alan Ashby, who caught for the Indians. When regular first baseman, Boog Powell was injured in 1976, Doug thought he would finally get his chance to be a regular player. Instead, player-manager,

Doug was a baseball All-American at BYU in 1970. He was also drafted by the NBA Chicago Bulls. In 1972, he batted .301, hit 24 homers, and drove in 109 runs in Triple A ball. He played for the Angels, Cardinals, and Indians.

Frank Robinson, penciled himself into the lineup on most occasions. Doug really felt betrayed when the Indians sent him back to the minors. He and Ashby were traded to the Toronto Blue Jays in November 1976. He went to spring training but did not make the team and retired from baseball.

While only seeing limited Major League playing time during five seasons, Doug is proud that he was able to hit against some of the best pitchers in baseball. He remembers well the excitement of witnessing no-hitters by teammate Nolan Ryan.

Initially Doug sold real estate in the San Francisco area. Later he used his college degree to become a high school science teacher and coach for high school baseball and basketball teams. His high school baseball teams have won over 150 games and played in the state championships several years. He still plays baseball in the Roy Hobbs league. He has served in a high council and as an Aaronic Priesthood teacher. His advice to young professional ballplayers is to chose good friends who share your positive values.

KEN HUBBS YEAR-BY-YEAR STATISTICS

Name: Kenneth Douglass Hubbs

Born: December 23, 1941
Riverside, CA

Hgt: 6′ 2″ Wgt: 180

Bats: Right Throws: Right

Died: February 15, 1964

Minor League: 1959-1961

Year	Club	L	POS	G	AB	R	H	2	3	HR	RBI	SB	AVG
1961	Chicago	NL	2	10	28	4	5	1	1	1	2	0	.179
1962	Chicago	NL	2	160	661	90	172	24	9	5	49	3	.260
1963	Chicago	NL	2	154	566	54	133	19	3	8	47	8	.235
	Lifetime			324	1255	148	310	44	13	14	98	11	.247

KEN HUBBS

In 1959, the *Los Angeles Examiner* awarded Ken a trophy for the "Best All-Around athlete in Southern California." It was an easy choice. In Little League, Ken's team played in the 1954 World Series in Williamsport. He was the winning pitcher in one game and hit a homer in another. He once had seventeen consecutive hits in Little League and four homers in one game. Ken was also a high school standout in football, basketball, and track. *The Sporting News* selected him to their All-American team as quarterback. He was an All-American pick in basketball and was recruited by John Wooden at UCLA. He competed in track but only in the conference championship where he won the high jump. He thought seriously about pursuing a basketball career; instead, he signed a bonus contract with the Chicago Cubs. By the way, Ken was president of his 2,100-student high school and regularly wrote a column that was carried by several newspapers.

As a seventeen-year old, Ken played his first year of pro ball, hitting .298 with 50 RBIs in 56 games. It was his fielding, however, that was especially noteworthy winning comparisons to Brooks Robinson. In 1960, his hitting faltered to .216, pointing out his need to learn how to hit good curveballs. He also had to learn a new position. In 1961, the Cubs moved him from shortstop to second base because at his height he would be strong enough to complete double plays despite runners trying to disrupt the second baseman's throw. He worked hard at his new position to the point that both elbows and knees were raw. He had a good season at the plate hitting .286. Although he was only playing Class B ball, the Cubs called him up to the Majors for the last ten games of the 1961 season. One of his five hits was a "never will forget" home run.

Ken's 1962 rookie season was unbelievable. No Church member would have as electrifying a first year until Wally Joyner's 1986 season. Ken hit .350 in spring training and won the starting role at second base. He played well through the year having two, five-hit games. It was in the field, however, where Ken made news--national news. He went errorless at second base from June 13 until September 5, taking 418 chances before making a throwing error. He played 74 games without a mistake, a Major League record for second basemen. The entire baseball world knew who twenty-year old Ken Hubbs was. One of the sports writers of the time wrote of Ken, "What makes the glue-gloved Hubbs click? They say he possesses the effervescence of an Evers, the competitive spirit of a Collins, the grace of a Gehringer, the daring of a Doerr, and the swift, strong hands of a Schoendienst." Ken easily won the Rookie of the Year award and a Gold Glove for his heroics. The Cubs gave him a new contract worth $12,000 a year.

He went to college in the off-season and treated himself to a new car. He handled his notoriety with his usual modesty. Ken said at the time, "All the big glory of the thing is over. Now I really have to knuckle down." The newspapers noted his Church membership and quoted his observance of the Word of Wisdom and that he regularly

On September 2, 1962, Ken Hubbs set a Major League record by going errorless in 74 consecutive game at second base, covering 418 chances. He was an easy pick for NL Rookie of the Year and Gold Glove second baseman.

attended Church services while on the road. He got teammate Ron Santo to give up smoking. Ernie Banks recounted at the time, "Lots of young players do something special and you can't talk to them anymore. Not Ken. One day, he got seven hits in a doubleheader. Pretty good for a rookie. But he didn't talk or act any differently than at times when he didn't get a hit."

The 1963 season must have seemed anti-climactic. His average dropped to .235. He played a steady second base but set no records. Ken's nickname was "Nutsy" according to one newspaper account because "he was young and his jokes were corny and maybe because he was a Mormon boy who preferred chocolate malts and donuts to beer and pretzels.

During flights on the Cubs chartered airplane, Ken became interested in flying, and he would often sit with the pilot. After the 1963 season, he purchased a Cesna 712 and began flying lessons. With 71 hours logged, he and a friend flew to Provo. He never returned. On February 13, 1964, his plane was caught in a downdraft during a snowstorm, and Ken was killed as it crashed into Utah Lake.

Jim Murray of the *Los Angeles Times* wrote, "Kenneth Douglas Hubbs was more than just another baseball player. He was the kind of athlete all games need. A devout Mormon, a cheerful leader, a picture book player, blond-haired, healthy, generous with his time for young boys; he was the kind of youth in short supply in these selfish times."

Reporter Bob Smith wrote, "Ken Hubbs was a fine, decent young man who hustled his way into a man's world because, more than anything, he wanted to be a big league baseball player. Tragedy is too small, too meaningless a word for Ken Hubbs. It doesn't explain that sick, burning lump in the hearts of people who knew him. There are no words for that."

A community leader said, "Ken was the kind of boy you would be proud to have as your own . . . the kind you would like your son to grow to be."

On May 4, 1964, the Dodgers-Cubs game at Dodger stadium was dedicated to the memory of Ken. His family was recognized at pre-game ceremonies behind second base.

KEN HUNT YEAR-BY-YEAR STATISTICS

Name: Kenneth Raymond Hunt

Born: December 14, 1938
Ogden, UT

Hgt: 6′ 4″ Wgt: 200

Bats: Right Throws: Right

Home: Morgan, UT

Minor League: 1958-60, 1962-63

Year	Club	L	POS	G	IP	W	L	SO	BB	H	ERA	SV	SHO
1961	Cincinnati	NL	P	29	136	9	10	75	66	130	3.96	0	0
	Lifetime			29	136	9	10	75	66	130	3.96	0	0

KEN HUNT

In 1953, future Hall of Famer, Frank Robinson, was toiling in the minor league in Ogden, Utah. Watching him play was fourteen-year old Ken Hunt. Robinson was Ken's favorite Major League player, and the Cincinnati Reds were his favorite team. Eight years later, Ken Hunt and Frank Robinson would be teammates on the Reds, playing in the 1961 World Series.

Ken lettered in four sports in high school. He played defensive tackle and offensive guard in football, competed in the high jump in track, won all-state honors as a forward in basketball, and excelled even more in baseball. As a high school pitcher, he lost only two games in three years. He pitched two no-hit, no-run games, striking out 21 batters in one game. Ken decided to attend Brigham Young University on a basketball scholarship and averaged eighteen points a game on the freshman team. He pitched two shutouts for the freshman baseball team against the BYU varsity team.

After a year at BYU, Ken signed a contract in June 1958 with the Cincinnati Reds. He played with Visalia, a class C team, in the California League during the 1958 and 1959 seasons. His combined record was 6-19. In 1959, he brought his ERA down from 9.00 to 6.66. He struck out 160 batters in only 150 innings in 1959, but he walked even more, 185. The Reds still believed in Ken and promoted him to Columbia, a class A team.

The Columbia manager, Max Macon, had pitched for six years in the National League. He worked with Ken extensively to help him control his fastball and develop consistency with his curveball. He had an all-star year in 1960, going 16-6, and striking out 221 batters in 211 innings. He had a 2.86 ERA. He walked 134 batters, still high, but acceptable. Ken was selected as the league's Most Valuable Player. A teammate that year was Pete Rose.

Ken was invited to join the Major League team for spring training. No one expected him to jump from the lowly class A level all the way to the Reds' 1961 Opening Day roster but that is exactly what he did. He was described as "the rookie sensation of spring camp." It would be a season of greatness and a season of despair. *The Sporting News* named Ken to its Rookie of the Year team. It was also his only year in the Major Leagues.

His first Major League game was as a relief pitcher on April 17. With two St. Louis Cardinals on base and none out, Ken retired the side without a run. As the starting pitcher on April 19, he won his first game in a 4-2 victory over Willie Mays and the Giants. On May 14, he beat the World Champion Pittsburgh Pirates 4-1, and he hit a double, driving in a run. The victory boosted his record to 3-1. By the All-Star break, Ken was 9-4 and was the leading candidate for Rookie of the Year honors. Unfortunately, he never won another game.

Ken had a 9-4 record and was the leading contender for NL Rookie of the Year in 1961 when he developed a finger blister that ruined his season. He pitched against the New York Yankees in the 1961 World Series.

Ken had developed a calloused tip on the middle finger of his pitching hand. He let it go too far and a blister formed underneath. He said, "The first time it popped, I was pitching against the Chicago Cubs in late July. The fingertip was raw, bleeding, and painful. Favoring the finger, I couldn't control my pitches." He also developed a sore shoulder. He ended the season with a disappointing 9-10 record. He pitched one inning against the New York Yankees in the World Series. He faced Elston Howard, Tony Kubek, and Roger Maris without a ball getting out of the infield. It gave him hope that he could still be a dominating pitcher.

He failed to make the Reds in 1962. His finger finally healed, but he could not regain his form. After the 1963 season in the minors, Ken decided to retire. Despite the obvious disappointment, he is glad he had the moments of success he enjoyed.

Ken returned to college and earned a teaching degree at Weber State. He teaches high school English. He enjoys fishing and is a high priest in his ward.

BRUCE HURST YEAR-BY-YEAR STATISTICS

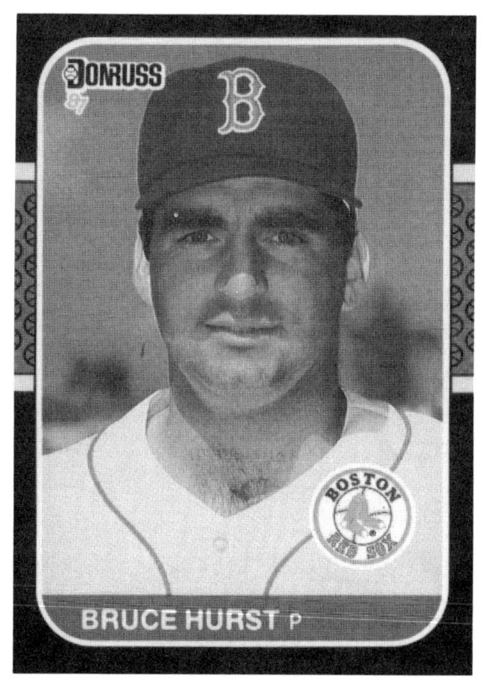

Name: Bruce Vee Hurst

Born: March 24, 1958
St. George, UT

Hgt: 6′ 3″ Wgt: 190

Bats: Left Throws: Left

Home: St. George, UT

Minor League: 1976-1981

Year	Club	L	POS	G	IP	W	L	SO	BB	H	ERA	SV	SHO
1980	Boston	AL	P	12	31	2	2	16	16	39	9.00	0	0
1981	Boston	AL	P	5	23	2	0	11	12	23	4.30	0	0
1982	Boston	AL	P	28	117	3	7	53	40	161	5.77	0	0
1983	Boston	AL	P	33	211	12	12	115	62	241	4.09	0	2
1984	Boston	AL	P	33	218	12	12	136	88	232	3.92	0	2
1985	Boston	AL	P	35	230	11	13	189	70	243	4.51	0	1
1986	Boston	AL	P	25	174	13	8	167	50	169	2.99	0	4
1987	Boston	AL	P	33	239	15	13	190	76	239	4.41	0	3
1988	Boston	AL	P	33	217	18	6	166	65	222	3.66	0	1
1989	San Diego	NL	P	33	245	15	11	179	66	214	2.69	0	2
1990	San Diego	NL	P	33	224	11	9	162	63	188	3.14	0	4
	Lifetime			303	1928	114	93	1384	608	1971	3.91	0	19

BRUCE HURST

During the past several years, Bruce has been one of the best left-handed pitchers in the Major Leagues. It was something he worked hard to obtain, having suffered through injuries, poor performances, homesickness, and despair on his way to the top. Even after he had played in the Majors, he experienced severe frustration and even retired from baseball for three days in 1981. While his journey wasn't easy, he achieved the star potential many had predicted for him.

Bruce spent the first eighteen years of his life almost entirely in St. George, Utah, usually only leaving to play baseball or basketball. As a youngster, he had two casts on his legs to correct the severe bow-leggedness he was born with. It worked and by the time he was nine, he was playing either baseball or basketball non-stop. He liked baseball a lot. He had 4,000 baseball cards--which he still has. His favorite players were Sandy Koufax and Don Drysdale. He liked basketball even more than baseball, and he dreamed of playing on the NBA's New York Knicks.

A turning point in Bruce's life occurred in 1971 when Kent Garrett moved to St. George. Kent recognized that Bruce had great potential. Garrett started an American Legion team in St. George to give Bruce more playing opportunity and the two of them worked out together nearly every day. Bruce had some wildness--he once walked thirteen hitters in a seven-inning game, but he kept improving. During his senior year in high school, he led his baseball team to the state playoffs and was selected to the all-state baseball team. At times, there were over twenty scouts watching him pitch. That same year, Bruce was selected to the all-state basketball team. He was planning to go to college when the Boston Red Sox made him their first choice in the June 1976 draft. He was the twenty-second person drafted in the entire nation, the highest ever for a Utah native. He talked to Church leaders about going on a mission. Afterwards, he felt he should give baseball a chance.

A week after high school graduation in St. George, Bruce was 2,000 miles away in Elmira, NY. It was a rude awakening. Bruce admits he was homesick and scared. Most of the players were two or three years older and most lived a very different lifestyle with smoking, drinking, and swearing. Accommodations were even worse than in high school: there were only three showers for 25 players and uniforms were washed only once a week. He played well, striking out 40 batters in 42 innings, but he also had control problems, walking 38. He had a good record in 1977, but his playing time was limited by elbow problems. His 1978 season was curtailed by a shoulder injury, and he played in only six games. In 1979 he was healthy and posted a 17-6 record and 2.88 ERA. In the off-season, he attended Dixie Junior College in St. George and played basketball, going to the Jr. College playoffs.

Bruce was invited to the Red Sox spring training in 1980 and made the team, becoming the first Red Sox player in three years to jump from a Double A team to the parent club. Unfortunately, he didn't stay with the Red Sox very long. His first game

Bruce won Game 1 and Game 4 of the 1986 World Series against the New York Mets. He became the first southpaw since Babe Ruth to win a World Series game at Fenway Park.

against the Milwaukee Brewers was a disaster. In one inning of relief, he gave up four hits and five runs. He won his first Major League game on April 26, but he was soon sent to Pawtucket, the Triple-A level club. There was some talk that Bruce was "too nice" and "too Mormon" to make it in the big leagues.

Despite walking as many as he fanned, he did well enough at Pawtucket, 8-6, to be called back to the Red Sox at the end of the year. There was no way he could have anticipated what was ahead. After not playing for two weeks, he came into a game with bases loaded and none out. He got the first batter to hit into a double play. So far, great. He then caught the runner at third base in a run down. Bruce was slightly out of position, but still thought he put the tag on the runner. The umpire called the runner safe. In the ensuing commotion, Bruce and his manager, Don Zimmer, got in a shouting match at each other. Zimmer chased Bruce off the field, yelling at him. It was humiliating and demoralizing.

After a rocky start to the 1981 season at Pawtucket with a 6.75 ERA, Bruce announced his retirement from baseball on May 2, and left the team which was playing in Charleston, West Virginia. Everyone in the Boston organization felt they had seen Bruce for the last time. So did Bruce, but after returning to Pawtucket he had a chance to talk to relatives and Kent Garrett. Bruce also called Elder Paul Dunn and shared his feelings with the general authority who could understand what Bruce was describing. Elder Dunn encouraged Bruce to give baseball three more years. Bruce reported in an interview at the time, "I love baseball. It's a hard life sometimes. I just want to bear down and make it to the big leagues." The Red Sox accepted Bruce back and he performed well, finishing with a 12-7 mark and a 2.87 ERA at Pawtucket. He finished the year with the Red Sox and won two games without a loss.

He started with the Red Sox in 1982 and initially pitched well; however, he failed to win a game after July 10, and was relegated to the bullpen in August. His arm was hurting but he didn't tell his coaches or manager. After the season, it was discovered that Bruce needed elbow surgery to remove three cartilage chips. In 1983, he was the team's number two starter and posted a 12-12 record. He could have won more games but on seven occasions he held the other team to three or less runs without earning a win. Opposition baserunners learned to respect Bruce's pickoff ability as he nailed nine would-be base stealers.

Bruce was the Opening Day pitcher in 1984 and pitched nine scoreless innings although he didn't win the game. On May 6, he had a no-hitter going into the eighth inning, when fellow Church member, Vance Law, ruined it with a home run. Bruce finished the year with a 12-12 record. His twelve victories tied for most on the team. The 1985 season began miserably. He had a 2-7 record and was being booed regularly. Finally, he recognized some mistakes and made the right adjustments. He won nine of his last 15 decisions and finished the season with 189 strikeouts, the most ever by a left-handed Red Sox pitcher.

In his second game in the National League, Bruce pitched a one-hitter. His manager said, "His forkball has guys talking to themselves and his curve freezes them."

The 1986 season was the year the baseball world learned that Bruce had arrived. On Opening Day he faced Church member, Jack Morris, in a pitcher's duel that ended in a no-decision for Bruce. On May 16, he struck out fourteen Texas Rangers. By the end of May, he was leading the American League in strikeouts. Then injury struck again. He was out for nearly seven weeks with a groin injury. During the last two months of the season, he led the Red Sox to the AL pennant and nearly to a World Series championship. He was the AL Pitcher of the Month for September. He was 5-0, struck out 41 batters in 42 innings, walked only six, and posted a 1.07 ERA. He finished the year with a 2.99 ERA, fourth-best in the AL. He won a playoff game against the California Angels. Bruce started the first game of the World Series against the New York Mets and got the win in an exciting 1-0 victory. He became the first left-handed pitcher since Babe Ruth to win a World Series game at Fenway Park. In the fifth game, he pitched a complete game victory, winning 4-2. In a recent interview, Bruce said he considered this game to be the best-pitched game of his career. He received plenty of good media coverage. For example, Bob Costas, the NBC announcer, told the nation, "Bruce Hurst pitched more strikeouts per inning during the season than did Cy Young winner Roger Clemens." The Red Sox lost the sixth game and then the Series even though Bruce came back on little rest to pitch the seventh game.

In 1987, he set career highs with 15 wins, 15 complete games, 238 innings, and 190 strikeouts. He was Pitcher of the Week in June when he pitched back-to-back shutouts. He was selected to the All-Star team. In 1988 he had a great 18-6 record despite being hampered by a blood disorder. He was 5-0 in August earning AL Pitcher of the Month honors. The Red Sox won the AL East but lost to Oakland in the playoffs. Because of the short distance to the "green monster" wall in left field, southpaws generally do poorly at Fenway Park. Bruce made it his favorite pitching haven, going 33-8 at Fenway during 1986-1988. But he would see Fenway no more. On December 7, he signed a three-year contract to pitch for the San Diego Padres.

Bruce established himself in the National League quickly in 1989. In his second game, he threw a one-hitter. His manager, Jack McKeon, said, "His forkball has guys talking to themselves and his curve freezes them." His 2.69 ERA was the best of his career and fifth-best in the NL. The Padres had a disappointing year in 1990. They didn't have the strong relief pitching they had in 1989. Bruce had four shutouts, the most since 1986, but his 11 victories were his lowest total since 1985. He started the 1991 season in fine fashion with a 5-1 record through the first two months.

Bruce enjoys fishing, tennis, and golf. He recently was serving as a Sunday School teacher in Church. When asked what advice he would give to a player who had just signed a pro contract, Bruce replied, "Understand the odds. Only the top one percent make it, so give it your all. Use your talent and keep a good mental attitude."

DANE IORG YEAR-BY-YEAR STATISTICS

Name: Dane Charles Iorg

Born: May 11, 1950
Eureka, CA

Hgt: 6′ Wgt: 180

Bats: Left Throws: Right

Home: Pleasant Grove, UT

Minor League: 1971-1978

Year	Club	L	POS	G	AB	R	H	2	3	HR	RBI	SB	AVG
1977	Phila-St. Louis	NL	1,O	42	62	5	15	2	0	0	6	0	.242
1978	St. Louis	NL	O	35	85	6	23	4	1	0	4	0	.271
1979	St. Louis	NL	O,1	79	179	12	52	11	1	1	21	1	.291
1980	St. Louis	NL	O,1	105	251	33	76	23	1	3	36	1	.303
1981	St. Louis	NL	O,1	75	217	23	71	11	2	2	39	2	.327
1982	St. Louis	NL	O,1	102	238	17	70	14	1	0	34	0	.294
1983	St. Louis	NL	O,1	58	116	6	31	9	1	0	11	1	.267
1984	St. L-Kan City	AL	1,O	93	263	30	64	18	2	5	33	0	.243
1985	Kansas City	AL	DH	64	130	7	29	9	1	1	21	0	.223
1986	San Diego	NL	O,3	90	106	10	24	2	1	2	11	0	.226
	Lifetime			743	1647	149	455	103	11	14	216	5	.276

DANE IORG

*D*ane grew up with the San Francisco Giants and from the time he was nine, he listened to nearly every game. He said he collected a "ton of baseball cards" and his idol was Willie Mays. He lettered in baseball, basketball, and football in high school. He attended Brigham Young University and led his team to the NCAA baseball playoffs. He set a BYU record by hitting .467, and *The Sporting News* named Dane to their 1971 college All-America team.

He was the first selection of the Philadelphia Phillies in the secondary phase of the June 1971 draft. He hit over .300 in four of his first six minor league seasons and was selected to all-star teams in 1971 and 1974. In 1974 he made a transition from outfielder to first baseman while at Toledo. He had a tough time in 1975 and gave some thought to quitting. He rebounded at Oklahoma City the next year, hitting .326. He had an excellent spring training and made the Phillies' roster. You know he was disappointed when the Phillies sent him back down to Oklahoma City. On June 15, 1977, he was traded to the St. Louis Cardinals and assigned to their Triple-A team in New Orleans. He batted .330 and was called up at the end of the season and hit .313 with the Cardinals.

Dane had good reason to think that 1978 would be the year to show what he could do in the Majors. He batted .379 in spring training but found himself sitting on the bench behind Keith Hernandez who was the starting first baseman. As a pinch-hitter Dane was hitting .182 and the Cardinals decided to return him to the minors. Dane was really upset. He felt he had paid his dues and had proven he could hit Major League pitching if given a chance to play regularly. He said, "Most people have no idea how hard pinch-hitting is. I might face a guy one time--one pitch even--and if he gets me out, I can't go back in there a couple innings later." He thought about calling it quits (he had three children then) but as disappointed as he was, he knew he had Major League capability. Accepting the demotion to Springfield, he literally murdered the ball, batting .371 with 20 doubles, 24 homers, and 87 RBIs in just 89 games. He returned to the Cardinals in September 1978 and was in the Majors to stay.

Over the next eight years, Dane was never an everyday starter on a regular basis, but he contributed much to his team's success by platooning in the outfield, pinch-hitting, and filling in at first and third. He hit his first Major League homer on May 8, 1979. As a pinch-hitter he had eight RBIs, and he had four game-winning RBIs as a starter. On April 18, 1980, he smacked two home runs in one game, and he led the team that year with 10 hits coming off the bench. In 1981 he led the team with a .327 average.

From beginning to end, 1982 was a great year. On opening day he had two doubles and two RBIs. On April 24, he went 4-for-4 in a 7-4 win over the Phillies--how sweet it is to do well against a team you once played for. The Cardinals won the 1982 National League Championship and played the Milwaukee Brewers in the World Series.

Dane is one of only a handful of players to win World Series rings on two different clubs. He was 9 for 17 in the 1982 World Series and had the key hit in the 1985 Series.

Manager Whitey Herzog chose Dane to be the designated hitter. It was the type of choice that has made Whitey one of baseball's most successful managers, because Dane surpassed everyone's expectation. He had a World Series batting average of .529, going 9-for-17 including four doubles. Dane said, "The 1982 World Series was the highlight of my career because I responded well to the pressure and felt that I was a real part of the team." Little did he know that his most dramatic World Series hit was yet to come.

Dane commented in discussing his experience as a Church member in baseball, "Living the gospel was never a hindrance. Teammates expect you to live up to your standards. You can still be a hard-nosed, tough ball player without sacrificing gospel principles." He liked his teammates and he felt they respected him. He enjoyed playing teams with other Mormon ballplayers--talking at the ball park and sometimes getting together afterwards.

In 1983, Dane played in only 58 games. He said, "St. Louis is the best baseball town and Herzog is a great manager, but I wanted a change and wanted to play in the American League." Early in the 1984 season, he was traded to the Kansas City Royals. He especially enjoyed playing against the Toronto Blue Jays and his brother Garth. He collected 22 extra base hits in 78 games, helping the Royals win their division in 1984.

The Royals won their division again in 1985 and Dane was primed for post-season play. First he would be playing against his brother in the AL playoffs. The Royals won the playoffs and their World Series opponent was none other than the St. Louis Cardinals. Dane said, "My most memorable hit in the Majors was in the sixth game of the World Series." With the bases loaded in the bottom of the ninth and behind 1-0, the Royals could either tie the series three games apiece or they could lose it all. Coming to the plate to pinch-hit for relief pitcher Dan Quisenberry was Dane Iorg. In this pressure-packed situation, Dane drove a single to right field, scoring two runs and breaking the back of his former team. The Royals won the next game and Dane picked up his second World Series ring. That hit was Dane's last as a Royal.

Dane played his last season with the San Diego Padres in 1986. Two of the games that year were quite different from any of the others in his career--he was the pitcher! On June 23 when the Padres were losing to the San Francisco Giants 14-1, Dane took the mound for the first time in an official game. Dane said of the inning he pitched, "I proved I can throw strikes." Two of his strikes went over the fence. The first one was a three-run homer by the Giants pitcher, Mike LaCoss. The second one was a solo homer by Mike Woodard. In both cases it was their first home run ever in the Major Leagues. Two months later on August 30, the Padres were behind 10-0 after seven innings. This time Dane was prepared. He said, "I developed a split fingered fast ball just in case I got another chance." He pitched the eighth and ninth innings against the Montreal Expos and held them to one hit and no runs.

He retired from baseball and worked for a pharmaceutical company. He has served in a number of church callings over the years including high councilor in one of the BYU stakes and more recently as Bishop of his home ward.

GARTH IORG YEAR-BY-YEAR STATISTICS

Name: Garth Ray Iorg

Born: October 12, 1954
Arcata, CA

Hgt: 5′ 11″ Wgt: 175

Bats: Right Throws: Right

Home: Blue Lake, CA

Minor League: 1973-1980

Year	Club	L	POS	G	AB	R	H	2	3	HR	RBI	SB	AVG
1978	Toronto	AL	2	19	49	3	8	0	0	0	3	0	.163
1980	Toronto	AL	2,3	80	222	24	55	10	1	2	14	2	.248
1981	Toronto	AL	2,3	70	215	17	52	11	0	0	10	2	.242
1982	Toronto	AL	3,2	129	417	45	119	20	5	1	36	3	.285
1983	Toronto	AL	3,2	122	375	40	103	22	5	2	39	7	.275
1984	Toronto	AL	3,2	121	247	24	56	10	3	1	25	1	.227
1985	Toronto	AL	3	131	288	33	90	22	1	7	37	3	.313
1986	Toronto	AL	3	137	327	30	85	19	1	3	44	3	.260
1987	Toronto	AL	3	122	310	35	65	11	0	4	30	2	.210
	Lifetime			931	2450	251	633	125	16	20	238	23	.258

GARTH IORG

*F*rom wiffle ball in the backyard to a contract with the New York Yankees, nineteen-year old Garth Iorg achieved his dream. As a youngster, he played wiffle ball everyday with his brothers. This activity seems to have been a bonding factor among the brothers notwithstanding the many games that ended in a fight. Garth was the youngest and for self-preservation he would run for the safety of a locked bathroom.

Garth was all-league in football, basketball, and baseball. He played basketball at the College of Redwoods in California, but it was baseball that he loved. He was noticed in American Legion baseball and the Yankees drafted him in the eighth round of the 1973 draft. He was the third Iorg to sign a contract with a Major League team. His brother Dane had signed earlier with the Philadelphia Phillies, and his brother Lee was in the New York Mets organization.

Garth started slowly hitting .237 and .215 in 1973 and 1974. He batted .250 in 1975 and was promoted to the Double A level. He progressed steadily in 1976 batting .275. In November 1976, the newly formed Toronto Blue Jays selected him in the fourth round of the expansion draft. He batted .294 in 1977 and was promoted to Syracuse, the Triple A farm club for the 1978 season. In 1978, he hit for more power but his average fell to .216. Nevertheless, the Blue Jays called him up at the end of the season. He got up 49 times and made only eight hits. But it was off the field as a brand new rookie that Garth made his biggest hit as he befriended teammate Luis Gomez and gave him a copy of *The Book of Mormon*. Luis joined the church between the 1978 and 1979 seasons.

All of the 1979 season was spent at Syracuse where he batted .281. He was playing well at Syracuse in 1980, hitting .299 when he was called up to stay by the Blue Jays. He hit a double in his first at bat of the season on May 24. He played four infield positions and left field during his rookie season. On September 4, he hit a triple that beat the Chicago White Sox. At the end of the 1981 season, he became the regular second baseman. Garth had a strong year in 1982, playing in 100 games at third base. In a game against the Detroit Tigers early in the year, he hit a double and triple, driving in two runs and scoring three runs in a 9-5 win. In May, he had three singles in a 7-0 win over the Yankees. On June 19, he had a pinch-hit double that beat the Oakland A's. He finished the year with a ten-game hitting streak in September. His seven sacrifice flies tied a club record. He had career highs with 119 hits, 5 triples, and a .285 average.

In 1983, Garth and Rance Mullinicks were platooned at third base. Garth would play against lefties and Rance would play against right-handed pitchers. This system was so successful that *Sports Illustrated* wrote an article in 1985 entitled, "Mullinorg: birds of a feather." In an August 1983 doubleheader against the Yankees, Garth delivered four hits, two RBIs, and three runs. In 1984, he had four game-winning RBIs. After the 1984 season, he signed a new three-year contract with the Blue Jays.

Between 1978 and 1985, Garth had seven Blue Jay teammates who were members of the Church. In 1985, his club-leading .313 batting average helped the Blue Jays win the AL East. Garth and Dane are the only brothers to play each other in the play-offs.

In his first five years with the Blue Jays, Garth held the distinction of having more Mormon teammates than any other Church member. In 1978, Garth's rookie year, Alan Ashby, Jerry Garvin, and Don Kirkwood were on the team, and Luis Gomez was soon to become a member. Garth roomed with Danny Ainge at Syracuse and Toronto. Barry Bonnell joined the team in 1980 when Luis Gomez was traded. Jim Gott was on the team in 1983 and 1984, making a total of seven members who were teammates at Toronto. Garth recalls going to the Washington Temple with Bonnell and Garvin in the early 1980s. Garth said he never found it a problem to be an active church member and ball player. He credits Vernon Law and Harmon Killebrew for paving the way.

Garth achieved his greatest baseball success in 1985 as did the Blue Jays. He led the team in hitting with a .313 average. His seven homers exceeded the total of the five previous years. He hit two homers off of Texas pitcher Charlie Hough. Garth remembers it was one of his biggest games. He said, "The 1985 season was my career highlight because Toronto won the American League East and I was an important part of it." In the AL Championship series, he played against his older brother, Dane, of the Kansas City Royals. It was the only time brothers played against each other in divisional play-offs. He wrote a daily column for *The Toronto Star* during the championship. Of his playing against Dane, Garth wrote in the *Star*, "It's like a dream come true, Dane and I in a play-off series against each other. It's astounding that two guys from a really small town with a gas station and a store could make it to the Major Leagues, let alone face each other in a play-off game." Only one brother could go to the World Series, and it was Dane as Kansas City won the play-offs in seven games.

In 1986, Garth knocked in a career high 44 RBIs but after a mediocre 1987 season, he decided to retire from baseball. He said, "I feel good about my career. I wasn't a star, but I performed the role I was asked to fill." He returned to his home town and bought a small steel company. He always enjoyed hunting and fishing. He has been a Scoutmaster and Sunday School teacher.

In 1989, he participated in the first year of the Senior League in Florida. With baseball back in his blood, he took on the job of managing Toronto's rookie team in Medicine Hat, Alberta, Canada. He and the team were featured in a July 23, 1990, issue of *Sports Illustrated* on minor league baseball. Garth is filling an important role again for the Blue Jays. *Sports Illustrated* reported, "On the field, he can correct a batter's swing or an infielder's positioning in an instant. Off the field, he will find common ground in music with players 15 years younger." Garth signed on to manage the Toronto Class A team at Myrtle Beach, South Carolina for 1991.

RAY JACOBS YEAR-BY-YEAR STATISTICS

Name: Raymond F. Jacobs

Born: January 2, 1902
Salt Lake City, UT

Hgt: 6′ Wgt: 160

Bats: Right Throws: Right

Died: April 5, 1952

Minor League: 1923-1939

Year	Club	L	POS	G	AB	R	H	2	3	HR	RBI	SB	AVG
1928	Chicago	NL		2	2	0	0	0	0	0	0	0	.000
	Lifetime			2	2	0	0	0	0	0	0	0	.000

RAY JACOBS

Ray played semi-pro baseball in 1921 and 1922 right out of high school. He signed with the Ogden Gunners in 1923 as a shortstop in the Utah State League. He was recognized as one of the best young infielders in the league and in August 1923, his contract was sold to the Los Angeles Angels of the Pacific Coast League. The Angels had intended for him to play with one of their affiliated teams in the lower minors, but Ray hit .356 with the Angels during the last month of the season and they decided he was ready to play in the PCL. A newspaper reporter wrote at the time, "This youngster is as good an infield prospect as the PCL has ever turned out. Jacobs is a youngster with courage, the like of which few kid ball players have."

He played steady ball in 1924 at third base and first. He hit nine homers and batted an acceptable .276. One of his career highlights occurred when the Angels came to play the Salt Lake City Bees. The Angels were behind by eight runs in the sixth inning when Ray entered the game as a pinch-hitter and hit a home run. He stayed in the game and the Angels rallied to tie the Bees. The game was still tied in the twelfth inning when he came to bat and hit another home run and won the game. Ray thought that was a pretty good way to say hello to friends and family who were at the game. His season ended prematurely on September 9 when he was hit in the head by a fast ball and knocked unconscious. He was literally carried off the field by his team mates.

Ray returned in 1925 for an even better year, batting .310 for the Angels while playing third base and shortstop. He hit 13 homers, a lot for that era of baseball and stole 18 bases, also a lot. His season ended early again when on Labor Day he hurt his ankle. In 1926, baseball players were rated principally on their batting average so his .255 average was considered pretty puny. On the other hand, only one player in the entire Major Leagues hit more home runs than the 21 homers Ray hit for the Angels and that was Babe Ruth. Today, Ray would have had an express ticket to the Majors, but not in 1926. His homers helped propel the Angels to win the PCL pennant that year.

In 1927, he combined average with power. He led the PCL in RBIs and had a .323 average at mid-season. Moreover, he had played well at all four infield positions. A reporter wrote, "Jacobs has been the most valuable member of the Los Angeles club this year--and perhaps the most valuable player in the league." The Brooklyn Dodgers had agreed verbally to give the Angels $15,000 and a player in exchange for Ray. Playing in a July 4th doubleheader, he hit two home runs, apparently cementing the trade. Then disaster struck. Sliding into third base in the sixth inning of the second game, he broke his leg. It was a bad injury, and he was out for the year. Reporter Stub Nelson wrote, "Jacobs may have lost his chance of ever going up as the accident may slow him up. It was the toughest break for a young player."

During spring training of 1928, the Chicago Cubs needed a third baseman and were impressed that Ray, who was often called "Jake," could play first, second, and shortstop

Ray hit more homers, 21, in the Pacific Coast League in 1926 than anyone did in the Majors except Babe Ruth. Notice the glove in his back pocket. Can you do that?

as well as third. The Cubs were concerned that Ray was favoring his leg with a slight limp. The trade was made and Ray began the season with the Cubs. Unfortunately, the ankle did not heal quickly enough to allow Ray to play all-out. He appeared as a pinch-hitter, but was released to Toledo of the American Association where he batted .333 in 40 games. By season's end he was back with the Angels. It must have been a disappointing year. There is no doubt that he would have been a Major League player for many years if he hadn't been injured. Reporter Bob Ray wrote in 1928, "Before he broke his leg, Jake would have made good with the Cubs."

He rebounded completely in 1929, hitting .332 and smashing 20 homers. He even showed he still had some speed by stealing eleven bases. In 1920, he led all first basemen in the PCL in fielding; he made only twelve errors in 1,835 chances. After the 1931 season, he was traded to Portland and then to the Hollywood Stars in 1933. In two successive games against the Angels, he had a total of eleven RBIs and three homers, demonstrating that he still had a lot of talent. He was leading the entire country in home runs with 36 when he broke his thumb, putting him out of action for eleven weeks. His last year in the PCL was 1936 at San Diego. He was still a dangerous hitter as noted by five RBIs he had in one game.

One of the movies of the time was *Elmer the Great*, starring comedian, Joe E. Brown. The movie was about a fictional baseball player who thought he was the world's best. Ray was one of the real baseball players who was in the supporting cast. He seemed to enjoy his brief encounter as an actor. He had several pictures taken with Mr. Brown.

The Yakima Pippins of the Western International League offered Ray the job of player-manager for the 1937 season and Ray accepted. Speaking of his new team, he said, "One thing the Yakima club will have is fight and hustle; we're not going to be licked until the last putout." Ray played first base and hit .325. His team came in second during the regular season, but won the five-game league championship for which each player received $155 in bonus money. His 1938 Yakima team was in first place every day of the year and won the pennant which was infuriating to the rest of the league who thought his team wasn't all that good because only two Yakima players batted over .300, and Ray was one of the two.

He retired from baseball after the 1939 season and moved his family to Salt Lake City to manage a service station. He didn't stay out of baseball long. After 60 games, the Twin Falls Cowboys were in the cellar of the Pioneer League and they wanted out. They called the right person. It wasn't an overnight success, but by season's end, Ray had everyone's admiration as the Cowboys won 22 of their last 32 games. Reporter Frank Baker commented, "The difference between the Cowboys under Ray's leadership and the punchless club at midseason represents one of the greatest transformations I've seen on a sports team of any kind."

Ray was slated to join the Brooklyn Dodgers in 1927 but he broke his leg on July 4 and the deal was cancelled. He was with the Chicago Cubs in 1928 but his leg was not fully healed, and he returned to the minors.

He managed the Spokane Indians of the Western International League in 1941 where they won the league's pennant. He managed at Spokane in 1942 and then returned to Utah to manage the Brigham City Peaches in 1943. From 1944 to 1952, he worked at a Standard Oil plant in Utah. He was an avid bowler and played on several area teams.

On a vacation in 1952 to California to visit a son and see old friends, he died in an automobile accident. Of the many obituaries that appeared, perhaps the words below are ones that Ray would have liked best.

> Ray, a gruff guy on the outside, could take the bitter with the sweet. He never balked when the scribes panned him, but made them eat their words with his hitting, hustling, and fielding.

WALLY JOYNER YEAR-BY-YEAR STATISTICS

Name: Wallace Keith Joyner

Born: June 16, 1962
Atlanta, GA

Hgt: 6′ 2″ Wgt: 185

Bats: Left Throws: Left

Home: Yorba Linda, CA

Minor League: 1983-1985

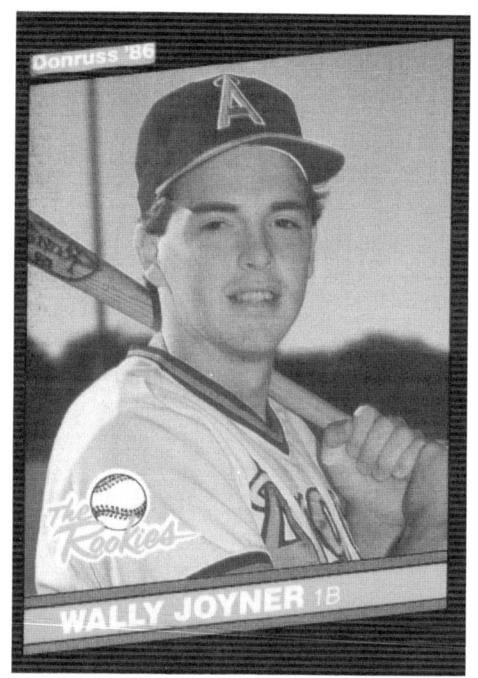

Year	Club	L	POS	G	AB	R	H	2	3	HR	RBI	SB	AVG
1986	California	AL	1	154	593	82	172	27	3	22	100	5	.290
1987	California	AL	1	149	564	100	161	33	1	34	117	8	.285
1988	California	AL	1	158	597	81	176	31	2	13	85	8	.295
1989	California	AL	1	159	593	78	167	30	2	16	79	3	.282
1990	California	AL	1	83	310	35	83	15	0	8	41	2	.268
	Lifetime			703	2657	376	759	136	8	93	422	26	.286

WALLY JOYNER

Wally gave everyone quite a scare when he was born. He was orange because of a blood disorder and had to undergo two complete blood transfusions before he was 48 hours old! When he was nine years old, he scared everyone by gaining fifteen pounds overnight. He would have died if his parents hadn't rushed him to the hospital where doctors detected a kidney disease that was causing fluids to be retained in his body. Despite these close calls, Wally was very active as a youth. One activity that helped him to develop quick reflexes was playing wiffle ball in the basement with his older brothers.

His favorite sport was basketball which he considered "more exciting" than baseball. He was an all-county basketball selection his freshman year in high school and excelled until he tore his right ankle ligaments in a basketball game at the beginning of his senior season. He saw his chances of a basketball scholarship disappearing so he sent a letter to Brigham Young University baseball coach, Gary Pullins, seeking a baseball scholarship. BYU sent a scout to see Wally, who played a great game and went on to be named the Georgia Baseball Player of the Year. Wally also attended an area sports banquet and met Dale Murphy of the nearby Atlanta Braves. They became good friends and Wally would help Dale out by driving the future Mrs. Murphy around Atlanta when Dale couldn't because of team conflicts.

BYU extended a scholarship to Wally which he accepted. Upon arriving at BYU, Wally went with his brother to meet the baseball coaching staff. The coaches hadn't met Wally before and they erroneously assumed that his bigger brother was the new player they were expecting from Georgia. Wally quickly corrected their impression and soon became a key member of the BYU Cougar baseball team from 1981 to 1983. He batted .445 his sophomore year and .462 his junior year in 1983. He broke the RBI and hit records at BYU with 95 RBIs and 113 hits in 64 games. His 23 homers were the second most by a BYU player, behind teammate Cory Snyder who hit 27 that year. Wally was selected to several All-America teams after his junior year, and he was picked by the California Angels in the third round of the June 1983 draft.

He performed well in his first minor league season hitting .327. At Waterbury in 1984, he was voted as his team's player of the year, and *Baseball America* selected him as the best defensive first baseman in his league. He was invited to the 1985 Angels spring training camp and played well. It was here that he first met Reggie Jackson and was "adopted" by Reggie as a future great player. The Angels assigned Wally to their Triple A team in Edmonton. He batted .285 and was very disappointed when the Angels did not call him up to the team at the end of the season.

He decided to play in the Puerto Rican Winter league to work on hitting left-hander pitchers. He hit every pitcher in the league becoming the first player in 25 years to win the Triple Crown. His team held a "Wally Joyner Day" to acknowledge the

Wally became the first player to be voted to start in the All-Star game as a rookie. In 1987, he became the first AL player since Ted Williams to drive in 100 runs in his first two seasons. He was on the 1991 AL All-Star team.

accomplishment. Unfortunately, Wally went 0-for-6, struck out three times, and made two errors. The fans showed their displeasure by tearing up the pictures of Wally that had been given out at the beginning of the game and throwing the pieces on the field. Even a Triple Crown winner can have an "off day."

Few players began their Major League careers as spectacularly as Wally did. He batted .387 in spring training earning the right to start the 1986 season at first base. Wally took the American League by storm, leading in nearly every hitting category before the All-Star break. In the first 87 games he had 20 homers, 78 RBIs, and a .313 average. His teammates led by future Hall-of-Famer Reggie Jackson and such baseball media as *Sports Illustrated* extolled Wally's capabilities and maturity. Baseball fans nationwide demonstrated their support by making Wally the first ballplayer ever voted to start in the All-Star game during his rookie season--no small accomplishment when you have to beat out a player the stature of Don Mattingly.

Unknowingly, Wally played the last two months of the season with a staph infection. During that time he hit only two homers and batted in only 22 runs. The Angels won the AL West, but after the third play-off game Wally was hospitalized, missing the last four games. It was then learned that he had been affected since early August. Undoubtedly, his illness cost him rookie of the year honors which he lost to Jose Canseco by only twelve points.

He proved that his rookie season was no fluke by performing even better in 1987. On July 12, he was leading the AL in RBIs when he collided at first base with Glenn Braggs. Resulting injuries caused him to miss several games. On August 26, he had a life-threatening scare. While leaving the field, he was hit in the left arm by a knife with a 5-inch blade that was thrown from the upper deck of Yankee Stadium. Although unhurt, he quickened his pace to get to the clubhouse. He made history on September 4, when he became the first AL player since Ted Williams in 1939-1940 to drive in 100 runs or more in his first two seasons. Only eight other players in all Major League history had amassed 100 RBIs or more in their first two years in baseball. He finished the 1987 season with a perfect 3-for-3 game on October 3--all three hits were home runs! He led all AL first basemen in putouts, assists, double plays, and games. His offensive numbers were also great placing third in homers and fourth in RBIs in the AL with 34 homers and 117 RBIs. He became the third best "Wally" ever in number of homers in a season behind Wally Berger (38) and Wally Post (40).

Wally played consistently solid baseball throughout 1988. He led the Angels in hits, tied a team record with three doubles in a game, was second on the team in RBIs, and had the lowest number of strikeouts in his career, 51 in 597 at bats. In 1988 he led all Major League first basemen with 1369 putouts, 143 assists, and 1520 total chances. In both 1988 and 1989, he displayed great range at first base by leading the Majors in starting double plays. Although he didn't hit homers at the rate he did his first two seasons, he was not concerned about it because he doesn't view himself as a traditional home run slugger. In a 1987 interview, he said, "I don't worry about homers or RBIs. If

Wally is an outstanding first baseman. In 1988, he led all Major League first basemen with 1369 putouts. In 1988 and 1989, he led all first basemen in starting double plays.

I hit line drives the rest of the year, that'd be fine. I'd be doing my job." With the close of the 1989 season, Wally became the first Angel player to go four consecutive seasons with at least 160 hits each year.

He was hampered quite a bit during the 1990 season because of a fractured knee injury that occurred in June. It reduced his playing capability until he finally went on the disabled list in August for the remainder of the season. Wally rebounded fully in 1991, tearing up the AL with a torrid hitting spree in May. He established a career-high sixteen-game hitting streak that earned him AL Player of the Week honors. On May 10, he hit a grand-slam home run and drove in five runs. On May 15, he hit his fourth homer of the season, a three-run blast. The next day, he hit another homer and drove in four runs. On May 18, he went 3-for-4 to raise his batting average to a league-leading .391. He hit his sixth homer and drove in all four Angel runs to defeat the Baltimore Orioles 4-2. On May 20, he hit another homer. Between May 10 and May 20, he was 22-for-44, smashed five homers, and drove in 21 runs.

HARMON KILLEBREW YEAR-BY-YEAR STATISTICS

Name: Harmon Clayton Killebrew

Born: June 28, 1936
Payette, ID

Hgt: 6′ **Wgt:** 210

Bats: Right **Throws:** Right

Home: Phoenix, AR

Minor League: 1956-1958

Year	Club	L	POS	G	AB	R	H	2	3	HR	RBI	SB	AVG
1954	Washington	AL	2	9	13	1	4	1	0	0	3	0	.308
1955	Washington	AL	3,2	38	80	12	16	1	0	4	7	0	.200
1956	Washington	AL	3,2	44	99	10	22	2	0	5	13	0	.222
1957	Washington	AL	3,2	9	31	4	9	2	0	2	5	0	.290
1958	Washington	AL	3	13	31	2	6	0	0	0	2	0	.194
1959	Washington	AL	3,O	153	546	98	132	20	2	42	105	3	.242
1960	Washington	AL	1,3	124	442	84	122	19	1	31	80	1	.276
1961	Minnesota	AL	1,3	150	541	94	156	20	7	46	122	1	.288
1962	Minnesota	AL	O,1	155	552	85	134	21	1	48	126	1	.243
1963	Minnesota	AL	O	142	515	88	133	18	0	45	96	0	.258
1964	Minnesota	AL	O	158	577	95	156	11	1	49	111	0	.270
1965	Minnestoa	AL	1,3	113	401	78	108	16	1	25	75	0	.269
1966	Minnesota	AL	3,1	162	569	89	160	27	1	39	110	0	.281
1967	Minnesota	AL	1,3	163	547	105	147	24	1	44	113	1	.269
1968	Minnesota	AL	1,3	100	295	40	62	7	2	17	40	0	.210
1969	Minnesota	AL	3,1	162	555	106	153	20	2	49	140	8	.276
1970	Minnesota	AL	3,1	157	527	96	143	20	1	41	113	0	.271
1971	Minnesota	AL	1,3	147	500	61	127	19	1	28	119	3	.254
1972	Minnesota	AL	1	139	433	53	100	13	2	26	74	0	.231
1973	Minnesota	AL	1	69	248	29	60	9	1	5	32	0	.242
1974	Minnesota	AL	DH	122	333	28	74	7	0	13	54	0	.222
1975	Kansas City	AL	DH	106	312	25	62	13	0	14	44	1	.199
	Lifetime			2435	8147	1283	2086	290	24	573	1584	19	.256

HARMON KILLEBREW

*I*n an interview soon after his election into the Hall of Fame, Harmon said, "I found out early in life I could hit the ball further than most players and that's what I tried to do." And he did it with great success hitting home runs every 14.2 at bats, more frequently than any players other than the immortal Babe Ruth and Ralph Kiner. Perhaps no player hit the ball as hard as Harmon did. He was the first player to clear the left-field roof of Tiger Stadium, which he did with a mammoth home run. In 1960, he hit the lights atop the Kansas City Stadium from where the ball bounced into the parking lot. When it came to crushing a baseball, his nickname of "Killer" was certainly applicable. No right-handed hitter in the American League has smashed more career home runs than Harmon despite his having only eleven homers in his first five years in the Majors! His 573 career homers are second in the AL behind the Babe.

Harmon began to gain some visibility as a twelve-year-old. He cracked into the starting lineup of the local American Legion team, where most players were sixteen and seventeen years old. He hit around .400 during his five years of Legion ball, playing shortstop and third base. In 1952, he helped his team win the Idaho American Legion title. But Harmon was not one-dimensional: he was an outstanding T-formation quarterback in high school. His legs were so strong that he was nearly impossible to tackle. He received a scholarship offer from the University of Oregon to play football.

Major league scouts were getting geography lessons in finding their way to Payette, Idaho, and all but four teams made offers to Harmon. He was seriously considering playing with the Boston Red Sox, mostly because of his great admiration for Ted Williams, who he later described as the greatest hitter he ever saw. If Harmon had known that the left-field fence at Fenway Park was only 315 feet from home plate he surely would have signed with Boston and the history books may have had Harmon breaking Ruth's record. As it was, Harmon thought all baseball diamonds were like the ones played on with the left-field fence 415 feet from home plate. He had never seen a Major League game in person.

Idaho's Senator Welker gave Clark Griffith, owner of the Washington Senators, a tip that Harmon was a tremendous player and that he ought to play in the nation's capital. The Senators sent their farm director to witness the last part of a tournament in which Harmon had already gone 12-for-12. In the next game, he smashed a 435 foot home run and a triple that hit the outfield fence so hard it bounced nearly all the way back to the infield. That was all the Senators needed to see; they made Harmon the best offer yet. In the 1950s if you got a signing bonus you had to stay on the Major League team for two years instead of going to the minors. Harmon thought he might get more chances to play on the lowly Senators than on other teams. Unfortunately one of the few good players the Senators had was Eddie Yost who played third base. So Harmon spent most of the next two years on the bench. Finally getting to play regularly in the minors in 1956 and 1957, he showed his hitting ability, but his fielding was still questionable.

In 1959, in his first season as a starter for the Washington Senators, Harmon became the second-youngest player to win the AL Home Run crown behind DiMaggio. He was always popular with fans. Even President Eisenhower brought his grandson to meet Harmon.

The 1958 season at Indianapolis began as a disaster. He couldn't get untracked and after 38 games he was batting only .215 with two homers. Discouraged, he was sent down to Chattanooga where he showed his determination by hitting .308.

In 1959, the Senators decided that Harmon would be their starting third baseman, and he didn't disappoint them. On opening day he hit a home run, in the last game of the season he hit a homer, and in between he hit 40 homers to tie with Rocky Colavito for the AL Home Run title with 42. He became the second-youngest person to win the AL Home Run crown. The youngest was Joe DiMaggio who was six months younger when he won the title in 1937. Harmon became a Washington celebrity with no less a person than President Dwight Eisenhower bringing his grandson to the ball park to meet Harmon.

It's hard to describe the next fifteen years--they are so full of achievements it could take the rest of the book to recite them all. As team owner, Griffith, said in 1974, "He kept us in business . . . Plus you have to remember the kind of man he has been and still is. He has been a great public relations man for us." The next few paragraphs just touch the surface of his achievements.

In 1961, the Senators became the Twins with their move to Minnesota, and Harmon set team records with a .606 slugging percentage and 107 walks. In 1962, he hit at least two homers in each AL park and on September 21, 1963, he smashed four homers in a doubleheader. In 1964, he won his third successive AL home run title, making him the only person other than Babe Ruth to win three in a row. In August 1965, he was well on his way to his fourth home run title which would have eclipsed Ruth's record when he dislocated his elbow and was out for seven weeks. He returned to the lineup in time to play in his first and only World Series where he hit a homer off Don Drysdale. During this time a writer commented on Harmon's attitude, "He carries his stardom with a dignity and a startling absence of egotism that few in any field can match." Harmon had his own television show where he would interview various baseball stars. Micky Mantle said after an interview, "A player feels at ease talking to a guy like Harmon." Another milestone for Harmon was his baptism into the Church in 1966. His demeanor and quiet positivism were widely recognized and created a good image of the Church in baseball upon which future players would build.

He played in thirteen All-Star games and hit three homers, but the All-Star game he certainly remembers most occurred in July 1968. When stretching for a ball at first base, he slipped and ruptured his left hamstring muscle. It looked like his career was over, but he worked hard to rehabilitate his leg and returned in 1969 to have his greatest season with 49 homers, 140 RBIs, and 145 walks. He led the Twins to first place in the AL West and was selected as the MVP by the Baseball Writers. He led the Twins to first place again in 1970 with 41 homers and 113 RBIs. *The Sporting News* named him their outstanding AL Player of the Year for the second year in a row.

Harmon was numbered among the best players of his era. He was a member of 13 All-Star teams; once an MVP; twice the AL Player of the Year; and in 1984, a member of the Hall of Fame. He hit more homers in the 1960's than anyone in baseball.

During the 1960s, he was the Major League's most prolific home run hitter with 393 homers. Never to be mistaken as a graceful gold glove fielder, he is nevertheless, the only AL player ever to be selected to the All-Star team in three different positions: outfield, first base, and third base. By the way, he played more games at first base than any other. In 1971 he led the AL with 119 RBIs and in 1972, he hit 26 homers making it the thirteenth year he had hit 25 homers or more. Only one player hit 40 homers more than the eight times Harmon did it. You're right-- it was Babe Ruth. When the Twins wanted to hold a Harmon Killebrew Day in 1974, his first reaction was, "No Way." The only way they could get him to agree was by donating all the gifts to charity. In August 1984, he was enshrined in the National Baseball Hall of Fame an honor he called "the biggest thrill of my baseball life."

Harmon stayed associated with baseball, broadcasting televised games for the Twins, Angels, and Athletics. He has been active in promoting Equitable Old-Timers games to help destitute former players. Recently he has been the victim of a double whammy. In 1989 an auto dealership and car-leasing company failed, placing him into heavy debt, and in 1990 he underwent several operations for stomach and lung problems. He is a star attraction at many baseball card shows and has a reputation for being warm and friendly to everyone.

A quote from Bob Fowler, who covered the Twins for many years and who wrote for *The Sporting News,* is a fitting way to end Harmon's biography:

> A game winner. A leader. An inspiration. Respected. A public relations man. A franchise. Harmon Killebrew has meant all of that to Minnesota. Now for the first time ever, his feats, which have been appreciated, will be publicly acknowledged. For charity. That seems appropriate. For the Killer is one of the game's true gentlemen, and one of its gentle men.

NEWT KIMBALL YEAR-BY-YEAR STATISTICS

Name: Newell W. Kimball

Born: March 27, 1915
Logan, UT

Hgt: 6′ 2″ Wgt: 190

Bats: Right Throws: Right

Home: Las Vegas, NV

Minor League: 1934-39, 1944-46

Year	Club	L	POS	G	IP	W	L	SO	BB	H	ERA	SV	SHO
1937	Chicago	NL	P	2	5	0	0	0	1	12	10.8	0	0
1938	Chicago	NL	P	1	1	0	0	1	0	3	9.00	0	0
1940	Brkln-St.Louis	NL	P	23	48	4	1	27	21	40	3.02	1	0
1941	Brooklyn	NL	P	15	52	3	1	17	29	43	3.63	1	0
1942	Brooklyn	NL	P	14	29	2	0	8	19	27	3.68	0	0
1943	Philadelphia	NL	P	39	101	2	7	35	47	94	3.84	3	0
	Lifetime			94	236	11	9	88	117	219	3.78	5	0

NEWT KIMBALL

*B*orn in Logan, Utah in 1915, Newt Kimball remembers being baptized as a youth in the Logan Temple. His family moved to Santa Monica, California, and he became a fan of the Hollywood Stars in the Pacific Coast League. In high school, he played basketball and baseball. He pitched his baseball team to two coast league championships in three years. He attended junior college, playing basketball one year. He then signed a contract with the Los Angeles Angels, part of the Chicago Cubs minor league organization.

Newt was assigned to Ponca City, Oklahoma, in the Class C, Western League. In his first professional baseball game, he pitched a no-hitter! In the next game, he pitched six innings of one-hit baseball. He was 20-12 his first year. He was still somewhat wild, walking four and five batters per game, but he could really bear down. On three occasions with bases loaded and none out, he struck out the side. He earned $150 a month and received $1.50 a day for meal money. Looking back, Newt said, "It was great!" Branch Rickey of the St. Louis Cardinals offered $25,000 to buy his contract along with several other players, but Los Angeles was not interested.

In 1935, he jumped to the Triple A level and played for Los Angeles in the PCL where he was 8-10. The next year he was 16-7 at Tulsa and was selected to the Texas league all-star team where he pitched three scoreless innings. He was called up to the Chicago Cubs at the end of the 1937 and 1938 seasons but pitched in only a few innings each year. In 1939, he spent the whole year in the minors with Milwaukee. In 1940, he posted an excellent 2.61 ERA and a low ratio of walks per inning. He was called up in August 1940 by the Brooklyn Dodgers where he was 3-1. In September, he was sold to the St. Louis Cardinals where he beat the Cincinnati Reds, 5-1.

While Newt was working his way to the Majors, he was also establishing a reputation as an outstanding golfer. He qualified for the Los Angeles Open twice as an amateur. He won the West Coast baseball players golf tournament several years in a row, and in 1940 he dethroned Wes Ferrell, three-year king of the Florida baseball golf league. At age 75, Newt was still an avid golfer although he said that he was thinking of giving it up--he hadn't played in three weeks. But four months later, Newt and his wife were departing for--can you guess? You're right if you said a three-day golf outing.

His sale to the Cardinals was cancelled by the Baseball Commissioner so he returned to the Dodgers in 1941. It was a blessing because the Dodgers were on their way to a National League pennant. Newt was used as a relief pitcher and had a 3-1 mark. The Dodgers lost to the Yankees in the World Series in five games, and although Newt did not make an appearance, he said, "Being on the Dodgers during the 1941 season was a great experience of my life." In 1966, he and his wife went to New York to participate in the 25th anniversary of the 1941 Yankee-Dodger World Series.

Newt pitched a no-hitter in his first pro game in 1934. He had a 3-1 record for the 1941 Brooklyn Dodgers as a relief pitcher, helping them win the NL pennant.

In 1942, he was 2-0. The Dodgers won 102 games but finished behind the Cardinals. During the 1943 season, he was traded to the Philadelphia Phillies. He spent 1944 to 1946 with the Hollywood Stars of the PCL. He had given some thought to managing and seized the opportunity to become part-owner and manager of the Class C minor league team in Las Vegas from 1947-50. He enjoyed it and felt he did a good job teaching young players.

Newt feels lucky to have been part of two first class organizations like the Cubs and the Dodgers. He recalls his Major League experience as "pleasant days." At 76, he has a sense of humor about himself that is refreshing. When asked if there were any particular batters he hated to see come to the plate, he said, "Most all of them." When asked if he was ever thrown out of a Major League game, he replied, "I was never in a game long enough to get thrown out!"

After baseball, he operated a gas station for a year and didn't enjoy it so he became a salesman for Westinghouse, selling such appliances as refrigerators directly to stores. Later he sold life insurance. He retired in 1977 which he called his "best move."

DON KIRKWOOD YEAR-BY-YEAR STATISTICS

Name: Donald Paul Kirkwood

Born: September 24, 1950
Pontiac, MI

Hgt: 6′ 3″ Wgt: 175

Bats: Right Throws: Right

Home: Troy, MI

Minor League: 1972-1974

Year	Club	L	POS	G	IP	W	L	SO	BB	H	ERA	SV	SHO
1974	California	AL	P	3	7	0	0	4	6	12	9.00	0	0
1975	California	AL	P	44	84	6	5	49	28	85	3.11	7	0
1976	California	AL	P	28	158	6	12	78	57	167	4.61	0	0
1977	Calif-Chicago	AL	P	29	58	2	1	34	19	69	5.15	1	0
1978	Toronto	AL	P	16	68	4	5	29	25	76	4.24	0	0
	Lifetime			120	375	18	23	194	135	409	4.37	8	0

DON KIRKWOOD

When interviewed, Don Kirkwood had just been watching a Tigers and Angels game on television: the perfect matchup since Don grew up rooting for the Tigers, and he was a pitcher for the California Angels for three years. His rise to big league pitcher was unusual because he never pitched until he was 19! Don played third, shortstop, and second base through high school and summer leagues. He was a good fielder and had a strong arm but was only an average hitter. He once asked to pitch for his high school team but his coach ignored his offer. What a mistake.

Don went to a small college where he could play baseball as a starting shortstop. Again, he volunteered to pitch and this time he got his chance. He developed quickly, and he also grew physically, becoming much stronger. In the spring of 1971, the Tigers offered Don a free agent contract as a shortstop. He declined. That summer, he pitched three no-hitters in a row, and a scout for the Angels saw two of them. In January 1972, Don signed with the Angels as a free agent, meaning all he got was an airplane ticket and the chance to try out.

Don had a great pro start in 1972 with a 6-2 record, nine saves, and a 2.81 ERA. After 17 games in 1973, he had a 1.26 ERA and was promoted to the Double A level team at El Paso in mid-season. In 1974, he gave up only one hit in eighteen innings at the Triple-A spring training camp, but was sent back to Double A ball because other pitchers had more experience. Disappointed, Don worked hard. He had a 9-4 record and was the team's ace relief pitcher with a 2.91 ERA. Then without an inning at the Triple-A level, Don was called up to pitch for the Angels. Was he excited! Don said that his first big league appearance was the most fabulous experience of his pro career. He struck out the first batter he faced--it was almost too good to be true for a fellow who loved the game but had been just an average 145-pound high school shortstop.

Don had married a Church member and joined the church in 1972. By coincidence when he joined the Angels in 1974, he was assigned to room with Doug Howard. Don said he was sure the Angels didn't do it because they were both Church members but more likely because they both seemed to keep high standards. Four years later, Don would join the Toronto Blue Jays where there were almost enough Church members on the team to form their own ward.

Determined to stay with the Angels, Don played winter ball in the Mexican league, leading the league in strikeouts. He completed 16 of 17 games, also a league high. With a high degree of confidence, he not only made the 1975 Angels but won six games and saved seven games, becoming their top relief pitcher.

Don loved baseball and was involved in every inning, even in ball parks where the relief pitchers sit far away in the bullpen. Don told of one year when the Angels had a rookie who would go to sleep in the bullpen because he was bored. Some of the

Don did not pitch until he played in college. In 1975, he was the top relief pitcher for the California Angels. The next year he was a starting pitcher in the same rotation with Nolan Ryan.

veterans got fed up and put a match to the rookie's shoelaces to teach him a lesson. The shoelaces must have been pretty dry because in no time, the rookie's pant legs were on fire. Fortunately the fire was put out without injury. Don said, "After that fire, the rookie always kept at least one eye open."

In 1976, the Angels asked Don to become a starter. He didn't want to, preferring to pitch at a moment's notice in tough situations instead of throwing 130 pitches every fifth day. Needless to say, Don did as he was asked. Although he had some good games, he really never adjusted, as his 6-12 record indicates. However, being a pitcher for the Angels in 1976 was no picnic. Just ask Nolan Ryan who lost 18 games with the Angels that year despite a respectable 3.26 ERA and 327 strikeouts.

The 1977 season started out with a blessing as Joe Rudi was traded to the Angels. Don explained, "Joe Rudi could always hit me even if I threw the ball behind him." Unfortunately, Don was traded on June 15 to the Chicago White Sox. He commented, "It really hurt to be traded by an organization that had signed you out of college and where you were really close to at least half the guys on the team." He was just beginning to learn that baseball is sometimes a tough business.

Just before the 1978 season started, Don was traded again, this time to the Toronto Blue Jays. He had no idea his career would start falling apart beginning with Opening Day. He pitched five innings in relief and won the game despite the 32 degree temperature and 20 mph snowy gusts of wind. His arm was unusually stiff afterwards. He pitched in two more games them felt a twinge and had to go on the disabled list for the first time in his career. His manager, Roy Hartsfield, told him he had better pitch soon or someone else would take his spot. Don was shocked that his manager and coaches showed so little concern for his welfare. Three games later, he tore his tricep muscle and was out for two months. His arm never would heal. He was released in spring training of 1979 and had to pay for his own surgery. He tried out with the Tigers in the spring of 1980 but hurt his shoulder, ending his baseball career.

When I asked Don if there was anyone in the game today that he admired, he immediately said, "I have the most respect for Nolan Ryan, not just because he's a great athlete but because he's a great person." Don continued, "The first day I was in the Angels' locker room as a starry-eyed kid only knowing four fellows, Nolan walked all the way across the room, stuck out his hand and said, 'Nice to have you on the team.' " Don mentioned that other players with nearby lockers didn't take the time to say anything to him. Don said that he decided then that he would follow Nolan's example to be a friend to newcomers whenever he had the chance.

Don owns a steel brokerage firm with three partners including his twin brother, Ron, who played briefly in the Angels minor league organization. Don enjoys hunting, fishing, and golf. He has helped out as "pitching coach" for high school and college teams over the past several years.

GARY KROLL YEAR-BY-YEAR STATISTICS

Name: Gary Melvin Kroll

Born: July 8, 1941
Culver City, CA

Hgt: 6′ 6″ Wgt: 220

Bats: Right Throws: Right

Home: Tulsa, OK

Minor League: 1959-1970

Year	Club	L	POS	G	IP	W	L	SO	BB	H	ERA	SV	SHO
1964	Phil/New York	NL	P	10	24	0	1	26	17	22	4.01	0	0
1965	New York	NL	P	32	87	6	6	62	41	83	4.45	1	0
1966	Houston	NL	P	10	24	0	0	22	11	26	3.80	0	0
1969	Cleveland	AL	P	19	24	0	0	28	22	16	4.13	0	0
	Lifetime			71	159	6	7	138	91	147	4.24	1	0

GARY KROLL

Gary's favorite players as a youth were Duke Snider and Willie Mays. He would later pitch against Mays and, according to Gary's account, he registered 17 strikeouts in their 24 faceoffs. In fact, one of the significant aspects of Gary's career is that he pitched against eleven players who hit more than 500 home runs plus Hall of Famers like Roberto Clemente, Willie Stargell, and Joe Morgan.

In high school, he played end in football and center in basketball. Both teams won their league titles, and he averaged 32 points per game in basketball. In baseball, he played third base and outfield, batting .438 and hitting nine homers as a senior. The Philadelphia Phillies liked his potential as a pitcher even though he had never pitched before. He signed a $1,000 bonus with them and reported to rookie camp in the minor leagues in 1959.

Despite his lack of pitching experience he performed well, throwing a no-hitter and finishing second in the league in strikeouts and third in ERA. His 1960 season was remarkable as he struck out 309 batters in 257 innings on the way to a 17-12 record and 2.91 ERA. No one in all of the minor leagues would exceed 300 strikeouts in a season until 1983 when Dwight Gooden did it. In 1961, Gary suffered through a 4-18 year with two teams, neither of which could hit a lick. He rebounded in 1962 with a 12-5 record. He had 11-7 records at the Triple A level in both 1963 and 1964. The Phillies called him up and then traded him to the New York Mets on August 7, 1964. He appeared sparingly for the Mets and decided to play winter ball in Venezuela to be primed to make the Mets' roster for 1965.

In 1962, Gary joined the Church after listening to the missionary lessons. He attended Brigham Young University during the off-season, concentrating on physical therapy courses. Even before it became fashionable, he was preparing his own high-protein meals. He continues to follow a regular exercise program.

He had an excellent spring training with the Mets in 1965, pitching no-hit baseball for six innings against the Pittsburgh Pirates in an exhibition game. Relief pitcher, Gordon Richardson, followed with three more no-hit innings. The game is still the only no-hitter in Mets history. In spring training, Gary experienced some of Casey Stengel's legendary humor. He was pitching against the Cincinnati Reds who were getting more than their share of hits. Manager Stengel came to the mound to switch pitchers. Gary protested, "I'm not even tired." Taking the ball, Stengel replied, "I know you aren't tired, but your outfielders are!"

Gary won his first Major League game on April 19, when he threw a four-hit, 7-1 victory over the power laden San Francisco Giants, striking out eight including Willie Mays. On June 13, he entered the game in the ninth inning before the largest crowd in Shea Stadium history, 57,175. Unfortunately a double by Wally Moon gave the

Gary struck out 309 batters in 1960. Gary and Gordon Richardson combined to throw a no-hitter; the only one in NY Mets history. He averaged a strikeout per inning during his career.

Dodgers the lead. Gary had a 3-5 record. Over the next seventeen days, he appeared in five games pitching fifteen scoreless innings. His record was 5-5 at the end of June. The Mets only had 26 victories. On July 4, he struck out seven batters in four innings of relief.

He continued to pitch well in July with a 6-6 record, but then he had two bad games that seemingly wrote his ticket back to the minors. On August 5, the Pirates' pitcher hit a three-run home and Gary was yanked. Three days later, he was assigned to an infrequent start and things went okay at first. Then Billy Williams hit a three-run homer and Gary was sent to the showers. Three days later, the Mets sent a perplexed and discouraged Gary Kroll to Buffalo. He was second on the Mets in appearances, third in strikeouts despite pitching mostly in relief, and fourth in ERA. His six victories was only one behind the club leader. In fact, he was the only pitcher in the four year history of the Mets to win as many as six games and not have a losing record. It was tough to play for such poor team and even worse to be treated so poorly.

He was traded to the Houston Astros after the 1965 season. He made the 1966 team and roomed on the road with fellow Church member and battery mate, Ron Brand. Gary pitched well early in the season, sporting an ERA under 2.00 through his first five appearances. He hurt his arm in June and had surgery on his elbow to remove bone chips. He was assigned to Amarillo where Gary said they employed an idiot for a manager. Obviously, they didn't get along and Gary was released by the Astros. He signed with the Cleveland Indian organization in 1967 and played on their minor league team at Waterbury where he regained his form, posting a 1.00 ERA and averaging two strikeouts per inning as a relief pitcher.

He pitched for Portland in the Pacific Coast League in 1968 and started the 1969 season at Portland. He was called up by the Indians in late April. Commenting on his biggest moments in baseball, he said, "Putting on a Major League uniform again and sitting in the dugout represented one of my greatest accomplishments because I worked so hard to get back. In the big leagues it is very difficult to return from an injury." He also commented that most of the pitching coaches in the 1960s were cronies of the manager and knew very little about how to teach pitching or to communicate well with players. Into early July, he had the best ERA on the team but with the Indians in last place by 27 games, management decided to bring along younger players. Gary had a terrible outing on July 12, giving up five runs in one inning. It was all the Indians needed and they sent him to Portland where he continued to pitch well, ending the year with the fourth lowest ERA in the PCL.

He was sold to Hawaii where he pitched in 1970. He went to spring training with the St. Louis Cardinals in 1971, but retired shortly after being assigned to a minor league team. Gary is one of only a few pitchers to average more than nine strikeouts per game through his pro career. He works as a life insurance broker.

VANCE LAW YEAR-BY-YEAR STATISTICS

Name: Vance Aaron Law

Born: October 1, 1956
Boise, ID

Hgt: 6′ 2″ Wgt: 185

Bats: Right Throws: Right

Home: Provo, UT

Minor League: 1978-1981

Year	Club	L	POS	G	AB	R	H	2	3	HR	RBI	SB	AVG
1980	Pittsburgh	NL	2,S	25	74	11	17	2	2	0	3	2	.230
1981	Pittsburgh	NL	2,S	30	67	1	9	0	1	0	3	1	.134
1982	Chicago	AL	S,3	114	359	40	101	20	1	5	54	4	.281
1983	Chicago	AL	3,2	145	408	55	99	21	5	4	42	3	.243
1984	Chicago	AL	3,2	151	481	60	121	18	2	17	59	4	.252
1985	Montreal	NL	2,1	147	519	75	138	30	6	10	52	6	.266
1986	Montreal	NL	2,1	112	360	37	81	17	2	5	44	3	.225
1987	Montreal	NL	2,1	133	436	52	119	27	1	12	56	8	.273
1988	Chicago	NL	3,O	151	556	73	163	29	2	11	78	1	.293
1989	Chicago	NL	3	130	408	38	96	22	3	7	42	2	.235
1990	Japan League												
	Lifetime			1138	3668	442	944	186	25	71	433	34	.257

VANCE LAW

*V*ance Law was the youngest of all the players written about in this book to regularly be in a Major League ball park. He turned four just a week before his father won two World Series games against the New York Yankees. His favorite player was Matty Alou, whom he rooted for to beat Pete Rose out in their yearly contest for the National League batting title. Vance frequently played catch with Willie Stargell who combined kindness with being a feared home run hitter.

In high school Vance played football, basketball, and baseball. He was on the Brigham Young University basketball team for three years, 1974-76, playing as a starting guard his last two years. He made the BYU baseball team and practiced for hours learning every aspect of the game. In his senior year he just played baseball. He played well in several college tournaments and hoped to be drafted during the first ten rounds. Imagine his dismay when he learned he was picked in the 39th round by the Pittsburgh Pirates, mostly as a good will gesture since his dad was a stellar Pirate pitcher.

Vance set out to show what desire and determination could do. He was assigned to the Class A team and surprised everyone by batting .319. Within the year, he was playing at the Triple A level at Portland and had impressed some key people in the Pirate organization. Portland manager, John Lipon, said of Vance in a 1979 interview, "I like his chances. He's very dedicated and intelligent." Vance said, "I know I don't have great speed, so I have to make up for it in hustle. I know I don't have the skills that some people have, so in order to make myself better than the next guy, I have to work twice as hard." Playing shortstop at Portland, Vance batted .310 learning how to hit a hard slider. No one dreamed that Vance would do so well, but he had still more surprises for those who doubted his capability.

Vance was invited to spring training in 1980 with the Pirates. He started the season at Portland and was hitting around .350 on May 31 when he was called up by the Pirates. In his first at bat on June 1, he hit a double. After the game, he called Japan to speak to his father who was coaching the Seibu Lions. Two days later, Vance started two rallies with hits and scored the winning run. He returned to the minors when the regular second baseman came off the disabled list. In 1981, he played with the Pirates and at Portland where he hit .277.

Just before the 1982 season started, Vance was traded to the Chicago White Sox. By mid-year he was the starting shortstop and finished the season batting .281 in 359 at bats. During a string of nine games in August, he drove in ten runs. On July 30, 1983, Vance had a memorable game, hitting a single, double, and triple. The White Sox won the American League West in 1983 with Vance's help. In 1984, he attained career highs in homers with 17 and RBIs with 59. He played third, second, shortstop, and outfield.

A 39th round draft pick, Vance is the only player to play in playoff games for both the Chichago White Sox and Chicago Cubs. In 1988, he was picked to the NL All-Star team. In 1990, he played baseball in Japan and hit 29 homers.

The White Sox traded Vance to the Montreal Expos on December 4, 1984. As the Expos starting second baseman in 1985, he responded with career highs--30 doubles, 6 triples, and 75 runs scored. He placed fourth in the National League with 86 walks. He had his first four-hit game on July 12. He had a so-so year at bat in 1986 but he demonstrated excellent athletic versatility by playing four infield positions, the outfield, and--are your ready for this?--pitching in three games. And he gave up only one run in four innings pitched. He spot pitched again in 1987, appearing in three games. His Major League ERA is 3.68, just a tad less than his father's.

When questioned about the highlight of his oareer, Vance's answer was immediate and unexpected unless you know that in 1986, it was learned that his four-year old daughter had a brain tumor. He and his family exercised faith and prayer on her behalf. Vance credits the power of the priesthood for her healing. After the operation and chemotherapy, she had to relearn her basic skills. Vance said that it was a tough, tough, situation. Her turnaround was a great testimony-builder in his life.

In 1987, Vance rebounded with a .273 average and a career high of eight stolen bases. His most exciting hit of the year was a grand-slam homer against the Pirates. On December 14, 1987, Vance signed a free agent contract with the Chicago Cubs. He had an excellent year in 1988 and was selected to the National League All-Star team. He had career highs with 163 hits, a .293 average, and 78 RBIs, only one less than team leader Andre Dawson. Vance had only one stolen base, but what a steal. He stole homeplate! On May 8, he drove in six runs against the Giants. The 1989 season was exciting because the Cubs were in the pennant race and won the NL East. He is the only player to play in play-off games for both the Chicago White Sox and the Chicago Cubs. Vance played with a painful bone spur in his neck during most of 1989. It caused muscle spasms and made it hard for him to turn his neck. It definitely hurt his performance.

Coming off a relatively unproductive year, Vance decided to play the 1990 season in Japan. He was one of the best American players, hitting 29 homers and batting .313. In January 1991, he signed a contract to play with the Oakland Athletics. He was on the disabled list early in the season. The game against the Baltimore Orioles on May 15 was quite memorable. First, Vance met President Bush and the Queen of England before the game; then he was the hitting hero of the game, going 3-for-4 and driving in two runs to lead the A's to a 6-3 victory.

Playing baseball and living the gospel are intertwined for Vance. He said, "A primary reason for playing baseball is to magnify the Church. Everyone knows you are a member. They expect you to live up to high standards. So do it!" During the off-season, he has served as an assistant priests quorum advisor. Vance enjoys cycling and golf. Like his father, he is an accomplished furniture maker. He has considered teaching in high school or coaching at the college level when he completes his baseball career. In the *1989 Scouting Notebook* published by *The Sporting News*, Tom Seaver described Vance as, "a consummate professional . . . a hard worker, he is a player everyone can pull for."

VERNON LAW YEAR-BY-YEAR STATISTICS

Name: Vernon Sanders Law

Born: March 12, 1930
Meridian, ID

Hgt: 6′ 2″ Wgt: 195

Bats: Right Throws: Right

Home: Provo, UT

Minor League: 1948-1950

Year	Club	L	POS	G	IP	W	L	SO	BB	H	ERA	SV	SHO
1950	Pittsburgh	NL	P	27	128	7	9	57	49	137	4.92	0	1
1951	Pittsburgh	NL	P	28	114	6	9	41	51	109	4.50	2	1
1954	Pittsburgh	NL	P	39	162	9	13	57	56	201	5.51	3	0
1955	Pittsburgh	NL	P	43	201	10	10	82	61	221	3.81	1	1
1956	Pittsburgh	NL	P	39	196	8	16	60	49	218	4.32	2	0
1957	Pittsburgh	NL	P	31	173	10	8	55	32	172	2.87	1	3
1958	Pittsburgh	NL	P	35	202	14	12	56	39	235	3.96	3	1
1959	Pittsburgh	NL	P	34	266	18	9	110	53	245	2.98	1	2
1960	Pittsburgh	NL	P	35	272	20	9	120	40	266	3.08	0	3
1961	Pittsburgh	NL	P	11	59	3	4	20	18	72	4.70	0	0
1962	Pittsburgh	NL	P	23	139	10	7	78	27	156	3.94	0	2
1963	Pittsburgh	NL	P	18	76	4	5	31	13	91	4.93	0	1
1964	Pittsburgh	NL	P	35	192	12	13	93	32	203	3.61	0	5
1965	Pittsburgh	NL	P	29	217	17	9	101	35	182	2.15	0	4
1966	Pittsburgh	NL	P	31	178	12	8	88	24	203	4.05	0	4
1967	Pittsburgh	NL	P	25	97	2	6	43	18	122	4.18	0	0
	Lifetime			483	2672	162	147	1092	597	2833	3.77	13	28

VERNON LAW

*I*n a 1954 interview as a Pittsburgh Pirate, Vern said, "When I finished high school all these scouts showed up talking about contracts. They all said I was good. Heck, I hadn't known I was any good -- I just liked to play ball." From this example of modesty, you can see why Vern is one of the most respected players to have worn a baseball uniform.

Vern earned twelve high school letters. He played center in basketball; quarterback in football; and pitcher in baseball. In track his events were pole vault and the shot put. In 1947, his American Legion team won the state and regional tournaments and was one of twelve teams to go to the nationals. He met Babe Ruth at the national tournament and got an autographed baseball which he still has today.

The Pirates got an edge on the competition in signing Vern in 1948, partly because Bing Crosby, who was one of the owners of the Pirates, called Vern's mother. She was an avid Bing Crosby fan and it's reported that's why she gave her permission for Vern to sign a contract with the Pirates. She was concerned, however, that pro baseball might not be a good environment. At the time, few Church members had played professional baseball. She didn't need to worry because Vern had a firm commitment to gospel values.

In Vern's first year in pro ball, 1948, he had a 8-5 record and struck out 126 batters in 110 innings. He had an agreement with the Pirates that he thought was permanent that he didn't have to pitch on Sundays. He didn't even go to the Sunday games in 1948. The next year his new manager told Vern he would have to play on Sundays since baseball is an everyday job during the season. Vern didn't like it, but he realized that it wasn't fair to his team mates for him to be off when everyone else had to be at all the games.

His ERA was 2.94 in 1949 at Davenport, Iowa. He started the 1950 season with New Orleans and had a 5-4 record and 2.67 ERA when the Pirates called him up to the Majors. On June 11, a Sunday, Vern pitched well in his first game. It was a complete game but he lost, not an uncommon situation with a team that at the time had lost 15 of their last 17 games. Pirate catcher, Clyde McCullough said, "I've caught a lot of youngsters . . . but Vernon Law is one of the best. He has a great curve and a fast ball that sails. And he knows what he's doing."

Vern won seven games in 1950 and six games in 1951. He spent the 1952 and 1953 seasons in the Army. He returned to the team in 1954 and won nine and saved three games. On July 19, 1955, Vern achieved a pitching feat that was astounding and will always be a standard of excellence. The game was against the Milwaukee Braves and Vern was the Pirates starting pitcher. Eighteen innings later, the score was tied 2-2. Five Braves pitchers had gone to the mound -- but Vern was still pitching for the

Bucs' Law Climbing Lofty 20-Win Ladder

Corsair Ace Hiked Victory Total Every Year Since '56

Pirate Biffers Support Vern With Hot Bats

Pride of Pittsburgh Pitched Eight Complete Games in First 13 Starts of Season

By LES BIEDERMAN
PITTSBURGH, Pa.

The least-publicized yet probably the best all-round pitcher in the game today is 30-year-old Vern Law, the pride of the Mormons and the pride of the Pirates.

Law enjoyed his biggest year in 1959, when he compiled an 18-9 record, and he expects an even greater season in 1960.

Vern became the first pitcher in the majors to win nine games when he posted a 15 to 3 victory over the Cards, June 12. With one-third of the season gone, the big righthander appears certain to win 20 games.

The Pirates take good care of Law and three times have scored in double figures for him. In his nine victories the Bucs tallied 66 times. In his ninth triumph, the Pirates gave Law six runs in the first inning before he threw a pitch.

"It's nice to have a big lead," Law said later, "but it can be a bad habit, too. When you get such a big lead, you have a tendency to merely throw the ball down the middle and let them hit it. You don't work the corners or try to set up a batter. You're sitting on a good cushion and you try to take advantage of the situation."

* * *

13 Starts, Eight Complete Games

In the Pirates' first 51 games, Law started 13 and went the distance eight times. He pitched two shutouts and beat the Phils four straight, the Cards and Reds twice each and the Dodgers once.

Law is the best-known Mormon in baseball and carries a notebook with him that serves as a guide. In this notebook, Law has a page titled, "Words to Live By," and he tries to follow the principles of quotations he has saved.

The quotations include:

"I have never met a man who is not my superior at something. A good timber never grows with ease; it needs a strong wind and storms to give it strength. A discouraged man is not a strong man. Don't be satisfied with mediocrity. Will Rogers once said: 'We're all ignorant, only we're ignorant about different things.' There is nothing wrong with youth. Actually only ten per cent of the youths are bad and these ten per cent get all the publicity."

* * *

Lives by Set of Rules

Law also is guided by a set of

Flashy Freebooter ∴ Scourge of Swatters

Danny Matched Vern's Fine—Gave It to Mormon Fund

PITTSBURGH, Pa.—It may be difficult to believe but Vern Law once was fined $25 by Danny Murtaugh. Law didn't break any law. It happened this way:

Two years ago Law looked at the traveling list in the clubhouse before practice and noticed his name was missing for the trip next day. However, before the players left the clubhouse, Murtaugh added Law's name but Vern didn't see it.

When the bus departed next day, Law wasn't aboard. The automatic fine is $25 and when the team returned, Law handed Murtaugh his check for $25.

"Would you do me a favor?" Law asked. "The Mormon Church in Fort Myers, Fla., is having a

Vern was featured in the June 22, 1960 edition of The Sporting News. It was his season. He won an All-Star game, two World Series games, and the Cy Young Award.

Pirates. He had struck out twelve Braves, allowed nine hits and two walks, and tossed fourteen straight scoreless innings. Vern said, "Manager Danny Murtaugh was going to pinch-hit for me in the 13th and 16th innings, but I convinced him to leave me in the game. I tried again in the 19th inning, but Murtaugh said he would be killed if something happened to my arm." The new Pirate pitcher let in a run in the 19th but the Pirates scored two runs in the bottom of the 19th to win 4-3 giving the relief pitcher the victory. Four days later, Vern pitched again and won in a twelve-inning game. Count them. That's 30 innings in five days!

In 1957 Vern had the fourth best ERA in the National League at 2.86. He showed improvement each year from 1956 through 1960 with 8, 10, 14, 18, and 20 victories. In 1959 he sported an enviable 2.98 ERA and had the second best winning percentage in the National League with an 18-9 record. Besides being recognized as a good pitcher, Vern was bringing favorable attention to the Church. *The Sporting News* carried a full page article on Vern in 1960 that began, "The least publicized yet probably the best all-round pitcher in the game today is 30-year-old Vern Law, the pride of the Mormons and the pride of the Pirates." The article, one of several over the years recounted Vern's belief in paying a full tithe; refraining from alcohol, coffee, tea, and cigarettes; and controlling his temper and speech. Vern hardly ever argued with the umpires; he must have been surprised when umpire Stan Landis threw him out of a game. It happened this way according to Landis's official report to the league office. The Pirate bench was riding Landis pretty hard and using "salty language." Landis went over to the dugout and told Vern to leave the ball game. In his report, Landis said, "I didn't want Law to have to hear the abusive language."

Vern was also known for carrying a notebook that he had entitled, "Words to Live By." The notebook contained sayings that he collected such as "A discouraged man is not a strong man," "We're all ignorant, only we're ignorant of different things," and "I'll always have a happy smile for everyone, especially those who like me least." Several of Vern's baseball cards note that he is an ordained Elder in the Mormon church. The backside of his 1955 Bowman card has "My Advice to Youngsters" where Vern encouraged kids not to smoke or drink, emphasized the development of a winning attitude, and advised youngsters to listen to their coaches.

The 1960 season belonged to the Pirates and Vern was a big reason. He had an outstanding 20-9 regular season record, becoming only the fifth Pirate pitcher in history to win 20 games. He was also the winning pitcher in one of the two All-Star games that were played. After the pennant-clinching game in Milwaukee, Vern was injured in the celebration when a player tried to take Vern's shoe off without untying his shoe laces and twisted his ankle. It was evident he was hurt as he pitched poorly in his next game. In the World Series against the powerful New York Yankees, he started three games, won two of them, and the team won the third game as the Pirates won the World Series. It was a great experience but he was in pain all three games, especially game four when he doubled and singled requiring him to run the bases. Vern was voted baseball's coveted Cy Young award for 1960.

A reporter called Vern, "One of the most highly respected persons in the game." Tom Seaver's <u>1989 Scouting Notebook</u> said, "Vance is a player everyone can pull for."

Unfortunately for Vern, pitching with the sprained ankle put severe stress on his shoulder and caused a rotator cuff injury. He pitched in only 59 innings in 1961. He struggled in 1962 and 1963 to regain his form. He said, "I loved the game and didn't want to quit despite the pain." Catcher and roommate, Smokey Burgess, said in a 1965 *Sporting News* interview about the 1961-1963 seasons, "I could see pain written all over his face every time he threw a ball. Many a night he walked the floor after pitching because of the pain." Trainer Danny Whalan said, "I never saw a fellow suffer as much as he did when he was trying to pitch his way back, yet he never once complained."

Just as the pain was finally ending in August 1963, the Pirates asked him to retire from baseball. Vern knew he could still pitch and was deeply discouraged when he was placed on the retired list. Not giving up, he worked through the winter and made the team in 1964. He won twelve games including a career high five shutouts. In 1965, he fully rebounded with a 17-9 record including eight wins in a row and a 2.15 ERA, winning the Comeback Player of the Year award. Les Biederman wrote in *The Sporting News*, "Vernon Law occupies a unique and envious position. He's an elder in the Mormon church, an elder statesman among the Major League baseball players and one of the most highly respected persons in the game."

During his career, Vern held his own in the batter's box. In three seasons he batted over .300. Hitting was important to him. He traces it back to a not-so-strong high school team. He said, "To win a game, I usually had to pitch a shutout and hit a home run." In 1954, he made three sacrifice hits in one game tying a record for pitchers. He said that his bunts helped win a number of ball games. He could also poke it over the fence. He is one of only seven pitchers, who pitched only after 1900 and who did not play other positions, to hit a home run in ten or more seasons. Of the seven pitchers, Vern had the highest lifetime batting average at .216.

Vern was the pitching coach at Brigham Young University from 1970 to 1979. He called the 1971 College World Series that BYU participated in a "real thrill." He was the pitching coach for the Seibu Lions in Japan during the 1980-81 seasons. He was the pitching coach for the Denver Bears in 1983 and then its manager in 1984 in the Chicago White Sox organization. He was also a sales representative for a company that made safety products for automatic braking systems for school buses and trucks. He is a accomplished cabinet maker and carpenter. In the church, he has held a number of positions including bishop and high councilor. He recently attended the thirty-year reunion of the 1960 World Champion Pirates.

JACK MORRIS YEAR-BY-YEAR STATISTICS

Name: John Scott Morris

Born: May 16, 1956
St. Paul, MN

Hgt: 6′ 3″ Wgt: 195

Bats: Right Throws: Right

Home: Orchard Lake, MI

Minor League: 1976-1977

Year	Club	L	POS	G	IP	W	L	SO	BB	H	ERA	SV	SHO
1977	Detroit	AL	P	7	46	1	1	28	23	38	3.72	0	0
1978	Detroit	AL	P	28	106	3	5	48	49	107	4.33	0	0
1979	Detroit	AL	P	27	198	17	7	113	59	179	3.27	0	1
1980	Detroit	AL	P	36	250	16	15	112	87	252	4.18	0	2
1981	Detroit	AL	P	25	198	14	7	97	78	153	3.05	0	1
1982	Detroit	AL	P	37	266	17	16	135	96	247	4.06	0	3
1983	Detroit	AL	P	37	294	20	13	232	83	257	3.34	0	1
1984	Detroit	AL	P	35	240	19	11	148	87	221	3.60	0	1
1985	Detroit	AL	P	35	257	16	11	191	110	212	3.33	0	4
1986	Detroit	AL	P	35	267	21	8	223	82	229	3.27	0	6
1987	Detroit	AL	P	34	266	18	11	208	93	227	3.38	0	0
1988	Detroit	AL	P	34	235	15	13	168	83	225	3.94	0	2
1989	Detroit	AL	P	24	170	6	14	115	59	189	4.86	0	0
1990	Detroit	AL	P	36	250	15	18	162	97	231	4.51	0	3
	Lifetime			430	3043	198	150	1980	1086	2767	3.73	0	24

JACK MORRIS

A teammate known for his own intense desire to win, Kirk Gibson, once said of Jack, "He's the fiercest competitor I've ever seen." His manager, Sparky Anderson, known for being one of baseball's best leaders, said of Jack, "He'll give me everything he's got every step of the way. He always has." These comments show the way Jack has approached most things in life since his early childhood.

He has fished and camped "since he was in diapers" and leaves for a fishing or hunting trip as soon as he can after the end of each season, usually within days. One of the reasons he went to Brigham Young University was because of the beauty of the country around the campus. Growing up, Jack enjoyed nearly all sports including ski jumping which he started at age ten when his father and uncle dared him to jump. Jack and his younger brother, Tom, played high school basketball and baseball together where they were noted for athletic ability and an overwhelming drive to win. Tom was the star pitcher winning 22 of 25 games. Jack was an excellent third baseman and shortstop. His hitting in high school was favorably compared with Dave Winfield and Paul Monitor. Although he had an extremely strong arm, he much preferred playing in every game to pitching. Besides, throwing hard was different than throwing with pinpoint control.

When the BYU baseball coaches saw how hard Jack could throw, he became their special project to develop into a pitcher. Jack is quoted as saying that it "was the end of my fun." It made winning even more personal, and, as a pitcher, if Jack had a bad outing he had to wait four or five days before he would have a chance to prove himself again. On the other hand, as an everyday player, he would know he'd be in the lineup the next day and could release his competitive energy by smashing the game-winning home run. This difference may explain some of the emotion Jack has displayed throughout his career when things weren't going as desired. Jack's hard work at BYU and the contribution of his coaches, including pitching coach Vernon Law, helped him to become a capable pitcher. He was picked by the Detroit Tigers in the fifth round of the June 1976 draft.

He was assigned to the Florida Instructional League and then to Montgomery where he had a so-so 2-3 record and 6.25 ERA. He was invited to the 1977 Tigers spring training and was then assigned to their Triple A team. He had a 6-7 record and 3.60 ERA when he was called up by the Tigers to replace the injured Mark Fidrych. His first Major League appearance was as a relief pitcher for four innings on July 26 against the Chicago White Sox. He won his first game on August 10 against the Milwaukee Brewers. He developed a sore arm in a game on August 26 that ended his year. He made the Tigers in 1978 but had limited success pitching in only 108 innings with a 3-5 record.

Jack began the 1979 season at Evansville but rejoined the Tigers in May to post a 17-7 record proving he could pitch and win in the Major Leagues. No right-handed pitcher

Jack was selected as the AL Pitcher of the Year in 1981. He pitched a no-hitter against the Chicago White Sox in 1984. Later in the year, he won two World Series games.

won more games in the American League in 1979. Moreover no pitcher in either league won more games than Jack did during the 1980s. He was the only pitcher to win at least 15 games for each of ten years from 1979 to 1988 excluding the strike-shortened 1981 season. He was outstanding in 1981 earning his first All Star team selection and starting the All Star game for the American League. *The Sporting News* picked him as the AL right-handed Pitcher of the Year. He signed a four-year contract after the 1982 season. He was a 20-game winner in 1983 and led the AL in strikeouts with 232. Attesting to his all-round athletic ability, he was used as a pinch runner on seven occasions in 1983.

The 1984 season was one of the greatest in Tiger history. For Jack it was a great year in many respects, yet it was a difficult year as well, mostly because he demanded so much of himself. He began the year by pitching a no-hitter against the White Sox (Vance Law went 0-for-1) in a game that was seen by a nationwide NBC Game of the Week audience. Baseball tradition is not to mention that a no-hitter is in progress for fear of jinxing it. Showing his competitive nature, Jack said to his pitching coach, Roger Craig, as he went out to pitch the ninth inning and in a voice loud enough to be heard by teammates, "I am going to do it!" And he did. By June 1, he had a super 10-1 record as the Tigers got off to an electrifying 35-5 record. He was selected to the All Star team and pitched two scoreless innings.

Then things went downhill. He experienced tendinitis in his right shoulder, fought off a month-long chest cold, had problems with the media, his coaches, and some teammates. His expectation that he should win every game was not practical and led to tremendous frustration as he had a 3-6 record after the All Star break. He was able to reconcile his feelings and played a dominant part in the Tigers winning the AL pennant and World Series. He won, 8-1, the opening game of a four-game sweep over the Kansas City Royals to win the AL championship. In the World Series against the San Diego Padres, he won the opening game, 3-2, and fourth game, 4-2. To realize how impressive Jack was, remember that in 28 World Series games that Sparky Anderson has managed, only two of them were complete games, and Jack was the pitcher in both games. Immediately after making a short speech to the celebrating fans in Detroit, Jack was off on a hunting trip with relatives.

He was selected to the All Star team in 1985. The first half of 1986, beginning with the first pitch of the season that Dwight Evans hit out of the park, was long and hard for Jack. He gave up three additional homers in the opening game, and on June 9 the Yankees hit four homers in the first three innings. In an interview at the time, he said, "You can't know what it feels like to have already given up four home runs and nearly the entire game is still ahead of you." In his first 17 games, he gave up 25 homers. Instead of getting down on himself, he responded to his problems with confidence that things would be better. He lost a game 3-1 on June 29, and 2-1 on July 4, and then threw three consecutive shutouts going 44 straight innings without giving up an earned run. He finished the season with an enviable 21-8 record and led the AL with six shutouts.

Jack won more games during the decade of the 1980s than any pitcher in the Major Leagues. In 1991, Jack won his 200th game and gained his 2000th strikeout.

With the expiration of his four-year contract, Jack decided to become a free agent, fully intent on playing elsewhere. Unbelievably, no team would make a serious offer. He had no choice but to stay with Detroit. He won his arbitration hearing, giving him one of the highest salaries for a pitcher in the Major Leagues. In 1987, he was selected to the All Star team, had more than 200 strikeouts, and at age 31 reached the mid-point toward 300 wins. In 1988 he got off to a slow start but won 15 games and had a 2.27 ERA after the All Star game. Despite being injured part of 1989 and having a below average record, Jack was second in the AL for complete games. In 1990 he tied with Dave Stewart for most complete games with eleven, more than the total of some teams. He finished second in innings pitched and came on strong going 6-3 at the end of the season. After the season, he was ruled to be a free agent because of collusion by the baseball owners to limit a player's free agency back in 1986 and 1987. From 1981 through 1990, Jack was the opening day pitcher for the Tigers, but not in 1991. In February 1991, he signed with his hometown team, the Minnesota Twins.

He kept his opening day tradition alive by starting in the Twins first game of 1991. Jack achieved two career milestones early in the 1991 season. On April 24, he became the 40th pitcher to strike out 2,000 batters; and on April 28, he won his 200th victory. He started slowly with a 0-3 record and then won 11 of his next 13 decisions, helping the Twins set a team record with 16 straight victories and surprising everyone by gaining first place in the AL West. On June 30, he pitched a six-hit shutout to win his eighth consecutive game and boost his record to 11-5.

In recounting some of his career highlights, Jack said, "The no-hitter was the most satisfying personal highlight and the 1984 World Series was my greatest team experience, but the game I remember most was a game I lost." He went on to explain that he started a game in the 1987 AL Championship Series against the Minnesota Twins in the Metrodome. He said, "The decibel level in the stadium was like an airport. As I stood on the mound, I realized how much I love the excitement and enthusiasm of the fans."

He is the pitcher's equivalent of Lou Gehrig, holding the AL record for pitching in 336 consecutive starting assignments. He holds the Tiger record for leading the team in victories for nine consecutive years. He has a 90+ mile per hour fastball, a great slider, and a forkball that often makes hitters talk to themselves.

Jack was taught as a youth to drive for victory and to despise losing. That's how he has lived his pro career. His goal, stated in an interview in 1987, is worthy of consideration for all important endeavors. He said,

> My ultimate goal in this game is that I don't want to walk away from it someday looking at myself in the mirror and saying, "You could have done this different" or "You could have worked harder here," I just want to be able to walk away from the game saying what you saw is what I gave and it was all I had. I don't want to cheat myself or anybody else.

DALE MURPHY YEAR-BY-YEAR STATISTICS

Name: Dale Bryan Murphy

Born: March 12, 1956
Portland, OR

Hgt: 6′ 4″ Wgt: 180

Bats: Right Throws: Right

Home: Roswell, GA

Minor League: 1974-1977

Year	Club	L	POS	G	AB	R	H	2	3	HR	RBI	SB	AVG
1976	Atlanta	NL	C	19	65	3	17	6	0	0	9	0	.262
1977	Atlanta	NL	C	18	76	5	24	8	1	2	14	0	.316
1978	Atlanta	NL	1,C	151	530	66	120	14	3	23	79	11	.226
1979	Atlanta	NL	1,C	104	384	53	106	7	2	21	57	6	.276
1980	Atlanta	NL	O,1	156	569	98	160	27	2	33	89	9	.281
1981	Atlanta	NL	O,1	104	369	43	91	12	1	13	50	14	.247
1982	Atlanta	NL	O	162	598	113	168	23	2	36	109	23	.281
1983	Atlanta	NL	O	162	589	131	178	24	4	36	121	30	.302
1984	Atlanta	NL	O	162	607	94	176	32	8	36	100	19	.290
1985	Atlanta	NL	O	162	616	118	185	32	2	37	111	10	.300
1986	Atlanta	NL	O	160	614	89	163	29	7	29	83	7	.265
1987	Atlanta	NL	O	159	566	115	167	27	1	44	105	16	.295
1988	Atlanta	NL	O	156	592	77	134	35	4	24	77	3	.226
1989	Atlanta	NL	O	154	574	60	131	16	0	20	84	3	.228
1990	Atl-Phila	NL	O	154	563	60	138	23	1	24	83	9	.245
	Lifetime			1983	7312	1125	1958	315	38	378	1171	160	.268

DALE MURPHY

*D*ale was always interested in sports and played football, basketball, and baseball in high school. In basketball, he was selected to the Portland, Oregon all-city second team as a guard. His high school team won three city titles, and he was the catcher on the all-state baseball team. In 1973, his American Legion team had a 54-8 record and went to the World Series. As a youth, Dale's baseball heros were Willie Mays and Johnny Bench. He would never have guessed that he would become a hero to thousands, perhaps millions, of baseball fans.

Arizona State offered Dale a scholarship, but he decided to sign with the Atlanta Braves who had made him their first choice in the 1974 draft. The Braves were impressed with his catching ability, particularly his strong arm. His progress in the minors began slowly. He hit .254 and .228 with five homers in each of his first two seasons. However, it was off-the-field that Dale made life-changing progress. During 1975, Barry Bonnell joined the Greenwood Braves. Dale noticed that Barry was frequently reading from the scriptures. He listened intently whenever he heard Barry explain his beliefs. One evening on the team bus ride home, Dale and Barry sat together. They were soon discussing the Church. Dale had already decided to stop drinking and to gain greater spirituality. Pretty soon he was seriously learning about the Church. He was baptized by Barry the day after the season ended.

In 1976, Dale played well at Savannah and made the league all-star team. He was called up to the Triple-A level Richmond team, and at the end of their season, he was called up to the Braves. He went 2-for-4 in his first game and batted .262 in nineteen games. During the off-season, he considered going on a two-year mission. In a February 1977 article, reporter Gary Caruso quoted Dale about his mission, "It is something that is really important to me." He thought a lot about it and discussed it with Church leaders. Dale decided that being a player is a mission in itself since you can talk to young people and be a positive example. He has been an excellent ambassador for the Church ever since.

Returning to Richmond in 1977, Dale had a really good year and showed some power, hitting 22 homers. He joined the Braves at the end of the 1977 season and batted .316. On the Braves from Opening Day in 1978, he hit his first grand-slam homer and smashed six homers in six consecutive games. In 1979, he started the year with a bang, posting a .348 average, 13 homers, and a league-leading 36 RBIs when he tore knee cartilage chasing an errant knuckleball. Right after the 1979 season, Dale was married in the Salt Lake Temple. Barry Bonnell and his wife attended the service.

As a catcher, Dale was known for his powerful arm, but during the 1977 season he became known for his erratic arm. Sometimes he threw the ball into the outfield and on occasion, his throws bounced before getting to the pitcher's mound. Finally after much frustration and embarrassment, Dale began the 1980 season as an outfielder. His

Dale was the NL's MVP in both 1982 and 1983. In the 1980s, only Mike Schmidt hit more homers and only Eddie Murray drove in more runs. No one had more total bases.

fielding was outstanding. His throwing accuracy reappeared and few runners dared to take an extra base for fear that Dale would throw them out. He was selected to the 1980 National League All-Star team. In August, he slammed eight homers and 25 RBIs to became the NL Player of the Month. He finished the year with 33 homers.

Just after the 1980 season ended, Dale had the honor of baptizing Curtis Patton into the Church in Atlanta. Curtis had first met Dale in June 1979 in the Braves clubhouse. Curtis was an editor with the Atlanta newspaper. He had several discussions with Dale about the Church. After one particular conversation, Curtis reported in a 1982 interview, "I felt the presence of the Holy Ghost in Dale. My heart was stirred." He accepted a copy of *The Book of Mormon* from Dale and attended church with him. Curtis later helped Dale to have a regular article in the newspaper called, "Ask Dale Murphy."

The 1981 season was curtailed by a players' strike and by injury. 1982 was a really big year--Dale led the Braves to the NL West pennant. His 36 homers and 109 RBIs plus standout fielding earned him the NL Most Valuable Player award. He was a repeat NL MVP winner in 1983, hitting 36 homers and 121 RBIs. He became the seventh player in Major League history to hit 30 homers and steal 30 bases in the same year. He played in the All-Star game in 1982 and 1983 and was the Gold Glove centerfielder both years. A particularly memorable day was June 12, 1982. In San Francisco, Dale visited in the stands with a six-year old girl who had lost a leg and both hands in an accident. He gave her a cap and a shirt, then the question--would he hit a home run for her? The Braves won the game 3-2 on the strength of two homers by Dale.

Dale tied for the NL lead in homers in 1984 with 36, and he hit a home run in the All-Star game. He was the NL Player of the Month in September. He began 1985 on a hot streak, tying a Major League record for the most RBIs in the month of April. He led the league with 37 homers and 118 runs scored as well as collecting 111 RBIs and batting .300. On July 9, 1986, the news was that Dale did not play. It was the first game he watched from the bench in 740 games, the eleventh longest consecutive game streak in Major League history. He played in his fifth straight All-Star game and won his fourth straight Gold Glove.

In 1987, August was a noteworthy month--in it he got his 1500th Major League hit and 300th home run. He also had a career high of 44 home runs, 115 walks, and a .580 slugging average. He moved from center to right field but still earned another Gold Glove. During the All-Star break in 1988, he was honored for his humanitarian efforts. He was presented with the Roberto Clemente award and rightly so. Among other activities, Dale has been a spokesman for the March of Dimes, Arthritis Foundation, American Heart Association, Huntington Disease Society, and Make-A-Wish Foundation. Dale had been previously honored by *Sports Illustrated* as one of the 1987 Sportsmen of the Year for his service to mankind.

After 17 years in the Braves organization, Dale joined the Philadephia Phillies on August 3, 1990. Dale said, "It was strange to look down at my feet and see red shoes.

Dale had played in over 12,000 innings, but he was not prepared for the game he experienced on July 27,1989. "I was totally flabbergasted," Dale explained when recounting what must be the favorite single inning of his career. He cracked two, three-run home runs in the same inning. As he rounded the bases the second time in the inning, he was thinking, "What's going on here?" His six RBIs and two homers tied a Major League record. Dale could easily be called the greatest Major League ball player of the 80s. Only Mike Schmidt hit more homers; only Eddie Murray drove in more runs; and no one had more total bases.

"City of Brotherly Love Is Perfect for Murphy" was the headline in *The Sporting News*. After seventeen years in the Braves organization, Dale was traded on August 3, 1990 to the Philadelphia Phillies. Showing the grace for which he is famous, he paid for a space in the *Atlanta Journal and Constitution* to thank the people of Atlanta. He wrote, "We will always consider it a privilege to have been associated with the people of Atlanta and the Atlanta Braves." Some reporters commented that the privilege was really all Atlanta's. In January 1991, the Braves 400 Club, a booster organization held a "Thank You Dale Murphy" party in his honor.

Sometimes when a player retires, a team will designate a game in his honor. But when a player is traded, it is highly unusual for the former team to organize a special day for the player. That's just what the Atlanta Braves did for Dale. On the Phillies' first visit to Atlanta on June 4, the Braves conducted a pre-game ceremony to recognize Dale's contribution to the team, which includes holding or sharing nineteen Atlanta Braves' batting records. Reporting on Dale's evening, Dick Polman of the *Philadelphia Inquirer* wrote, "He was cheered for stepping into the batting cage. He was serenaded with hosannas when he jogged to right field. He couldn't go near the dugout without drawing a phalanx of fans 20 feet deep. All the while, he flashed the aw-shucks grin and quiet charisma of the gentle giant--and everyone was reminded of why they missed him." Demonstrating the humility for which he is reknown, Dale said, "I know that every night I played here in Atlanta wasn't exactly like those highlight films you just saw."

During the 1991 season with nearly each home run, Dale passed former stars in the number of career home runs. He recently passed Tony Perez, Orlando Cepeda, and Johnny Bench. Dale, Eddie Murray, and Dave Winfield are the leaders in lifetime home runs among active players with each taking turns being the career leader.

Dale has pursued a number of interests over the years including sailboating, photography, and drawing. His favorite class in high school was art and he hopes to learn more about drawing. He enjoys golf when he has time. He has served in several Church callings including early morning seminary instructor and counselor in the stake mission presidency.

SCOTT NIELSEN YEAR-BY-YEAR STATISTICS

Name: Jeffrey Scott Nielsen

Born: December 18, 1958
Salt Lake City, UT

Hgt: 6′ 1″ **Wgt:** 190

Bats: Right **Throws:** Right

Home: Salt Lake City, UT

Minor League: 1983-1991

Year	Club	L	POS	G	IP	W	L	SO	BB	H	ERA	SV	SHO
1986	New York	AL	P	10	56	4	4	20	12	66	4.02	0	2
1987	Chicago	AL	P	19	66	3	5	23	25	83	6.24	2	1
1988	New York	AL	P	7	20	1	2	4	13	27	6.86	0	0
	Lifetime			36	142	8	11	47	50	176	5.45	2	3

SCOTT NIELSEN

Scott's nickname is "Scooter" which his dad gave him as a youngster. Jim "Catfish" Hunter was his favorite baseball player. Scott played high school football, basketball, and baseball. He was a pretty good quarterback and received several football scholarships. He turned these offers down partly because he realized he wasn't going to grow much bigger, but the linemen who would be trying to crush him were going to be a lot bigger and stronger. Besides he enjoyed baseball more than football. He pitched and played shortstop in high school and in the Senior Babe Ruth league. Scott said, "If I had known I wouldn't be able to hit much as a pitcher in the American League, I might have tried harder as a shortstop."

Scott went to Brigham Young University on a baseball scholarship and made the varsity team as a freshman in 1977. After his second year, he decided to go on a mission and was called to serve in Argentina. At the time he did not have much hope of ever playing any level of pro ball, much less becoming a New York Yankee. Looking back, Scott said, "My mission was hard work. There were a lot of ups and downs which helped me become more mature." He feels his mission experience has helped him deal with some of the disappointments of trades, injuries, and roster cuts as well as keeping in balance his moments of success.

He was redshirted upon his return to BYU in 1981. Because of his three-year separation from baseball, Scott definitely had an uphill battle. He was successful beyond his wildest dream. In his last two years at BYU, he won 26 straight games--an NCAA record. He was selected to All-American teams in 1982 and 1983. The Seattle Mariners drafted Scott in the sixth round. He started in their farm system in 1983 at age 24, six years older than the kids signing right out of high school.

Because of his age, Scott felt that he had to do well right away. And he did. He was 2-0 at Bellingham and was promoted to Double A level ball. In February 1984, the Mariners traded him to the New York Yankees. Scott was not happy since the Yankees had a reputation for spending big bucks on free agents instead of developing players through the farm system. He had a combined 13-8 record in 1984 making it to Columbus at the Triple A level by the end of the season. He got off to an outstanding 6-1 record in 1985 but saw the season end early when he had surgery to correct an elbow injury.

He began the 1986 season back at A level ball so he could come along slowly from his injury. He clicked off four quick victories and was promoted to Columbus where he was 11-7. He joined the Yankees in July and won his first start against the Texas Rangers on national TV. His second start was against the Minnesota Twins and he pitched a complete game shutout. Scott remembers his third game as a personal highlight, not because of what happened during the game--he suffered his first defeat. However, before the game he met former Yankee greats Whitey Ford, Mickey Mantle,

Scott was a NCAA All-American in 1982 and1983, setting a college record by winning 26 consecutive games. He won his first Major League start against the Texas Rangers on national televison.

and Joe DiMaggio who attended the Equitable Old-Timers' game. Scott was sent back to Columbus and then returned at the end of the season. Amazingly, his two shutouts led the entire Yankee pitching staff.

On January 5, 1987, the Yankees traded Scott to the Chicago White Sox. He began the year on the Triple A team in Hawaii. After pitching in ten games, he was called up and spent the rest of the year with the White Sox. He had a complete game shutout among his three victories.

Unfortunately for Scott, he was traded back to the Yankees and started the 1988 season in Columbus. He had a great year. He pitched a no-hitter on June 8, the first by a Columbus pitcher in 43 years. He pitched in the Triple A level All-Star game, led the International League with 13 victories, and pitched for the Yankees at season's end. Scott said, "I did everything the Yankees asked me to do." With that, the Yankees did not even invite him to their Major League spring training camp--a super letdown. He had a further letdown when he missed pitching another no-hitter with Columbus in the last inning. He was surprised when the Yankees traded him in mid-season from Columbus to the New York Mets' Triple A team, the Tidewater Mets. Scott holds the record for most career victories as a Columbus Clipper. This is a record he did not want. He was frustrated that he didn't have a better chance with the Yankees. "One or two mistakes and you're back in the minors," Scott said. The 1990 season was difficult because of shoulder problems that required surgery. He began spring training in 1991 with Tidewater but his shoulder was not fully healed so he started the season on the disabled list.

With a degree in accounting, Scott works as an accountant during the off-season. He enjoys golf and fishing.

JOHN NORIEGA YEAR-BY-YEAR STATISTICS

Name: John Alan Noriega

Born: December 20, 1944
Ogden, UT

Hgt: 6′ 4″ Wgt: 185

Bats: Right Throws: Right

Home: Kaysville, UT

Minor League: 1966-1971

Year	Club	L	POS	G	IP	W	L	SO	BB	H	ERA	SV	SHO
1969	Cincinnati	NL	P	5	8	0	0	4	3	12	5.63	0	0
1970	Cincinnati	NL	P	8	18	0	0	6	10	25	8.00	0	0
	Lifetime			13	26	0	0	10	13	237	7.27	0	0

JOHN NORIEGA

John's mother said that John set three goals as a child and accomplished them all. His goals were to be a high school all-state baseball player, to play on the University of Utah baseball team, and to play in the Major Leagues. John stated that his primary motive for going to school was so he could play sports and that he thought the letter 'A' was for Athletics. He was a football end, a basketball forward, and a baseball pitcher. In 1961, his high school basketball team won the state championship. He was an all-state selection in basketball and baseball. In the ninth inning of the state all-star game with bases loaded, he struck out the side, which John felt was appropriate since he had loaded the bases himself. Sandy Koufax was his idol.

John played freshman basketball in 1962 at the University of Utah and pitched from 1963 through 1965. He led the Western Athletic Conference in strikeouts in 1965. He was drafted by the Atlanta Braves in June 1965 but did not sign. He played summer ball in 1965, striking out 75 batters in 69 innings. John signed with the Cincinnati Reds in February 1966.

He started his pro career with a 2-6 record at Knoxville in 1966. The following year he was 7-8 with a 2.50 ERA. In 1968, he had a super year with a 9-3 record and 2.66 ERA , striking out 116 batters in 122 innings. He made the league all-star team. His manager was Sparky Anderson. John played winter ball in South America where he developed a sidearm delivery. He finished with a 9-4 record and 2.17 ERA. He recalled that some of the winter ball games were frightening because fans would throw beer bottles at players who made mistakes. He played winter ball in South America during three years but did not learn much Spanish because he was able to rely on the English of many Major Leaguers such as Dave Concepcion and the Alou brothers.

He had a good spring training in 1969 but was sent to Indianapolis. It was a surprise when he was called up to Cincinnati on April 28--his wife's birthday. The first two games he saw were no-hitters. Reds pitcher Jim Maloney threw a no-hitter on Friday night and then Don Wilson of Houston threw a no-hitter against the Reds. John pitched in relief for the Reds so he quipped, "I pitched in a no-hitter!" On a more serious note, John was excited that Sandy Koufax was announcing the game on television and he was able to get an autographed ball from him. John was a relief pitcher in four more games before returning to Indianapolis.

In 1970, he joined the Reds during the All-Star break. Sparky Anderson was now the manager and it was the year the Reds went to the World Series. John roomed with Pete Rose for three days in New York City and Pete was paying for everything wherever they went. Finally John said, "Really Pete, I have some money and should pay some of the tabs." Rose replied, "After you've been around, rookie, you help someone else." Unfortunately, John was optioned to the minors before the season ended, but he was voted a partial share of the World Series money by his teammates.

John pitched in eight games for the 1970 Cincinnati Reds. He was awarded a partial share of the Reds' World Series pool. He roomed with Pete Rose during one road trip.

He was particularly cxcited to have his dad, a former minor leaguer, attend a game in San Francisco; his grandparents came to a game in Los Angeles. Perhaps most exciting for John was his first and only Major League hit.

John was admired for his grit--very few players make the Major Leagues with any physical handicaps much less a paralyzed left eye. Because he could not move his left eye, he would occasionally make a fielding error. Once when covering first base, he thought he was going to step on the base to make a force out on the batter but instead he stepped an inch off the bag and the runner was safe. He also took some teasing but most of all he was recognized for his love of the game. In a 1970 interview John said, "I feel happy that I'm good enough to make this club. You can't take any job on a big league club and say its a bad job." He played the 1971 season at Eugene and Portland in the minor leagues with an 8-11 record for the whole year. He felt he would be an "up and down" player and his oldest son was starting school so he decided to retire. He referred to his baseball career as his "six-year paid vacation." He said that pitching to players like Ernie Banks, Joe Torre, and Willie McCovey was a "dream come true."

John had earned his college degree in physical education and biology. He worked for five years as the Tribal Enterprise Director on an Indian reservation in Texas. He was a sales representative for a publishing company. Most recently he has worked for the Davis County Utah Mental Health agency, helping clients to learn how to cope with their problems through such recreations as rafting and mountain climbing. His children say he is "paid to play." He served in a Singles Ward Bishopric for a year. John mentioned that one of his sons was serving on a mission in Costa Rica when the United States invaded Panama to overthrow the Noriega regime, but pointed out that he was no relation of Manuel's.

JERRY NYMAN YEAR-BY-YEAR STATISTICS

Name: Gerald Smith Nyman

Born: November 23, 1942
Logan, UT

Hgt: 5′ 10″ **Wgt:** 165

Bats: Left **Throws:** Left

Home: Helena, MT

Minor League: 1965-1969

Year	Club	L	POS	G	IP	W	L	SO	BB	H	ERA	SV	SHO
1968	Chicago	AL	P	8	40	2	1	27	16	38	2.01	0	1
1969	Chicago	AL	P	20	65	4	4	40	39	58	5.29	0	1
1970	San Diego	NL	P	2	5	0	2	2	2	8	16.20	0	0
	Lifetime			30	110	6	7	69	57	104	4.58	0	2

JERRY NYMAN

*F*rom 1951 through 1956, the New York Yankees and Cleveland Indians fought tooth and nail for the American League pennant. Jerry rooted for the Indians while his father rooted for the Yankees. There must have been some interesting moments at home as the Indians finished second each year to the Yankees except in 1954 when they won 111 of 154 games while the Yankees won "only" 103 games. When asked who his favorite player was, Jerry said, "The Big Three at Cleveland," meaning pitchers Early Wynn, Bob Lemon, and Mike Garcia. Early on, Jerry identified with pitchers and envisioned himself as a pitcher. He said, "In high school and American Legion, I was normally an outfielder. I only pitched when they ran out of people who could throw strikes." When he did pitch, the results were sometimes amazing, like when he struck out 22 batters in a seven-inning game. Jerry explained, "I threw really hard, but I was so wild the hitters would swing to get out of the batter's box as fast as they could."

Jerry played halfback and quarterback in high school. He said that his team got "beat up pretty bad" in most games. In a scrimmage his senior year, he got beat up, breaking his leg. In track, he ran the 440 and in baseball he was one of the best hitters on the team. He attended a try-out camp held by the Philadelphia Phillies and had his "good stuff." Watching the try-out was Glen Tuckett, then coach of the Brigham Young University baseball team. He offered Jerry a scholarship that he accepted. Over 30 years later Jerry commented, "Tuckett probably hated the day he gave me a scholarship." Jerry was on the team during the 1962-1964 seasons but he didn't pitch in many games. Despite his lack of pitching time and some disagreements with his coach, he credits his experience at BYU as a big help in "growing up" and credits Tuckett for not throwing him off the team.

He had a good record pitching in the college summer league in Western Canada in 1964. He tried out with the Los Angeles Dodgers who told him to "take a hike." Instead Jerry attended a try-out with the Chicago White Sox and struck out nine batters in three innings. He was signed to a contract in September 1964 and pitched in the Florida State League in 1965, winning 16 games and striking out 226 batters in 192 innings with a 2.81 ERA. Jerry said of his season, "It was more victories than I had in high school, American Legion, and BYU combined." In 1966, he was on three different teams and had an ERA under 2.90 at each of them. He was 7-4 at Evansville playing Double A ball in 1967 and had a 2.76 ERA.

Jerry was promoted to Triple A ball in 1968 at Hawaii. It was perfect for him as he took up surfing and was on the waves everyday except his pitching day. He even traded his courtesy tickets to the Islander games in exchange for a surf board. He was doing well on the mound too with a 7-5 record and 3.09 ERA in mid-August. On August 22, the Detroit Tigers and White Sox got in a brawl that put Tommy John on the disabled list so the White Sox called Jerry up. Pitcher Joel Horlen developed a stiff neck and could not start on August 28. To Jerry's surprise he was picked just before game time to

On August 28, 1968, Jerry pitched a four-hit, complete game shutout over Mickey Mantle and the New York Yankees in his first Major League game.

start and the opposing team was none other that the "hated" Yankees. He said he was so scared and excited that he went to the men's room so he could be alone and say a prayer that he might be calm and confident. He pitched a complete game, four-hit shutout, winning 3-0. He even got a single in the third inning to start a three-run rally, and he held Mickey Mantle to only one hit. Immediately after the game, he telephoned home to tell his dad that he had just beaten his Yankees. On September 5, he pitched seven innings against the Washington Senators to win his second game.

During the first six weeks of the 1969 season, Jerry pitched in only one inning. Finally on May 17, he started against the Senators and blanked them 6-0, allowing only one hit. Jerry was also the hitting hero, smashing a bases-loaded double to drive in three runs. His manager, Don Gutteridge, said, "The wonderful thing about Jerry was that he never once complained that he was being overlooked." Reporter Edgar Munzel wrote an article that described Jerry as "a sound youngster with solid Mormon virtues." He won his next start against the Tigers and had a no-decision against the Yankees. He then lost four straight games that by coincidence all occurred on Sundays. By mid-July, he was in the bullpen and things weren't going much better. He was one of five White Sox pitchers to take a 17-0 beating from the Baltimore Orioles. He was sent down to Tucson for a month. Upon his return, he started two games and won both of them giving up only three runs in seventeen innings to finish the season with a 4-4 record.

In 1970, he had made the White Sox roster and was concluding spring training when he was shocked to learn he had been traded to the San Diego Padres for Tommie Sisk. He was even more shocked when he was assigned to their Triple A team in Salt Lake City. He pitched well and despite the Padres being terrible, losing 102 games, he wasn't called up. Jerry felt embarrassed to be playing in front of his friends at the minor league level when he knew he was a Major League player. He had a good spring training in 1971, but was again assigned to a Triple A team. Before the season was over, he was playing 'A' level ball and not very well. He lacked concentration, was thoroughly discouraged with himself, and was disgusted with the Padres. He arranged for trades to several teams but the Padres always demanded too high a price, nixing the deals. At this time Jerry learned from a former teammate about a baseball school in Missouri that needed a director so he took the job and retired from baseball.

For over ten years, he directed the summer youth baseball camp for eight- to nineteen-year-olds that in a typical year was attended by 700 boys. In the fall he would hunt and in the winter he skied. In 1989, he took a job as pitching coach for an A-level team in the San Francisco Giants organization. In 1990 and 1991, he was pitching coach in the Pittsburgh Pirates organization in the New York--Penn league. He said, "I enjoy it a lot. The players are really great. I would be willing to adopt some of them. And the Pirates let me make all of the pitching decisions for the team." In the off season, he is a ski guide, taking clients on remote skiing expeditions. He recently served as gospel doctrine teacher in his ward in Helena.

MONTE PEARSON YEAR-BY-YEAR STATISTICS

Name: Montgomery Marcellus Pearson

Born: September 2, 1909
Oakland, CA

Hgt: 6′ Wgt: 175

Bats: Right Throws: Right

Died: January 27, 1978

Minor League: 1929-1933

Year	Club	L	POS	G	IP	W	L	SO	BB	H	ERA	SV	SHO
1932	Cleveland	AL	P	8	8	0	0	5	11	10	10.13	0	0
1933	Cleveland	AL	P	19	135	10	5	54	55	111	2.33	0	0
1934	Cleveland	AL	P	39	255	18	13	140	130	257	4.52	2	0
1935	Cleveland	AL	P	30	182	8	13	90	103	199	4.90	0	1
1936	New York	AL	P	33	223	19	7	118	135	191	3.71	1	1
1937	New York	AL	P	22	145	9	3	71	64	145	3.17	1	1
1938	New York	AL	P	28	202	16	7	98	113	198	3.97	0	1
1939	New York	AL	P	22	146	12	5	76	70	151	4.49	0	0
1940	New York	AL	P	16	110	7	5	43	44	108	3.69	0	1
1941	Cincinnati	NL	P	7	24	1	3	8	15	22	5.18	0	0
	Lifetime			224	1430	100	61	703	740	1392	4.00	4	5

MONTE PEARSON

At age twelve, Monte moved to Fresno, California where he participated in the high school football, basketball, baseball, and track teams. His basketball team won the state championship all four years he played on the team. He excelled in baseball, initially playing third base and catcher. He was the star hitter on his team and possessed an exceptionally strong arm. He said, "My delight was to rear back and buzz the ball over to first base with all the speed I could command, in high hopes of separating the first baseman from his glove." He could throw strikes to second base from his catching position without standing up to throw. He was called upon to pitch in his first game when his team was already far behind in only the first inning. Everyone was excited that the team rallied and that Monte was the winning pitcher. He gave up 18 hits and walked 16 batters, but his team won 18-16, and Monte found out that he liked pitching. He also learned in high school that he could make an extra $5 or $10 playing semi-pro games. In 1926, he played for the Fresno Auto Parts team and in 1927, he played for the Valley Body and Radiator Works.

In 1929, Monte's semi-pro team played an exhibition game against the Oakland Oaks of the Pacific Coast League, and he pitched five innings of shutout ball and struck out eleven. The Oaks wanted to sign him but Monte didn't want to leave home. Finally they offered a contract he couldn't refuse. Reminiscing in 1941, he said, "Mister, don't think I wasn't scared when I hit Oakland." Nobody on the team talked to him or paid him any attention. After several days he wanted to go back to his farm. He noticed that during hitting practice the pitchers just lobbed the ball to the plate. He decided that if he got to pitch hitting practice he would fire the ball to the plate, making everyone mad and thus, getting sent home. He got his chance and nobody could touch him. He was sure he had just earned his pink slip off the team. The next day when he wasn't fired, he left anyway. He told his Mom that he wasn't good enough. The Oaks general manager located Monte and told him that all the players were raving about what a great pitcher he was. Monte said, "I went back and from then on forgot all about the farm." But he never forgot the cold shoulder he received and always made it a point to pay a lot of attention to newcomers, especially rookies.

In 1930, he made the Oakland team and had a 3-2 record with a hefty 5.78 ERA when he was sent to Phoenix in July to play more frequently. He was also a good hitter so he played outfield when he wasn't pitching. He spent all of 1931 with Oakland where he appeared in 40 games and had a 17-16 record. He began to develop a curve ball for which he became well-known later in his career. The Cleveland Indians purchased his contract in 1932, and he started the season with them. After eight games, he had a 10.13 ERA, and he was sent to Toledo where he struggled through a 3-9 season. The next year was a complete turnaround. He compiled an 11-5 record at Toledo and was called back to Cleveland on July 4. He had a 10-5 mark for the Tribe and his 2.33 ERA was the lowest in the American League in 1933. One of his ten wins was a no-hitter until the last out of the game against the Washington Senators.

MAKING MARSE JOE'S JUDGMENT STAND UP

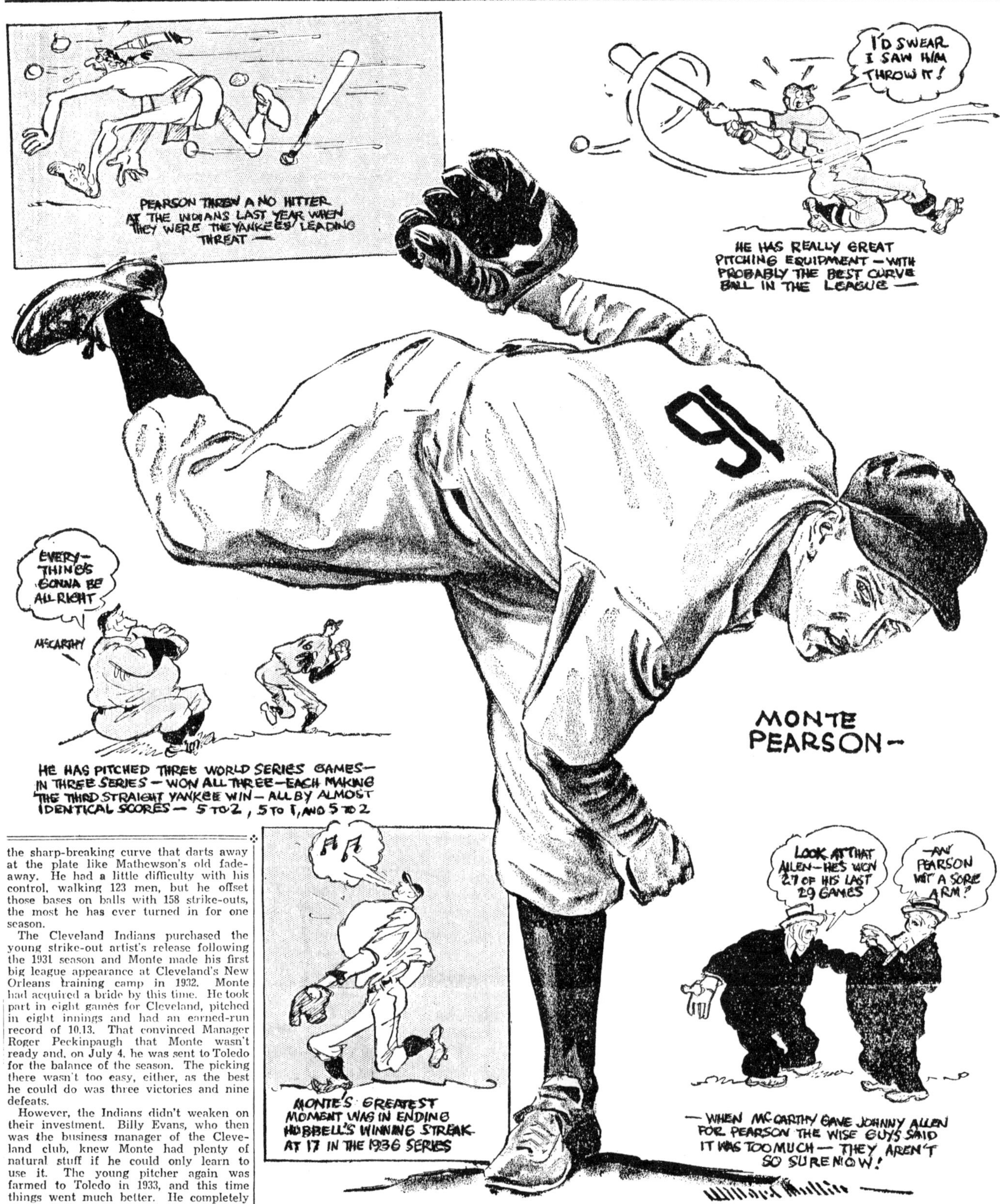

the sharp-breaking curve that darts away at the plate like Mathewson's old fade-away. He had a little difficulty with his control, walking 123 men, but he offset those bases on balls with 158 strike-outs, the most he has ever turned in for one season.

The Cleveland Indians purchased the young strike-out artist's release following the 1931 season and Monte made his first big league appearance at Cleveland's New Orleans training camp in 1932. Monte had acquired a bride by this time. He took part in eight games for Cleveland, pitched in eight innings and had an earned-run record of 10.13. That convinced Manager Roger Peckinpaugh that Monte wasn't ready and, on July 4, he was sent to Toledo for the balance of the season. The picking there wasn't too easy, either, as the best he could do was three victories and nine defeats.

However, the Indians didn't weaken on their investment. Billy Evans, who then was the business manager of the Cleveland club, knew Monte had plenty of natural stuff if he could only learn to use it. The young pitcher again was farmed to Toledo in 1933, and this time things went much better. He completely

In his rookie season in 1933, Monte led the AL with the lowest ERA, 2.33. On August 27, 1938, he pitched the first no-hitter in Yankee stadium history.

In 1934, he had an 18-13 record. A writer for *The Sporting News* said that his performance "stamped him as one of the coming great pitchers in the league." Unfortunately, he had a terrible season in 1935 with a dismal 8-13 record. Cleveland put him on the trading block and the New York Yankees offered Johnny Allen who had a 13-6 record in 1935. The Indians accepted immediately, but the Yankees never had any regrets. One of the reason given for the Yankees' interest was that in his three years with the Indians, Gehrig and Ruth had only a home run apiece off him. Another reason the Indians traded Monte was because he missed pitching assignments. Some in baseball felt that he was a hypochondriac and whiner. The Yankees manager, Joe McCarthy, dealt directly with the issue by having Monte examined by a doctor. The physician reported, "That fellow has no more right to be pitching than I have. He has the worst-looking arm I've ever examined. It's full of bone chips and calcium deposits and most of the time it hurts like the devil. But there will be days when he won't have a twinge." So the Yankee manager never assigned Monte in advance. Monte would test his arm each day and if he said it was okay, McCarthy would put him on the mound, replacing whoever was scheduled. It paid off.

Monte was a big part of the Yankees winning the pennant in 1936. His 19-7 record was the best winning percentage in the AL, and his 3.71 ERA and 118 strikeouts were the best on the Yankee pitching staff. He also showed he could hit in the big leagues, collecting 23 hits in 91 at bats for a .253 batting average. Pitchers like to talk about their hitting exploits, so Monte must have had a great time after the June 17 game since he went 4-for-4 with four RBIs! He had a sore arm in 1937 that limited his year although he recovered in time to be a factor in the World Series. On August 27, 1938, he pitched the first no-hit shutout in Yankee Stadium history, beating his old teammates, the Indians, 13-0. He faced the minimum number of 27 batters, as two Indians who had walked were erased on double plays. He was 12-5 in 1939 and his batting average was .321. He compiled a winning percentage of over 70 percent in his four years on the Yankees and was selected to the AL All-Star team in 1936 and 1940.

Reggie Jackson earned the nickname of Mr. October for his 1978 World Series heroics when he led the Yankees to victory by hitting five homers in six games. The next year he hit two homers and drove in eight runs during the World Series. But Monte Pearson was the original Mr. October as he won a World Series game in each of four successive World Series, 1936-1939, without incurring a loss. He is the only pitcher in the history of the game to hold such a record. And they were great games.

In 1936, the best pitcher in the National League was Carl Hubbell of the New York Giants, with a 26-6 record and a 2.31 ERA. Hubbell had won 17 straight games including a 6-1 victory over the Yankees in the first game of the World Series. Over 66,000 fans turned out, the largest attendance in the 33-year history of the Series, to see Hubbell go against Monte in Game Four. Hubbell left the game after seven innings, while Monte won a complete game victory, 5-2. He also had a double and a single off Hubbell showing that he was a complete ball player. Of the game, Monte said, "I never wanted a game so much in my life and I don't think I ever had more stuff . . . When I saw Gehrig's home run, I knew I would win."

Monte is the only pitcher to win a World Series game in four consecutive years without losing a game. His 1.01 ERA is the seventh lowest of all World Series pitchers.

The 1937 World Series was a rematch between the Yankees and Giants. The result was the same: a win for Monte and another Series Championship for the Yankees. Monte did add a little suspense to his five-hit, 5-1 victory, by loading the bases in the ninth. With two outs, relief pitcher, Johnny Murphy, came in to get the last out. There was no suspense in the 1938 Series as the Yankees swept the Chicago Cubs in four games. Monte won Game Three by a 5-2 score on five hits. After the game, Cubs manager Gabby Hartnett said, "Where does that guy get all that stuff? I've seen some pretty good curve ball pitchers, but that fellow certainly can make the ball duck over the corners." Monte saved his best for 1939. The Yankees swept the Cincinnati Reds and so did Monte with a 4-0 shutout that was a no-hitter through the first seven innings. Along with his 4-0 Series record, he struck out 28 batters, walked only seven, had an incredibly low 1.01 ERA, and batted .250. He had three complete games and nearly completed the fourth game. He allowed an average of only 4.79 hits per nine innings, just about the lowest in World Series history. The winner's share for the four World Series totaled less than $23,000, not much today, but no one in today's game has earned four World Series rings. He was recognized as a star of his time--he appeared on the front of Wheaties, "the breakfast of champions."

Monte tore a shoulder ligament in 1939, fielding a routine grounder in the fifth inning of a game. He stayed in the game despite the pain to gain a victory over Bob Feller and the Indians--in fourteen innings. It demonstrated toughness and courage, but he never fully recovered from the injury. In 1940, he started well but was used less and less frequently and was finally sold to the Reds. In 1941, he pitched in only seven games. His only win was a five-hit victory over the Philadelphia Phillies. He was released to the minors where he pitched in only one game. His 1940 baseball card referred to Monte as a future Hall of Famer, but his arm was shot and so was his career.

World War II had begun and Monte worked at an airbase fire department where they would ferry damaged airplanes to repair them. On several occasions, the planes crashed upon landing and Monte rescued the pilot before the plane exploded. In 1944, he was player-manager of the Lockheed team in the San Joaquin Valley league. He was an all-star at second base. In one stint as pitcher, he struck out twelve batters in five innings, but gave up eleven hits. From 1949-1952, he directed a baseball school in Fresno. For many years he helped outfit local Little League teams with baseball mitts. He was elected to the Fresno Athletic Hall of Fame in 1967. In 1977, he was the Special Honoree at the Fresno Hot Stove Dinner, attended by Johnny Bench, Joe Morgan, and Tom Seaver. He died in 1978 of cancer.

Speaking of baseball in 1933, Monte expressed feelings that are true for most players, even today. He said,

> A player may get weary and worn out by the grind toward the end of the season and heartily wish he could get home and forget about it. He may even think that it is high time to quit a most uncertain profession but by the first of February the next year his 'dogs' are just tickling to romp out on that diamond. Nothing else seems so desirable as baseball then.

"RED" PEERY YEAR-BY-YEAR STATISTICS

Name: George Allen Peery

Born: August 15, 1906
Payson, UT

Hgt: 5′ 11″ Wgt: 160

Bats: Left Throws: Left

Died: May 6, 1985

Minor League: 1923-1932 ?

Year	Club	L	POS	G	IP	W	L	SO	BB	H	ERA	SV	SHO
1927	Pittsburgh	NL	P	1	1	0	0	0	1	0	0.00	0	0
1929	Boston	NL	P	9	44	0	1	3	9	53	5.11	0	0
	Lifetime			10	45	0	1	3	10	53	5.00	0	0

RED PEERY

*A*s a youth, Red would play baseball nearly every day. When he didn't have anyone to play catch with, he would throw against the side of his family's brick home. He must have had a strong arm because the house was peppered with chip marks from Red's pitches. A relative reported that Red's catchers regularly inserted a cut of beef into their gloves to cushion the impact of his pitches. By the time he was fourteen, Red was a key player on local semi-pro teams in the Ogden, Utah area.

In 1923, Red was pitching for Magna in the old Utah Copper League that had many great players with Major League capabilities. That year Magna played an exhibition game against the Salt Lake City Bees of the Pacific Coast League. The Bees roster contained several players who would play in the big leagues including Tony Lazzeri of the New York Yankees whom Red struck out twice in the game. Tony was being hassled by his manager for letting a sixteen-year old kid get the better of him. He retorted, "If you think he's so easy, get a bat and try hitting against him yourself." Soon after the game, Red was signed to a pro contract.

A baseball authority of the time, Floyd Sullivan, reported, "George (Red) Peery may have been the best all-around baseball player developed in Utah. He was a terrific pitcher, a great fielder--maybe the best I ever saw--and a good hitter who could play the outfield." Red was selected as a first-team all-star pitcher in 1926 in the Western League where he played for St. Joseph. In 1927, he pitched for Wichita in the Western League and was called up at the end of the season by the Pittsburgh Pirates. It was an exciting time to be with the Pirates as they were in the thick of a pennant race with the St. Louis Cardinals and New York Giants. With so much on the line, Red was able to get into only one game. On September 22, with the Pirates beating the Giants 5 to 2, he entered the game to pitch the ninth inning. Before the largest crowd in Pirates history, he pitched no-hit, no-run relief. The Pirates won the pennant by a game and one-half and played the Yankees in the World Series. Red had joined the team too late to be on the post-season roster. As a momento of winning the National League pennant, the team gave Red a diamond-studded cigarette lighter. He was upset with the choice of the gift; nevertheless, when he accidentally threw the lighter out the window of a moving automobile, he spent over an hour looking for it without luck.

In 1929, Red was in the Boston Braves farm system and was assigned to Providence in the Eastern League. He had ten victories by mid-July and was promoted to the parent team to serve as a relief pitcher. His first game on July 17 was against his former teammates, the Pirates. He held them to one hit in five innings. On August 16, he pitched six innings against the Pirates. On August 20, he pitched three innings of shutout baseball against the Cincinnati Reds and at the plate, he was one for one and scored a run. On September 2, he pitched three innings against the Brooklyn Dodgers. Four days later, he pitched four innings against the Chicago Cubs. He pitched six

Red was the first LDS player to pitch in the Major Leagues. He pitched in one game for the 1927 Pittsburgh Pirates and nine games for the 1929 Boston Braves.

innings against the Reds on September 15, giving up only one run and getting a hit himself. His appearance on September 20 was disappointing as he took a loss against the Pirates. He pitched three innings against the Philadelphia Phillies on September 27.

Red experienced arm problems and was unable to remain in the Majors. In 1930, he appeared in five games for San Antonio and posted a disappointing 0-3 record. John Mooney, sports editor of the *Salt Lake City Tribune*, quoted Occie Evans, who played a lot of ball in the late 1920s and throughout the 1930s, regarding Red, "Peery had hurt his arm and come back down from the Majors. He had lost his fast ball, but he had all the pitching guile in the world." Among his cherished memories was pitching to Lou Gehrig and Babe Ruth during spring training.

As his nickname implies, Red had reddish hair, and he possessed the fiery temperament often associated with redheads. He had a quick temper and although he was not a large person, he would take on anyone regardless of size. An example of his fiestiness as told by relatives occurred after a game that he lost. He went to get a hair cut and shave at a barber shop where he was not well-known. Some fans came into the shop and started complaining to the barber about the poorly-pitched game they had witnessed that day. Red was in the barber's chair with his face lathered up so the fans couldn't recognize him. He was quickly fed up so he got out of the chair and started for the door. The barber said, "Aren't you going to pay?" and Red replied in stronger language than this quote, "No way, I'm the guy you people have been griping about."

After baseball, he worked for the Utah Department of Transportation, repairing radiators. He enjoyed being outdoors and would take motorcycle trips to neighboring states even when he was in his early 70s.

WALLY RITCHIE YEAR-BY-YEAR STATISTICS

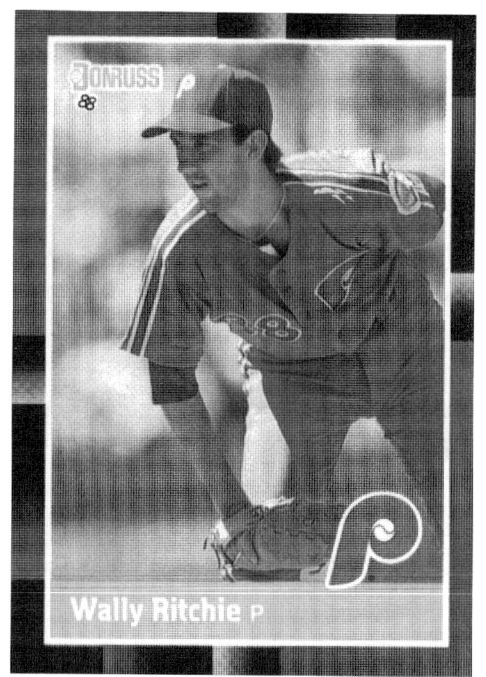

Name: Wallace Reid Ritchie

Born: July 12, 1965
Glendale, CA

Hgt: 6′ 2″ **Wgt:** 180

Bats: Left **Throws:** Left

Home: Glendale, CA

Minor League: 1985-1991

Year	Club	L	POS	G	IP	W	L	SO	BB	H	ERA	SV	SHO
1987	Philadelphia	NL	P	49	62	3	2	45	29	60	3.75	3	0
1988	Philadelphia	NL	P	19	26	0	0	8	17	19	3.12	0	0
	Lifetime			68	88	3	2	53	46	79	3.57	3	0

WALLY RITCHIE

Wally was a high school star pitcher leading his team to a division pennant with a 12-1 record. He earned all-area honors and accepted a baseball scholarship to attend Brigham Young University. As a relief pitcher, he helped BYU win the Western Athletic Conference title in 1984. The next year, he transferred to Glendale Junior College near his home. He was a starting pitcher and had a 12-3 record. The Philadelphia Phillies selected him in the fourth round of the June 1985 draft.

Wally began as a starting pitcher in the minors. He had a 4-1 record in 1985. He switched to relief pitching in 1986 and had a great year. He was promoted in mid-year to Reading in the Double A Eastern League. He had a total of 60 appearances with an 8-2 record and 14 saves. He had an impressive spring training in 1987 with the Phillies. In one relief appearance, he struck out four of the six Toronto Blue Jays he faced. He also threw two scoreless innings against the New York Mets. Pitching coach Claude Osteen said, "Wally's performance against the Blue Jays was the best outing by a pitcher I saw all spring."

He began the 1987 season at Maine, the Phillies Triple A team. On May 1, he was in a Phillies' uniform ready to pitch against the Cincinnati Reds. In the seventh inning, he entered the game and struck out Dave Parker and Buddy Bell to end the inning. Wally said that his first appearance was the most memorable game of his career. He faced the Reds again two days later, pitching two innings and recording three strikeouts including one against the hot-hitting Eric Davis. In his first four appearances, he pitched shutout baseball, striking out seven batters in five innings. He won his first game on June 3. He returned to the minors briefly but was back in the lineup on July 30 to register his first Major League save, pitching three shutout innings against the Pittsburgh Pirates. He appeared in 49 games with three wins and three saves.

In 1988, Wally started with the Phillies; however, he developed control problems, walking 17 batters in 26 innings--real trouble for a relief pitcher. He was used less frequently, which made it harder to be sharp when he did pitch. Finally, he was assigned to Maine. In 1989, the Phillies Triple-A team was located in Scranton, where Wally pitched in both starting and relief roles. One of his teammates in 1988 and 1989 was Church member, Tommy Barrett.

Wally had a 4-3 record as a starter in Scranton in 1990, when he developed arm trouble and was placed on the disabled list. He underwent surgery in August to remove bone chips and calcium deposits. He worked out at BYU and looked forward to pitching his way back to the big leagues. He said, "I know I have the ability to play in the Major Leagues. If I get the right opportunity, I'll make it."

Wally got off to a good start in 1991 at Scranton as a starter. After the first month, he had a 1-0 record with 16 strikeouts in 18 innings. He was disappointed when the

Wally pitched middle relief for the Philadelphia Phillies, appearing in 49 games in 1987 and 19 games in 1988. He rejoined the team in May 1991.

Phillies decided to move him to the bullpen to strengthen their relief pitching. In the next eight innings, he struck out nine batters and earned a save. He got his opportunity to rejoin the Phillies on May 6 when starting players Len Dyksta and Darren Daulton were involved in an automobile accident. Wally pitched to one batter on May 7 against the San Diego Padres. He got the out; it was a great feeling to be back in the Majors. On June 4, he entered the game against the Atlanta Braves to pitch the eighth inning. It was an inning that he probably wishes he could forget. The first batter was Otis Nixon who in the sixth inning had stolen a base despite the Braves being ahead by several runs. Wally nearly hit Nixon and then his next pitch landed on Nixon's leg. Nixon felt Wally was throwing at him on purpose and charged the mound, kicking Wally in the ribs and landing several punches. A full-scale brawl ensued with the result that Wally went on the disabled list for bruised ribs and was suspended for a game. Nixon was suspended for four games.

In comparing starting and relief pitching, Wally said, "I enjoy starting assignments because you have more control of your outcome than coming in when there are already men on base." His best pitch is his changeup. He considers Tony Gywnn of the San Diego Padres the toughest man to get out since he waits on the ball and is hard to fool.

Wally has been a Church member all his life. His advice to fellows entering pro ball is to keep high standards and work very hard--don't cheat yourself. Wally feels he has been supported by everyone in his efforts to keep Church standards. He reads a lot, especially adventures and mysteries.

FRED SANFORD YEAR-BY-YEAR STATISTICS

Name: John Frederick Sanford

Born: August 9, 1919
Garfield, UT

Hgt: 6′ 1″ **Wgt:** 200

Bats: Right **Throws:** Right

Home: Salt Lake City, UT

Minor League: 1939-43; 1946; 1952-53

Year	Club	L	POS	G	IP	W	L	SO	BB	H	ERA	SV	SHO
1943	St. Louis	AL	P	3	9	0	0	2	4	7	1.93	0	0
1946	St. Louis	AL	P	3	22	2	1	8	9	19	2.05	0	2
1947	St. Louis	AL	P	34	187	7	16	62	76	186	3.71	4	0
1948	St. Louis	AL	P	42	227	12	21	79	91	250	4.64	2	1
1949	New York	AL	P	29	95	7	3	51	57	100	3.87	0	0
1950	New York	AL	P	26	113	5	4	54	79	103	4.55	0	0
1951	NY-Wash-St.L	AL	P	27	91	4	10	29	75	79	6.82	0	0
	Lifetime			164	744	37	55	285	391	768	4.45	6	3

FRED SANFORD

Fred's American Legion team won the Utah State Championship in 1935 and 1936. His combined pitching record was 14-2. He recorded 20 strikeouts in one nine-inning game. After three years of semi-pro ball, Fred signed a contract in 1939 with the St. Louis Browns, now the Baltimore Orioles, and went to Youngstown, Ohio. He was 14-12 in 1940, had a 2.84 ERA in 1941, and pitched at the Triple A level at Toledo in 1942. Fred began the 1943 season with the Browns but on May 20, he was sent back to Toledo where he would get more pitching time. He won a 12-inning game, 1-0, and retired the last 27 batters in order--the equivalent of a nine-inning no-hitter! He also got a single in the bottom of the twelfth inning that led to the winning run. He entered the Army in October 1943 and spent the 1944 and 1945 seasons serving in the South Pacific and Japan.

Returning from the military, Fred pitched for Toledo in 1946 and had a great year leading the league in complete games, strikeouts, and victories. He was the leading vote-getter in the league's all-star balloting. He joined the Browns at the end of the season, and his first start on September 15 was against the mighty New York Yankees. Fred said, "The game was one of my career highlights." He pitched a five-hit shutout, winning 1-0. A week later, he threw another shutout, winning 2-0 against the Chicago White Sox . He also got a single and drove in one of the two runs. In 1947, he won seven games with the Browns. In a game against the Red Sox, the batter bunted a pitch. It was bouncing foul and just to make sure it stayed foul, Fred threw his glove at the ball. Now throwing your glove at a hit ball is against the rules, but do you know what the penalty is? Well, Fred must have not known either, because the batter gets a triple! In this case, it must have been one of the shortest triples in history.

He was the Opening Day pitcher for the Browns in 1948, facing Hall of Fame pitcher, Bob Feller, before 73,000 Cleveland fans. He lost that game but won four games in April and May toward a career high twelve victories. He led the Browns in victories but he also endured 21 defeats. For fans who don't remember the St. Louis Browns, they were not very good as their 59-94 record in 1948 demonstrates. While in St. Louis, Fred became good friends with Hall of Famer, Dizzy Dean, who was the radio announcer for the Browns.

During the off-season, Fred stayed in shape by refereeing college basketball games. He also worked as a deputy sheriff. Imagine Fred's surprise when he learned he had been traded from the lowly Browns to the powerhouse Yankees. It was not an ordinary trade. The Yankees gave the Browns three players plus $100,000 in cash. That doesn't sound like so much today but in 1949 not even the best players like Ted Williams made $100,000. So the trade in today's terms would read, "Yankees give Browns $6,000,000 in cash plus three players worth over $1,000,000 each for Sanford." Obviously the Yankees expected big things from Fred. One of the people who encouraged the Yankees to make the deal for Fred was Joe DiMaggio, whom Fred usually got out.

In 1948, Fred led the St. Louis Browns with twelve victories. He was traded to the New York Yankees in 1949 for the equivalent of $9,000,000 in today's money.

He was on a better team, made more money, and got two World Series rings, but he was not very happy. The New York media was very demanding, expecting all-star caliber pitching. He needed to work every four or five days to stay sharp, but sometimes he went two weeks between starts. The Yankees' new manger, Casey Stengel, and the new pitching coach had not participated in the trade decision and felt no urgency to play Fred regularly. To compound matters, Fred stepped on a water sprinkler head while running in the outfield and was out for three weeks. He pitched less than half the innings he had with the Browns. He was 7-3 in 1949, and won three games in a row during the last month of the season to help the Yankees win the AL pennant by one game over the Red Sox. In 1950, he was 5-4. Forty years later, Fred described being on two World Series teams as career highlights, but not having a good chance to live up to what the Yankees hoped for as a major disappointment.

His last year in the Majors was 1951 when he played for New York, and for the Washington Senators before going back to the Browns. His record was 4-10. In 1952 and 1953, he pitched for Portland in the Pacific Coast League, going 17-9 and 7-11, respectively. He hurt his arm in 1953 and retired from baseball.

Fred's parents had joined the Church in England and migrated to Utah. He was raised in the Church and married in the Salt Lake Temple. People in baseball knew that Fred was a "family man" and lived by positive values. He was one of the first Church members to be noted as a Mormon in the press. His St. Louis manager, Zack Taylor, said "Fred is one of the cleanest-living boys I have ever seen in the big leagues."

After baseball, Fred worked as a construction inspector for Salt Lake City checking street work, viaducts, and reservoirs. He continued to referee basketball and football games, and he worked as ticket manager with the minor league Salt Lake Bees for eighteen years. He retired in 1982. He and his wife like to travel and have been to Europe four times, sailed through the Panama Canal, and seen most of the U.S. He is an avid golfer, playing nearly every day the weather permits. He receives a couple of letters a week asking him to autograph baseball cards. He is a member of the Utah Baseball Hall of Fame.

ELMER SINGLETON YEAR-BY-YEAR STATISTICS

Name: Bert Elmer Singleton

Born: June 26, 1920
Ogden, UT

Hgt: 6′ 2″ Wgt: 190

Bats: Both Throws: Right

Home: Plain City, UT

Minor League: 1940-42; 1944-46; 1949-63

Year	Club	L	POS	G	IP	W	L	SO	BB	H	ERA	SV	SHO
1945	Boston	NL	P	7	37	1	4	14	14	35	4.82	0	0
1946	Boston	NL	P	15	34	0	1	17	21	27	3.74	1	0
1947	Pittsburgh	NL	P	36	67	2	2	24	39	70	6.31	1	0
1948	Pittsburgh	NL	P	38	92	4	6	53	40	90	4.97	2	0
1950	Washington	AL	P	21	36	1	2	19	17	39	5.20	0	0
1957	Chicago	NL	P	5	13	0	1	6	2	20	6.75	0	0
1958	Chicago	NL	P	2	5	1	0	2	1	1	0.00	0	0
1959	Chicago	NL	P	21	43	2	1	25	12	40	2.72	0	0
	Lifetime			145	327	11	17	160	146	322	4.83	4	0

ELMER SINGLETON

*E*lmer's father was hopeful that his son would become a professional baseball player. Each year as a child, Elmer received a ball more and more like a baseball until as a seven-year old, he played catch and hit using a regulation baseball. His father insisted that he play the infield although his goal was for Elmer to become a pitcher. He wasn't allowed to pitch until he was sixteen. He did not play baseball in high school but participated in organized leagues during the summers. He was signed by the Cincinnati Reds in 1939 after he struck out five of six batters at a baseball tryout in Salt Lake City. He was soon released but then signed with the New York Yankees when they saw him pitch a no-hitter and hit a grand slam homer in a semi-pro tournament in Ogden. He won his first minor league game 2-1 in 1940. Overall it was a learning season as he gave up 218 hits and 111 walks in 165 innings, registering a 7.69 ERA.

In the 1941 season, he showed much improvement as he struck out 71 batters in 70 innings and walked only 28 while cutting his ERA in half to 3.21. Unfortunately his season was shortened because of an arm injury. He tried to enlist in the military but was rejected because of a knee injury. In 1942, he was promoted to Double A ball at Oklahoma City. The team was nearly bankrupt so instead of travelling by train, they went by car and Elmer was one of the regular drivers. On one occasion, after driving all night (750 miles from Tulsa to Houston), he was the starting pitcher. He posted an 11-15 record with a 3.04 ERA. It wasn't until after Thanksgiving that he was fully paid. Elmer said at the time, "The door of the club office was always locked on pay day." He voluntarily sat out the 1943 season because he wanted to be with his wife who was pregnant. Doctors had told them they wouldn't have children so he was really excited.

He returned to baseball in 1944 playing at the Triple A level. In a play-off game, he came in during the second inning with bases loaded and none out and pitched shutout ball for the rest of the game, winning the game. He started another play-off game, shutting out Baltimore 5-0. Again with Kansas City in 1945 in the minors, he pitched the best game of his career to that point by tossing a no-hitter until the last out in the ninth inning. After winning his first three games, he tore tendons in his heel from sliding too hard into second base. He had a 7-6 record and a great 2.43 ERA when his contract was bought by the Boston Braves on August 15, and he joined the big league team. In posting a 1-4 record, he beat the Reds 3-2 and lost three close games: to the Pirates 3-2, to the Cubs 2-0, and to the Cardinals 4-2. He performed principally as a relief pitcher for the Braves in 1946.

He played the 1947 and 1948 seasons with the Pittsburgh Pirates, appearing in 74 games over the two years. On April 30, 1947, he treated his teammates to celebrate his first victory as a Pirate. What is interesting is that later he learned he had not won the game. Here is what happened; you be the judge. With the Pirates losing to the Philadelphia Phillies 4-1, Elmer entered the game in the fifth inning with men on base and two out. He did his job by getting the third out without anyone scoring. He was

On April 24, 1952, Elmer pitched no-hit baseball for 12 and 1/3 innings. Unfortunately his own team couldn't score any runs and he lost the game 1-0.

lifted for a pinch hitter who started a rally that put the Pirates ahead 5-4. The next relief pitcher, Eric Bonham, started the sixth inning and finished the game, pitching four scoreless innings. It was a happy time in the club house as the Pirates celebrated their come-from-behind victory. They left to continue their celebration with Singleton as the winning pitcher since he was the pitcher of record when the team went ahead and with Bonham credited with a save. The next day in the papers they learned that the official scorer had a different idea and had decided that Bonham did more to earn the win and listed him as the winning pitcher. After discussing his decision with some players and coaches, the scorer changed his mind and gave the win to Elmer, but over a month later, the scorer reversed himself again and gave the win to Bonham. What do you think? In any case, it sounds a lot like, "Who's on First?"

He played the 1949 and 1950 seasons in the Pacific Coast League at San Francisco and earned a relief-pitching role with the Washington Senators during the latter part of 1950. Between 1951 and 1958, Elmer was one of the best pitchers in the PCL. In 1952, he won 17 games for the San Francisco Seals. One of the games he didn't win was a show-stopper. On April 24, he pitched no-hit baseball for 12 and 1/3 innings. Unfortunately his own team couldn't score any runs and he lost the game 1-0. It is recognized as one of the best-pitched games in minor league history. He won 15 games in 1953, 13 in 1954, and 19 games for Seattle in 1955. On July 24, 1955, he won the seven-inning nightcap of a double header, pitching no-hit ball. In 1956, he was selected by *Look* magazine to the all-PCL team with an 18-8 record and the league's lowest ERA.

In 1957, he made the Chicago Cubs roster but developed a sore arm and saw limited action. He won 13 games at Portland in 1958, and joined the Cubs at the end of the season. He pitched five scoreless innings in two games, winning one of them. 1959 was his last year in the Majors, pitching in 20 games for the Cubs with a 2-1 record and 2.72 ERA. Elmer continued in baseball, appearing in 85 games during the 1960-1963 seasons in the PCL compiling a 32-25 record. He was sometimes accused of throwing a spitball and in a 1961 game against Portland, the opposing manager protested five times to the umpire that the ball was sinking six inches straight down because of the spitter. Elmer retorted that he had great stuff that game, especially his sinker. He said later in an interview, "You know, as long as you've left the impression that you throw a spitball, it's as good as having an extra pitch."

Elmer didn't put up his pitching glove until age 43, having played in 671 pro games and pitched in at least 150 innings in thirteen seasons. He had 195 professional victories and many more of them would have been in the Majors if there had been 26 teams instead of the sixteen that existed during the 1950s. He was a playing coach in the 1960s at Seattle and Tacoma. He said. "The only year I was perfect was my last year, 1963, with a 1-0 record." He was the pitching coach and Tacoma was being routed by five runs, so instead of using another pitcher for the ninth inning, he put himself in the game and retired the side. To everyone's amazement including his own, Tacoma rallied to score six runs and he won the game!

Elmer pitched until age 43, playing in 671 pro games. Elmer quipped, "I helped a lot of players get to Cooperstown." Then seriousnessly, he said, "I cherished every time I went to the mound."

In reminiscing, Elmer told of facing Ted Williams in an exhibition game at Fenway Park when the wind was blowing about 40 miles per hour into Williams. Despite the adversity, Elmer said that Williams creamed one of his pitches twenty rows over the right-field fence. When Elmer sat down in the dugout, the player next to him said, "Gee whiz Elmer, he sure got hold of that one." Three innings later this same player was pitching and the wind was still blowing as hard when Williams came up. Williams smashed the ball forty rows over the right-field fence. You can imagine the fun Elmer had when the pitcher came into the dugout. Elmer quipped, "I helped a lot of players get to Cooperstown." Then in a moment of seriousness, he stated, "I cherished every time I went to the mound."

After leaving baseball, he worked in road construction with his son. He returned to Plain City, near Ogden, to retire in 1978.

TOMMIE SISK YEAR-BY-YEAR STATISTICS

Name: Tommie Wayne Sisk

Born: April 12, 1942
Adrmore, OK

Hgt: 6′ 3″ Wgt: 195

Bats: Right Throws: Right

Home: Orem, UT

Minor League: 1960-1964

Year	Club	L	POS	G	IP	W	L	SO	BB	H	ERA	SV	SHO
1962	Pittsburgh	NL	P	5	18	0	2	6	8	18	4.00	0	0
1963	Pittsburgh	NL	P	57	108	1	3	73	45	85	2.92	1	0
1964	Pittsburgh	NL	P	42	61	1	4	35	29	91	6.16	0	0
1965	Pittsburgh	NL	P	38	111	7	3	66	50	103	3.40	0	1
1966	Pittsburgh	NL	P	34	150	10	5	60	52	146	4.14	1	1
1967	Pittsburgh	NL	P	37	208	13	13	85	78	196	3.34	1	2
1968	Pittsburgh	NL	P	33	96	5	5	41	35	101	3.28	1	0
1969	San Diego	NL	P	53	143	2	13	59	48	160	4.78	6	0
1970	Chicago	AL	P	17	33	1	1	16	13	37	5.45	0	0
	Lifetime			316	928	40	49	441	358	937	3.92	10	4

TOMMIE SISK

Tommie's favorite book as a youth was *How to Pitch* by Bob Feller. When he wasn't reading the book, he was playing baseball. It must have helped since he was voted the California American Legion Player of the Year in 1958, pitching his team to the Southern California championship. In 1959, he pitched a nine-inning no-hitter for the American Legion All-Stars against the Los Angeles Dodgers rookie team. In 1960, he not only continued to wow the baseball scouts with a three-year 34-0 record; he led his high school basketball team to the Southern California championship. He scored 48 points in one basketball game and was named Southern California's High School Athlete of the Year in 1960. He received numerous basketball scholarship offers, including one from Brigham Young University even though he wasn't a Church member at the time. But how could someone who read *How to Pitch* all his life do anything other than become a baseball pitcher? He signed a bonus contract with the Pittsburgh Pirates in June 1960.

Reflecting on his success in athletics, Tommie recently said, "I wouldn't have become what I did in sports without the dedicated support of my Mom and Dad. From the time I was ten, my Dad would spend hours playing catch with me after work, and my Mom was at every one of my games." He also gives a lot of credit to his first pro manager, Harding Peterson, a former catcher. Peterson was a good teacher and helped Tommie with his control problems. In his first year he walked 87 batters in 96 innings, but he had good stuff as evidenced by a no-hitter against a Dodger rookie team. The next year, he was 12-3 and was promoted during the season to the Triple-A level. He started the 1962 season with Columbus and pitched well enough to be called up by the Pirates in July to pitch in a doubleheader and to join the team at the end of the season. His first complete game was on September 2--a foggy, rainy, cold afternoon. He pitched well enough to win but lost 2-0 against the Milwaukee Braves. In his second year in the minors in Asheville, Tommie became a good long-time friend with future Hall of Famer, Willie Stargell.

Any time a pitcher leads his team in relief appearances you know he is pitching well, and that is what Tommie did in his rookie year with the Pirates in 1963. He had a 2.92 ERA in 57 games. He had a so-so year in 1964 but rebounded in 1965 with a 7-3 record. In 1966 he became a key pitcher in the Pirate starting rotation with a 10-5 record. He had a few troublesome games at the beginning of the year as he gave up six homers in his first 22 innings. He settled down to have a 4-2 record going into August. Then he experienced the best month of his career as he earned five victories without a defeat. He pitched a complete game victory over the Cincinnati Reds on August 6. On August 12, the Pirates were engaged in a slugfest with the Reds with the score tied 11-11 after eleven innings. Tommie entered the game as the Pirates sixth pitcher and shutout the Reds for two innings . He was credited with the victory as the Pirates scored in the thirteenth. He won his seventh game on August 16 when he held the New York Mets to two hits. On August 19, he beat the Chicago Cubs and on September 3, he beat the Cubs again in a complete game victory that raised his record to 9-2.

In 1966, Tommie was a key member of the Pittsburgh Pirates pitching corps with a 10-5 record. The next year, he led the team in complete games, innings pitched, and shutouts.

For Tommie, the highlight of his pro career was combined with a personal celebration in August 1965. He attended the birth of his son at 9 o'clock that morning and then went to the ball park and beat the San Francisco Giants in an afternoon game. About five years later, he enjoyed the Father and Sons game the White Sox sponsored. He recounted with some pride that it was really neat to see his two sons running around the field with 'Sisk' on the back of their uniforms. Other highlights included pitching to some of baseball's greatest hitters. He remembers Hank Aaron doing well against him, but recalls Willie Mays getting only a single off him.

Tommie possessed a classic pitcher's lifetime batting average of .094. In one game in 1966 against the Mets, he hit like "Robeto Clemente," smashing two hits and collecting two RBIs. When asked about his batting, he laughed and said, "I was a good hitter in high school, hitting around .500. In the minors, I hit .280 but I went to pot in a hurry when I got to the Major Leagues." The game he remembers most as a hitter was when he struck out four times in a row trying to bunt. Manager Harry Walker had him taking bunting practice every day for the next two weeks. Tommie said, "My hands hurt so much from bunting practice that I could hardly pitch."

In 1967, he led the team in complete games, innings pitched, and shutouts. The 1968 season was not very kind to Tommie. New manager, Larry Shepherd, decided to use a three-pitcher rotation to start the year and then Tommie injured his ankle. When his ankle healed, there wasn't a spot in the rotation--not quite the treatment Tommie expected after doing well for three consecutive years. Although he had a 3.28 ERA, he was very disappointed that he pitched in less than 100 innings.

In the 1969 spring training, the Pirates used him so infrequently that Tommie was delighted when he learned he had been traded to the San Diego Padres. He could not have possibly guessed that 1969 would be a very long year. He did not win a game until September 6. He ended the season with a 2-13 record and 4.78 ERA. He was traded to the Chicago White Sox in March 1970 and pitched in relief. It was his last year in baseball.

His advice to players who are planning a pro career is to be dedicated to your profession. He reflected with some regret that instead of working hard to be a great ball player, he was satisfied to have made the Majors. He said, "I did just enough work and practice to get by, relying on my talent instead of magnifying it."

Tommie's family became active in the Church in the late 1960s. He joined the Church in 1970 and has since served in a bishopric and high council. After baseball, he entered the land title insurance business. He played in city basketball leagues until 1989. He is an avid golfer and has won a number of amateur titles.

CORY SNYDER YEAR-BY-YEAR STATISTICS

Name: James Cory Snyder

Born: November 11, 1962
Inglewood, CA

Hgt: 6′ 3″ Wgt: 175

Bats: Right Throws: Right

Home: Laguna Hills, CA

Minor League: 1985-1986

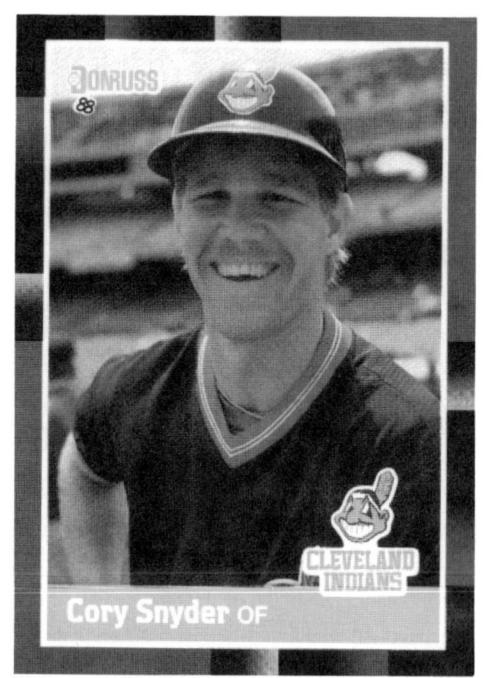

Year	Club	L	POS	G	AB	R	H	2	3	HR	RBI	SB	AVG
1986	Cleveland	AL	O,S,	103	416	58	113	21	1	24	69	2	.272
1987	Cleveland	AL	O,S	157	577	74	136	24	2	33	82	5	.236
1988	Cleveland	AL	O	142	511	71	139	24	3	26	75	5	.272
1989	Cleveland	AL	O	132	489	49	105	17	0	18	59	6	.215
1990	Cleveland	AL	O	123	438	46	102	27	3	14	55	1	.233
	Lifetime			657	2431	298	595	113	9	115	340	19	.245

CORY SNYDER

*I*f anyone ever grew up expecting to be a major league baseball player, it was Cory Snyder. His father worked with him every day during his little league years and used his own knowledge from playing in the minors to help Cory. A strong father-son relationship was created that would be important to Cory throughout his life. Unlike most gifted high school age athletes, Cory only played baseball, but he played it year round. As a junior in high school, he batted .450 playing shortstop and as a senior he was used mainly as a pitcher, compiling a 14-2 record and a 1.54 ERA.

Cory said, "I was supposed to go to Brigham Young University," meaning that special circumstances resulted in attending BYU. Cory sent flyers to USC, UCLA, ASU, and other colleges with strong baseball programs including BYU. Almost immediately he received a four-year full scholarship offer from BYU even though he had not been scouted by BYU. Disappointingly, none of the other schools even responded. Later, as Cory tore apart pitching of opponents as a freshman, coaches from schools he had sent flyers asked him, "Why didn't you even contact us and give us a chance to recruit you?" "What do you mean? I did send you flyers," was Cory's reply. It is hard to explain, but the result is history.

Cory started at BYU thinking he was going to be a pitcher, but the team had a strong pitching staff in 1982 so he battled for a starting spot at third base. In the season opener against UNLV, he hit three homers in his first three at bats! That game ended his pitching career and started his NCAA record of hitting 73 homers in three seasons. He was the first player in NCAA history to collect 20 homers or more in three consecutive seasons. His .900 single season slugging percentage was also an NCAA record, and he set seven BYU records. He capped his collegiate experience by playing on the 1984 U.S. Olympic baseball team, batting .400 with seven RBIs. He was selected to everyone's All-America team. Speaking of his years at BYU, Cory said, "My life was directed in a good way that has helped me a lot."

The Cleveland Indians considered Cory to be the best amateur player in America and picked him over Mark McGwire in the June 1984 draft. He won the Triple Crown at the 1985 Florida Instructional League with a .390 batting average, 14 homers, and 53 RBIs in only 46 games. Cory invited his dad to spring training in 1985. Cory said, "My dad knows my swing better than I do. I've listened to his advice since little league." His dad bought a satellite dish and video tape recorder with slow motion replay to be able to follow his son.

He was assigned to the Eastern League in 1985 and won the MVP award with 28 homers and 94 RBIs. He was promoted to Maine at the AAA level, but didn't stay there long. On June 12, 1986 Cory was called up by the Indians. He played four positions well and hit 24 homers in barely 400 at bats. It was the most homers by a Cleveland rookie since 1950. He ended the season in great style with a 17-game hitting streak, a

Cory was a college All-American and star of the 1984 U.S. Olympic team. He is one of the best outfielders in the game, especially noted for his "cannon arm." He had more assists during 1987-1989 than anyone in the Majors Leagues.

6-RBI game, and 14 RBIs in his last 20 games. If he had played a full year, he might have been Rookie-of-the-Year. The Indians director of minor leagues said, "Cory Snyder is the best draft choice ever made by the Cleveland Indians."

Cory continued his power hitting with 33 homers in 1987, leading the Indians. His 1987 exploits included two grand-slam homers and three homers in a game against the Twins. He started the 1988 season well, smashing 18 homers and 53 RBIs before the All-Star game. He was hampered by an injury but played anyway and his power dropped off. His hitting in 1989 was adversely affected by a painful back injury that resulted from a diving catch in May. Cory plays at 110% intensity even if his team is 30 runs behind, and he hates to sit out even when hurt. Consequently, he plays hurt frequently--something you rarely see in baseball anymore.

Cory is recognized as one of the best fielders in baseball. His "cannon arm" is already legendary. During 1987-1989, he made 50 outfield assists, more than anyone else in the Majors. In a poll of managers, he received the most votes for being the outfielder to gun down a runner . Cory said, "Throwing a runner out at the plate is as satisfying as hitting a homer since I am preventing the opponent from scoring." In 1990, Cory took a homer away from Wally Joyner with an "over-the-wall" catch.

During the off-season, he was traded to the Chicago White Sox. When the 1984 Olympic team was training they played a game in old Comisky Park in Chicago. In the game, Cory hit a mammoth homer, becoming the only amateur player to hit a ball over the left-field roof. Despite this "good omen," he got off to a very slow start in 1991. He didn't hit his first homer with the White Sox until May 28.

Cory enjoys playing golf and being with his family. He collects all of his baseball cards with his Topps Olympic card being his favorite. He receives about 75 cards each day to autograph and signs them all. In the last few years, he has only done one or two card shows a year and those were for charity. He said, I'd rather sign for free for kids, anyway." His advice to young players is to play hard. He said in an interview with *Sports Collectors Digest*, "You've got to have the gut drive to play baseball and the determination. Give 100 percent on and off the field. Do your best--nobody can ask more if you do your best."

BOB USHER YEAR-BY-YEAR STATISTICS

Name: Robert Royce Usher

Born: March 1, 1925
San Diego, CA

Hgt: 6′ 1″ **Wgt:** 185

Bats: Right **Throws:** Right

Home: San Jose, CA

Minor League: 1943,1947-1949
1952-1956; 1958

Year	Club	L	POS	G	AB	R	H	2	3	HR	RBI	SB	AVG
1946	Cincinnati	NL	O	92	152	16	31	5	1	1	14	2	.204
1947	Cincinnati	NL	O	9	22	2	4	0	0	1	1	0	.182
1950	Cincinnati	NL	O	106	321	51	83	17	0	6	35	3	.259
1951	Cincinnati	NL	O	114	303	27	63	12	2	5	25	4	.208
1952	Chicago	NL	O	1	0	0	0	0	0	0	0	0	.000
1957	Clev-Wash	AL	O	106	303	37	78	7	1	5	27	0	.257
	Lifetime			428	1101	133	259	41	4	18	102	9	.235

BOB USHER

Bob is probably the only person to go to the American Legion National Championship two years in a row, once as a catcher and the next year as a pitcher! In 1940, he was the backup catcher for Post 6 from San Diego. His team's regular catcher was a black who was disqualified because of his race from playing in the Championship series held in North Carolina, so Bob caught during the series. The next year, Bob led his team winning two of their three victories in the National Championship. He attended the 1940 World Series between Detroit and Cincinnati as well as the Yankee-Dodger World Series in 1941. Not bad for a fifteen and sixteen- year old.

Bob did not go unnoticed by pro scouts, especially Pat Patterson of the Cincinnati Reds who tried to sign Bob on several occasions during 1941-1943. Finally after high school, Bob signed with the Reds. He played for their minor league team at Birmingham in 1943 as an outfielder and batted .273. Then he went into the Navy for 30 months serving in Hawaii.

Upon discharge from the Navy in 1946, the Reds bought Bob's contract from Birmingham. He made the team as the fourth outfielder and played in 92 games. Bob spent the following three years in the minors. During spring training in 1948, he met Babe Ruth, his favorite player from childhood. The Babe personalized an autograph for Bob. Another career highlight happened in a spring training game when he slammed two homers off of pitching great, Warren Spahn. Bob said, "Those were the last hits I ever got off Spahn as he shut me down the rest of the year." In 1949, Bob had a good year at Syracuse hitting .287 with 14 homers and 81 RBIs.

1950 was Bob's best year in the Majors. He started the year right with a home run on Opening Day. He played in 106 games for the Reds, mostly against left-handers and batted .259 for the season. He felt that being platooned was not using his abilities to their best advantage since it is hard to stay sharp when you're not playing nearly every day and besides, he had some of his best days when he faced tough right-handers like Sal Maglie. In 1951, Bob had the misfortune to hit into a triple play. He was recognized as one of the best defensive outfielders in the National League. During the 1952 season, the Reds traded him to the Chicago Cubs who assigned him to their Pacific Coast League team in Southern California. During the off-season, Bob attended college classes at various schools including Miami University, San Diego State, and Syracuse.

After several so-so years, Bob was picked up by the Cleveland Indian organization in 1956. They assigned him to play with San Diego, his hometown. One week into spring training he had the scare of his life and feared that his career was ending as he experienced excruciating pain in both heels. Fortunately, he responded to cortisone shots and went on to have an outstanding season, batting .350. He was playing winter ball in the Dominican Republic when he learned that the Indians had added him to their

Bob played in two consecutive American Legion World Series. His best years in the Majors were 1950 with Cincinnati and 1957 with Washington. He hit a homer on opening day, 1950.

Major League roster. He started the 1957 season on the Cleveland Indians, and felt ecstatic that at age 32, which in the 1950s was considered old for a ball player, he had made it back to the Majors. After 10 games, he was traded to the Washington Senators where he played 96 games hitting .261. According to Bob, the picture on his 1958 baseball card shows him in a Cleveland uniform but wearing a Senators' hat. His last pro year was 1958 with a minor league team in Miami.

From 1958-1960, Bob worked as a bank collection manager. From 1962-1971, he worked as a counter intelligence investigator for the U.S. Navy. He served in the Department of Interior from 1971-1986 as a Protective Officer and Safety Manager. He was awarded his college degree in 1966 and attended law school for two years.

Bob owns a 32-foot power cabin cruiser and has been a Director of the Pacific-Inter-Club Yacht Association representing over 90 boat clubs. He was elected to the post of Rear Admiral of the Yacht Association for 1991, representing over 25,000 boaters in the northern California recreation boating area. He was also selected to fill a three-year term as Director of Recreation Boaters of California. Bob receives about 125 baseball card autograph requests per year. He is a life member of the Association of Professional Baseball Players.

JAY VAN NOY YEAR-BY-YEAR STATISTICS

Name: Jay Lowell Van Noy

Born: November 4, 1928
Garland, UT

Hgt: 6′ 1″ Wgt: 200

Bats: Left Throws: Right

Home: Logan, UT

Minor League: 1950-1956

Year	Club	L	POS	G	AB	R	H	2	3	HR	RBI	SB	AVG
1951	St. Louis	NL	O	6	7	1	0	0	0	0	0	0	.000
	Lifetime			6	7	1	0	0	0	0	0	0	.000

JAY VAN NOY

Jay's nickname in high school should have been "Captain" since he captained the football, basketball, track, and baseball teams two years in a row! Many high school stars have scouts watching their games but few have had Jay's experience. After only three high school baseball games, at age sixteen, he signed a contract with his favorite team, the St. Louis Cardinals. The contract required that after he completed college he would be obligated to the Cardinals for at least one year. Since Jay was considered a pro, he was not allowed to play baseball at college, but he sure played everything else, especially football.

Declining offers from Big Ten schools and the military academies, Jay decided to stay close to home by attending Utah State. He put them on the map. As a freshman in 1945, he scored three touchdowns in a game against Denver. He played as a running back and defensive back. For three years, he led the Big Seven Conference in total yards gained and in interceptions! In one game, he scored six touchdowns! He was selected as an All-American in 1948 and was the first draft choice of the Los Angeles Rams in 1950. On the track team, he threw the discus, heaved the shot, high jumped, and ran the 100-yard dash in 9.9 seconds. He played guard on the basketball team for two years. Besides all of this, Jay participated in the Army reserve program at college.

During college Jay was offered a $35,000 baseball contract by the New York Yankees that he turned down because of his commitment to the Cardinals. Now the Rams wanted him to sign with them. If it had been 1990, Jay could have played both like Bo Jackson, but it was 1950 and the sports world could not imagine it. Jay chose to stick to his contract with the Cardinals.

He was signed with the intent of being a pitcher. During his first batting practice, he hit eight or so balls over the fence and was immediately assigned as a starting outfielder. He batted .304 with 30 doubles, 15 homers, and 78 RBIs in only 106 games during his first minor league season. Jay said that an unexpected yet important event occurred in a game at Meridian, Mississippi. He was at the plate and the opposing team's catcher asked, "Are you from Utah?" Jay said, "I am." The catcher said, "I'm from Florida." Then he asked, "Are you a Mormon?" Jay said, "I am." The catcher replied, "So am I. My family and I are saving all our money so we can go to the Salt Lake Temple." Jay doesn't remember the catcher's name, but he does remember it as a special moment in his life to feel how important going to the Temple was to this player.

In 1951, the Cardinals jumped him all the way to the Triple-A level. It was too fast. He swung for the fences and struck out frequently. He got down on himself, but was soon called up to the Cardinals, partly to offset attempts by the Rams to sign him. Jay remembers his first Major League game distinctly. He didn't start. He was sitting on the bench in the seventh inning when Harry "the Cat" Brecheen, a pitcher from Broken Bow, Oklahoma, said, "Here kid, don't be a sissy, have a chew." Jay took it. The next

Jay was signed by the St. Louis Cardinals when he was sixteen to play baseball after college. In college, he became an All-American in football and was the first draft pick of the Los Angeles Rams in 1950.

thing he knew he was being called to pinch-hit with that awful-tasting chew still in his mouth. At bat against Sal Maglie, he swallowed--yes, swallowed-some of the chew. He was walked and then advanced to second. The score was tied. On the next hit, he knew he had to score. Rounding third base, he nearly tripped, but kept his balance and scored what became the winning run. He went to the club house and threw up! He said, "I never did anything stupid like that again." He got up several more times without a hit, but he had a taste of where he wanted to be.

In 1952, he had a good spring training and made the Cardinals. Then he was told by the Army to expect his reserve unit to be called up because of the Korean War. The Cardinals decided to send him to Columbus because of his pending assignment in the Army which never came. Despite his frustration, Jay would play pepper and catch with youngsters before the games, particularly to a boy and girl for whom he would buy hamburgers and sodas. The next year, his disappointment was even worse because he was sent to the lowly Texas League where he batted .240. After the 1954 spring training, he decided to give up baseball and get ready for football. His parents convinced him to give baseball another try. During the last two months of the 1954 season, he was "strictly a plus player" according to his manager.

Jay spent his last two seasons at the Triple-A level at Rochester in 1955 and Phoenix in 1956. It was in the 1956 season that one of Jay's most memorable moments took place. Playing against Spokane, Jay reached first base and the first baseman who was new to the league said, "Do you know who I am?" Jay said, "Sure, you're Frank Howard." The first baseman replied, "Yes, but do you know who I really am?" Jay was stumped. Frank said, "I'm the kid you played pepper with back in Columbus!" Recounting the story, Jay said, "Those are real things." Frank Howard went on to hit 382 homers in the Majors.

Jay coached baseball at Brigham Young University for a couple years. He has been the superintendent of parks and recreation at Logan, Utah; owned a construction company; owned a clothing store; and sold clothing directly to stores. He enjoys horses and dogs and spends many hours hunting and fishing. He has been the time keeper at Utah State basketball games for many years.

COLBY WARD YEAR-BY-YEAR STATISTICS

Name: Robert Colby Ward

Born: January 2, 1964
Lansing, MI

Hgt: 6′ 2″ Wgt: 185

Bats: Right Throws: Right

Home: Springville, UT

Minor League: 1986-1991

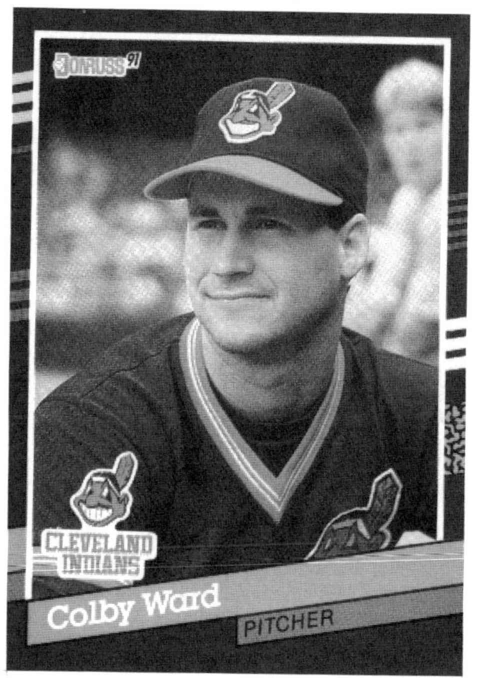

Year	Club	L	POS	G	IP	W	L	SO	BB	H	ERA	SV	SHO
1990	Cleveland	AL	P	22	36	1	3	23	21	31	4.25	1	0
	Lifetime			22	36	1	3	23	21	31	4.25	1	0

COLBY WARD

Not too many seventeen-year olds are starting players in the Houston Astrodome, but Colby was in a football play-off game on his high school team. He made the all-district team as a defensive back in football. He was one of the top Houston area high school pitchers in 1981 and 1982, leading the city in strikeouts his senior year. In the Connie Mack league, he helped take his team to the world series.

After his junior year in high school, Colby's family moved to Utah, where his father worked as a professor for Brigham Young University. Colby attended BYU and graduated with a degree in business communications. He also established himself as a mainstay of the BYU pitching rotation for four years with a 35-10 combined record. He won more games at BYU than any pitcher in Cougar history. He went to the NCAA regionals twice and won a play-off game in the 1985 regionals. He was drafted by the Milwaukee Brewers after his junior year but decided to stay at BYU. He signed with the California Angels after a 7-1 senior year at BYU.

In the rookie league, the Angels assigned Colby to a relief pitching role which he enjoyed because of the possibility of playing in so many games. He responded to pressure situations in his first minor league season, being credited with nine saves, a 3.21 ERA, and 74 strikeouts in 53 innings in the rookie league. He had a great 1987 season, winning seven games, saving 18, and posting a 2.54 ERA in 54 Class A games. The next year in Double A ball, he had a 9-2 record and 2.68 ERA, earning a mid-season promotion to the Angels' Triple A team. In 1989, he was traded by the Angels to the Cleveland Indians and had a combined 4-2 minor league record.

In November 1989, while working at his off-season job, Colby nearly chopped off a finger on his pitching hand. He was one player who was happy the player's strike delayed the starting of spring training since he couldn't even throw until March. At Colorado Springs, he was the team's top relief pitcher going over two months without allowing a run to score. In 43 appearances he had a 2.00 ERA when the Indians beckoned him to the Major Leagues.

On July 29, he heard his name announced for the first of 22 times in the 1990 season as a relief pitcher for the Indians. In his first game, he pitched three innings against the New York Yankees. He held them scoreless while striking out four. He and former BYU teammate Cory Snyder became the first pair of BYU players to play concurrently on the same Major League team.

He had another successful outing against the Yankees on August 4, pitching one inning of shutout baseball. The game on August 7 against the Texas Rangers was one of the shortest, yet most rewarding for Colby, at least statistically. In the eighth

Colby holds the record for most victories at BYU with 35. In his first Major League game on July 26, 1990, he held the New York Yankees scoreless in three innings of relief.

inning with two out and the score tied at four, Colby entered the game. He did his job, getting the third out. The Indians scored four runs in the bottom of the eighth, making him the pitcher of record. Another Indian player pitched the ninth inning. So Colby notched his first career victory by pitching to only one batter. Interestingly, his first loss came on a no-hit performance. On August 24, against the Baltimore Orioles, he entered the game in the middle of the sixth inning with the score tied. He held the Orioles hitless into the ninth inning when, to his dismay, he lost control of his pitches, walked several batters, and was charged with the loss as the Orioles won 5-4.

He played winter ball in Puerto Rico and pitched well, helping his team with the league title. In 1991, he was hampered in spring training by a knee injury that finally required surgery to correct. After a recuperative period, he was assigned to Colorado Springs.

Colby enjoys hunting, fishing, camping, and being with his family.

JIM WESSINGER YEAR-BY-YEAR STATISTICS

Name: James Michael Wessinger

Born: September 25, 1955
Utica, NY

Hgt: 5′ 11″ Wgt: 170

Bats: Right Throws: Right

Home: Liverpool, NY

Minor League: 1976-1980

Year	Club	L	POS	G	AB	R	H	2	3	HR	RBI	SB	AVG
1979	Atlanta	NL	2	10	7	2	0	0	0	0	0	0	.000
	Lifetime			10	7	2	0	0	0	0	0	0	.000

JIM WESSINGER

Since he is from New York, it isn't surprising that Jim's favorite team as a youth was the Yankees. His favorite player was Yankee catcher Thurman Munson, because he played hard and was a leader. In high school, Jim was a defensive back on the junior varsity football team and a starter on the varsity baseball team where he hit .405 his senior year and was selected to the league all-star team. In his first year of American Legion baseball in 1971, his team won the state championship. He went to Le Moyne college in Syracuse, New York where he knew he would be an everyday starter. His team played in the NCAA division II tournament two of the three years he was at college. As a contact hitter, his overall batting average was .349, and he played several infield positions. He was selected in the sixth round of the June 1976 draft by the Atlanta Braves.

After signing, he spent a week working out with the Major League team in Atlanta and was then assigned to Kingsport in the rookie league. He played shortstop and third base, but batted only .205 in over 200 at bats. In 1977, he performed well at Greenwood at the Class A level, hitting .296 and being named to the league's all-star team. He led the league's shortstops in double plays in both 1976 and 1977, and he led the league in sacrifice hits with sixteen in 1977.

Jim recounted an amusing story about himself from when he played at Greenwood. He hit a hard line drive to right center and was running hard with his head down hoping to get a double when he looked up and realized he had hit a home run. He slowed down and rounded the diamond making sure he touched each base. When he crossed home plate, he expected the normal "high fives" but no one in the dugout congratulated him. He decided his teammates were pulling a stunt on him by ignoring his home run. When he sat down, the person next to him said, "You really think you hit a home run, don't you? Well, you didn't--the fielder caught it." Jim didn't believe it. He thought it was part of the team's gag; however, he did notice when he went out to his shortstop position that a '0' instead of a '1' was on the scoreboard, much to his embarrassment.

At Greenwood, he lived near an LDS family and was soon dating one of the girls in the family. He learned about the Church and was baptized and married between the 1977 and 1978 seasons. A year later his marriage was solemnized in the Washington Temple.

The Braves promoted Jim to their Double A club at Savannah in 1978 where he played shortstop and third base and batted .279. In mid-season he was called up to the Triple A team at Richmond. He had some difficulty with the higher quality of pitching as noted by a .185 average in 148 at bats. He started 1979 at Savannah and after 83 games he was hitting .299 and warranted another call up to Richmond. This time he was batting .286 in 49 at bats when he was summoned on August 1 to join the Braves roster because of an injury to one of the team's infielders. He started one game playing

Jim joined the Atlanta Braves on August 1, 1979 and played in ten games as a defensive, late-inning replacement. Teammates were Dale Murphy and Barry Bonnell.

second base against the Houston Astros and went 0-for-3 facing Doc Ellis. He played in nine other games as a defensive replacement and pinch-runner. Jim and his wife lived at Dale Murphy's house during the last two months of the season. On a road trip to Cincinnati, Jim accepted teammate Barry Bonnell's invitation to go flying. He was surprised to learn that the plane had an open cockpit and that it was located in a field, not a real airport. He became concerned when once in the air, Barry turned the plane upside down. He was glad to be back on the ground even though they dodged power lines and trees to land.

He played the entire 1980 season at Richmond and batted .246. The Braves released him in the spring of 1981. Jim wishes he had been given more of a chance to play at the Major League level. He noted that he had a history of struggling when first going to a higher level of play. He felt he could have been a good player in the big leagues. Despite not achieving his ultimate goal, Jim said, "I'm glad I did it. I met all sorts of people. It was a great experience that I wouldn't trade for anything."

He works as an accountant in a grocery warehouse and enjoys golf. He has recently served in the Church as a Sunday School teacher.

***Mormons in the Major Leagues* should be available at your local book store or baseball card store; however, you may order additional copies through the mail. Photocopy and complete this form or write this information on a separate piece of paper and mail to Action Sports.**

ORDER FORM

NAME (Please Print) ______________________________
ADDRESS ______________________________________
CITY ___________________________ STATE _____________________ ZIP ________
TELEPHONE (______) _______-__________

MAILING ADDRESS (if different than above address)
Name (Please Print) ______________________________
Address ______________________________________
City ___________________________ State _____________________ ZIP ________

Please send additional copies of *Mormons in the Major Leagues* as indicated on this form:

Check one please	Your Price (includes postage)	
_____One Copy	$ 17.95	
_____Two Copies	$ 33.90	($ 16.95 per copy)
_____Three Copies	$ 47.85	($ 15.95 per copy)
_____More than Three $ 14.95 X ________	= $______	

Your Signature ______________________________ Date __________________

Send Check or Money Order with Order Form to: ACTION SPORTS
P.O. Box 54162
Cincinnati, OH 45254

SECTION 2

SINGLE SEASON

AND

LIFETIME STATISTICS

This section is full of statistics sliced every way you can imagine. For each player, you see the best single season statistic in each hitting and pitching category. Lifetime statistics are also listed for each player, hitters first and then pitchers. You can see how your favorite player stacks up with others. Of course, the number of innings played and the longevity of a player are big factors in how a player did relative to others. Just a few of many interesting statistical facts are noted below.

Harmon Killebrew, Wally Joyner, and Dale Murphy have season highs that included 100 runs and 100 RBIs. Those three plus Cory Snyder have seasons with more than 30 homers with Killebrew leading the pack by twice hitting 49 home runs in a year. Ken Hubbs leads in triples with nine, and Murphy was the speediest on the base path with 30 stolen bases. Dane Iorg leads all hitters with a .327 batting average with his brother Garth, Barry Bonnell, and Murphy also having .300 seasons. Killebrew leads in most career statistics with Murphy leading in career doubles, triples, and stolen bases.

For pitchers, Jim Gott leads in game appearances in a single season with 67. Jack Morris, Vernon Law, and Dennis Eckersley have been 20-game winners. Morris and Eckersley have 200-strikeout seasons. Eckersley and Gott are the save leaders with 48 and 34, respectively. Monte Pearson and Law led their leagues in lowest ERA, and Eckersley has one of the lowest ERA's ever at 0.61. Morris leads in career wins and strikeouts. Eckersley has the most career saves, and Law has the most career shutouts.

SEASON HIGH BATTING STATISTICS

(only players with more than 25 games)

PLAYER	G	AB	R	H	2B	3B	HR	RBI	SB	AVG
ADAMS	88/27	259/27	32/27	69/27	11/27	3/27	0/27	29/27	2/23	.273/25
AINGE	87/79	308/79	26/79	73/79	7/79	2/81	2/79	19/79	8/81	.243/80
ASHBY	125/87	396/77	53/87	111/87	19/80	3/77	14/87	63/87	3/75	.288/87
BARRETT	36/88	54/88	5/88	11/88	1/88	0/89	0/89	3/88	0/89	.222/89
BONNELL	140/82	463/80	59/82	128/82	26/82	4/84	13/80	56/80	14/82	.318/83
BRAND	117/65	391/65	27/65	92/65	12/69	3/70	2/65	37/65	10/65	.288/63
GOMEZ	153/78	413/78	39/78	92/78	7/79	3/78	0/81	32/78	2/78	.246/77
HOWARD	39/76	90/76	7/76	19/76	4/76	1/74	1/75	13/76	1/76	.263/72
HUBBS	160/62	661/62	90/62	172/62	24/62	9/62	8/63	49/62	8/63	.260/62
IORG, D.	105/80	251/80	33/80	76/80	23/80	2/84	5/84	39/81	2/81	.327/81
IORG, G.	137/86	417/82	45/82	119/82	22/85	5/83	7/85	44/86	7/83	.313/85
JOYNER	159/89	597/88	100/87	176/88	33/87	3/86	34/87	117/87	8/88	.295/88
KILLEBREW	163/67	577/64	106/69	160/66	27/66	7/61	49/69	140/69	8/69	.288/61
LAW	151/88	556/88	75/85	163/88	30/85	6/85	17/84	78/88	8/87	.293/88
MURPHY	162/85	616/85	131/83	185/85	35/88	8/84	44/87	121/83	30/83	.316/77
SNYDER	157/87	577/87	74/87	139/88	27/90	3/88	33/87	82/87	6/89	.272/88
USHER	114/51	321/50	51/50	83/50	17/50	2/51	6/50	35/50	4/51	.259/50

LIFETIME BATTING STATISTICS

PLAYER	G	AB	R	H	2B	3B	HR	RBI	SB	AVG
ADAMS	180	395	61	101	16	5	0	38	5	.256
AINGE	211	665	57	146	19	4	2	37	12	.220
ASHBY	1370	4123	397	1010	183	13	90	513	7	.245
BARRETT	50	81	8	17	1	0	0	4	0	.210
BONNELL	959	3017	359	823	141	24	56	351	63	.273
BRAND	568	1345	108	322	34	7	3	106	20	.239
GOMEZ	609	1251	108	263	26	5	0	90	6	.210
HANSEN	3	0	2	0	0	0	0	0	0	.000
HOWARD	97	217	19	46	5	1	1	22	2	.212
HUBBS	324	1255	148	310	44	13	14	98	11	.247
IORG, D.	743	1647	149	455	103	11	14	216	5	.276
IORG, G.	931	2450	251	633	125	16	20	238	23	.258
JACOBS	2	2	0	0	0	0	0	0	0	.000
JOYNER	703	2657	376	759	136	8	93	422	26	.286
KILLEBREW	2435	8147	1283	2086	290	24	573	1584	19	.256
LAW	1138	3668	442	944	186	25	71	433	34	.257
MURPHY	1983	7312	1125	1958	315	38	378	1171	160	.268
SNYDER	657	2431	298	595	113	9	115	340	19	.245
USHER	428	1101	133	259	41	4	18	102	9	.235
VAN NOY	6	7	1	0	0	0	0	0	1	.000
WESSINGER	10	7	2	0	0	0	0	0	0	.000

SEASON HIGH PITCHING STATISTICS

PLAYER	G	IP	W	L	SO	BB	H	ERA	SV	ShO
DOWNS, D.	4/72	23/72	1/72	1/72	5/72	3/72	25/72	2.75/72	0/72	1/72
DOWNS, K.	41/87	186/87	13/88	9/88	137/87	67/87	185/87	2.75/86	1/87	3/88
ECKERSLEY	63/90	268/78	20/78	14/80	200/76	90/75	258/78	0.61/90	48/90	3/82
FETTERS	26/90	68/90	1/90	1/90	35/90	20/90	77/90	4.12/90	1/90	0/90
GARVIN	61/80	245/77	10/77	18/77	127/77	85/77	247/77	2.28/80	8/80	1/77
GOTT	67/88	177/83	9/87	14/83	121/83	68/83	195/83	2.90/90	34/88	1/84
HUNT	29/61	136/61	9/61	10/61	75/61	66/61	130/61	3.96/61	0/61	0/61
HURST	35/85	245/89	18/88	13/87	190/87	88/84	243/85	2.69/88	0/90	4/90
KIMBALL	39/43	101/43	4/40	7/43	35/43	47/43	94/43	3.02/40	3/43	0/43
KIRKWOOD	44/75	158/76	6/76	12/76	78/76	57/76	167/76	3.11/75	7/75	0/78
KROLL	32/65	87/65	6/65	6/65	62/65	41/65	83/65	3.80/66	1/65	0/69
LAW	43/55	272/60	20/60	16/56	120/60	61/55	266/60	2.15/65	3/58	5/64
MORRIS	37/83	294/83	21/86	18/90	232/83	110/85	257/83	3.05/81	0/90	6/86
NIELSEN	19/87	66/87	4/86	5/87	23/87	25/87	83/87	4.02/86	2/87	2/86
NORIEGA	8/70	18/70	0/70	0/70	6/70	10/70	25/70	5.63/70	0/70	0/70
NYMAN	20/69	65/69	4/69	4/69	40/69	39/69	58/69	2.01/68	0/70	1/69
PEARSON	39/34	255/34	19/36	13/35	140/34	135/36	257/34	2.33/33	2/34	1/40
PEERY	9/29	44/29	0/29	1/29	3/29	9/29	53/29	5.11/29	0/29	0/29
RITCHIE	49/87	62/87	3/87	2/87	45/87	29/87	60/87	3.12/88	3/87	0/88
SANFORD	42/48	227/48	12/48	21/48	79/48	91/48	250/48	1.93/43	4/47	2/46
SINGLETON	38/48	92/48	4/48	6/48	53/48	40/48	90/48	2.72/48	2/48	0/59
SISK	57/63	208/67	13/67	13/67	85/67	78/67	196/67	2.92/63	6/69	2/67
WARD	22/90	36/90	1/90	3/90	23/90	21/90	31/90	4.25/90	1/90	0/90

LIFETIME PITCHING STATISTICS

PLAYER	G	IP	W	L	SO	BB	H	ERA	SV	ShO
DOWNS, D.	4	23	1	1	5	3	25	2.74	0	1
DOWNS, K.	113	588	36	32	399	190	541	3.55	1	6
ECKERSLEY	604	2815	169	140	1938	659	2625	3.49	145	18
FETTERS	27	71	1	1	39	21	82	4.31	1	0
GARVIN	196	607	20	41	320	219	648	4.42	8	1
GOTT	307	811	38	53	574	344	791	4.07	53	3
HUNT	29	136	9	10	75	66	130	3.96	0	0
HURST	303	1928	114	93	1384	608	1971	3.91	0	19
KIMBALL	94	236	11	9	88	117	219	3.78	5	0
KIRKWOOD	120	375	18	23	194	135	409	4.37	8	0
KROLL	71	159	6	7	138	91	147	4.24	1	0
LAW	483	2672	162	147	1092	597	2833	3.77	13	28
MORRIS	430	3043	198	150	1980	1086	2767	3.75	0	24
NIELSEN	36	142	8	11	47	50	176	5.45	2	3
NORIEGA	13	26	0	0	10	13	37	7.27	0	0
NYMAN	30	110	6	7	69	57	104	4.58	0	2
PEARSON	224	1430	100	61	703	740	1392	4.00	4	5
PEERY	10	45	0	1	3	10	53	5.00	0	0
RITCHIE	68	88	3	2	53	46	79	3.57	3	0
SANFORD	164	744	37	55	285	391	768	4.45	6	3
SINGLETON	145	327	11	17	160	146	322	4.83	4	0
SISK	316	928	40	49	441	358	937	3.92	10	4
WARD	22	36	1	3	23	21	31	4.25	1	0

Top Five Performers

Single Season Batting

Hits		Doubles		Home Runs		RBIs		Average	
Murphy	185	Murphy	35	Killebrew	49	Killebrew	140	Iorg, D.	.327
Joyner	176	Joyner	33	Murphy	44	Murphy	121	Bonnell	.318
Hubbs	172	Law	30	Joyner	34	Joyner	117	Murphy	.316
Law	163	Killebrew	27	Snyder	33	Snyder	82	Iorg, G.	.313
Killebrew	160	Snyder	27	Law	17	Law	78	Joyner	.295

Lifetime Batting (as of July 1, 1991)

Hits		Doubles		Home Runs		RBIs		Average	
Killebrew	2086	Murphy	323	Killebrew	573	Killebrew	1584	Joyner	.290
Murphy	2023	Killebrew	290	Murphy	389	Murphy	1208	Iorg, D.	.276
Ashby	1010	Law	191	Snyder	118	Ashby	513	Bonnell	.273
Law	966	Ashby	183	Joyner	103	Joyner	473	Murphy	.268
Joyner	850	Joyner	153	Ashby	90	Law	440	Iorg, G.	.258

Single Season Pitching

Wins		Strikeouts		ERA		Saves		Shutouts	
Morris	21	Morris	232	Eckersley	0.61	Eckersley	48	Morris	6
Eckersley	20	Eckersley	200	Sanford	1.93	Gott	34	Law	5
Law	20	Hurst	190	Nyman	2.01	Garvin	8	Hurst	4
Pearson	19	Pearson	140	Law	2.15	Kirkwood	7	Downs, K	3
Hurst	18	Downs, K	137	Garvin	2.28	Sisk	6	Eckersley	3

Lifetime Pitching (as of July 1, 1991)

Wins		Strikeouts		ERA		Saves		Shutouts	
Morris	209	Morris	2058	Downs, D	2.74	Eckersley	167	Law	28
Eckersley	170	Eckersley	1973	Eckersley	3.47	Gott	54	Morris	25
Law	162	Hurst	1457	Downs, K	3.60	Law	13	Hurst	19
Hurst	123	Law	1092	Ritchie	3.60	Sisk	10	Eckersley	18
Pearson	100	Pearson	703	Morris	3.74	2 with	8	Downs, K	6

SECTION 3

LEAGUE CHAMPIONSHIP

AND

WORLD SERIES RECORDS

Church members have played important roles in League Championship and World Series games. For instance, Alan Ashby had a game winning homer in the 1986 National League Series, and Harmon Killebrew had two homers in the 1970 American League Series. Dennis Eckersley pitched in all four games of the 1988 AL Series and saved each game. Twelve members have been on World Series rosters.

In 1925, Spencer Adams became the first Mormon to play in a World Series. As a matter of fact, he played in the World Series in 1926, making him the only Church member to play in two consecutive World Series on different teams. Can you name the two teams?

Dane Iorg also played on two World Series teams and they both won. Dane was the batting hero of the 1982 World Series, and he made the key hit in the sixth game of the 1985 World Series that drove in the game winning run. Can you name the two teams he played for?

Monte Pearson was the original "Mr. October," winning a game in four successive World Series, 1936-1939, for the New York Yankees. Bruce Hurst, Vernon Law, and Jack Morris have each won two World Series games. LDS starting pitchers have a combined 10-0 record in the Series. Kelly Downs made the cover of *Sports Illustrated* carrying his nephew off the earthquake shaken field in 1989 at Candlestick Park. And Dennis Eckersley has played in three World Series in a row, 1988-1990.

Who will be the next post-season hero?

BATTERS IN CHAMPIONSHIP SERIES GAMES

Player	Year	Club	L	G	AB	R	H	2B	3B	HR	RBI	SB	AVG
Alan Ashby	1980	Houston	NL	2	8	0	1	0	0	0	1	0	.125
Alan Ashby	1986	Houston	NL	6	23	2	3	1	0	1	2	0	.130
		Lifetime		8	31	2	4	1	0	1	3	0	.129
Dane Iorg	1984	Kansas City	AL	2	2	0	1	0	0	0	0	0	.500
Dane Iorg	1985	Kansas City	AL	4	2	0	1	1	0	0	0	0	.500
		Lifetime		6	4	0	2	1	0	0	0	0	.500
Garth Iorg	1985	Toronto	AL	6	15	1	2	0	0	0	0	0	.133
Wally Joyner	1986	California	AL	3	11	3	5	2	0	1	2	0	.455
Harmon Killebrew	1969	Minnesota	AL	3	8	2	1	1	0	0	0	0	.125
Harmon Killebrew	1970	Minnesota	AL	3	11	2	3	0	0	2	4	0	.273
		Lifetime		6	19	4	4	1	0	2	4	0	.211
Vance Law	1983	Chicago	AL	4	11	0	2	0	0	0	1	0	.182
Vance Law	1989	Chicago	NL	2	3	0	0	0	0	0	0	0	.000
		Lifetime		6	14	0	2	0	0	0	1	0	.143
Dale Murphy	1982	Atlanta	NL	3	11	1	3	0	0	0	0	1	.273

BATTERS IN WORLD SERIES GAMES

Player	Year	Club	L	G	AB	R	H	2B	3B	HR	RBI	SB	AVG
Spencer Adams	1925	Washinton	AL	2	1	0	0	0	0	0	0	0	.000
Spencer Adams	1926	New York	AL	2	0	0	0	0	0	0	0	0	.000
		Lifetime		4	1	0	0	0	0	0	0	0	.000
Dane Iorg	1982	St. Louis	NL	5	17	4	9	4	1	0	1	0	.529
Dane Iorg	1985	Kansas City	AL	2	2	0	1	0	0	0	2	0	.500
		Lifetime		7	19	4	10	4	1	0	3	0	.526
Harmon Killebrew	1965	Minnesota	AL	7	21	2	6	0	0	1	2	0	.286

PITCHERS IN CHAMPIONSHIP SERIES GAMES

Player	Year	Club	L	G	IP	W	L	SO	BB	H	ERA	SV	ShO
Kelly Downs	1987	San Francisco	NL	1	1	0	0	0	00	1	0.00	0	0
Kelly Downs	1989	San Francisco	NL	2	9	1	0	6	6	8	3.12	0	0
		Lifetime		3	10	1	0	6	6	9	2.70	0	0
Dennis Eckersley	1984	Chicago	NL	1	5	0	1	0	0	9	8.44	0	0
Dennis Eckersley	1988	Oakland	AL	4	6	0	0	5	2	1	0.00	4	0
Dennis Eckersley	1989	Oakland	AL	4	6	0	0	2	0	4	1.59	3	0
Dennis Eckersley	1990	Oakland	AL	3	3	0	0	3	0	2	0.00	2	0
		Lifetime		12	20	0	1	10	2	16	2.66	9	0
Bruce Hurst	1986	Boston	AL	2	15	1	0	8	1	18	2.40	0	0
Bruce Hurst	1988	Boston	AL	2	13	0	2	12	5	10	2.77	0	0
		Lifetime		4	28	1	2	20	6	28	2.57	0	0
Jack Morris	1984	Detroit	AL	1	7	1	0	4	1	5	1.29	0	0
Jack Morris	1987	Detroit	AL	1	8	0	1	7	3	6	6.75	0	0
		Lifetime		2	15	1	1	11	4	11	4.20	0	0

PITCHERS IN WORLD SERIES GAMES

Player	Year	Club	L	G	IP	W	L	SO	BB	H	ERA	SV	ShO
Kelly Downs	1989	San Francisco	NL	3	5	0	0	4	2	3	7.71	0	0
Dennis Eckersley	1988	Oakland	AL	2	2	0	1	2	1	2	10.80	0	0
Dennis Eckersley	1989	Oakland	AL	2	2	0	0	0	0	0	0.00	1	0
Dennis Eckersley	1990	Oakland	AL	2	1	0	1	1	0	03	6.75	0	0
		Lifetime		6	5	0	2	3	1	5	5.79	1	0
Ken Hunt	1961	Cincinnati	NL	1	1	0	0	1	1	0	0.00	0	0
Bruce Hurst	1986	Boston	AL	3	23	2	0	17	6	18	1.96	0	0
Vernon Law	1960	Pittsburgh	NL	3	18	2	0	8	3	22	3.44	0	0
Jack Morris	1984	Detroit	AL	2	18	2	0	13	3	13	2.00	0	0
Monte Pearson	1936	New York	AL	1	9	1	0	7	2	7	2.00	0	0
Monte Pearson	1937	New York	AL	1	9	1	0	4	2	5	1.04	0	0
Monte Pearson	1938	New York	AL	1	9	1	0	9	2	5	1.00	0	0
Monte Pearson	1939	New York	AL	1	9	1	0	8	1	2	0.00	0	1
		Lifetime		4	36	4	0	28	7	19	1.01	0	1

WORLD SERIES ROSTER

YEAR	PLAYER	TEAM	RESULT
1925	Spencer Adams	Washington Senators	Lost to Pittsburgh Pirates in 7 games
1926	Spencer Adams	New York Yankees	Lost to St. Louis Cardinals in 7 games
1936	Monte Pearson	New York Yankees	Beat NY Giants in 6 games
1937	Monte Pearson	New York Yankees	Beat NY Giants in 5 games
1938	Monte Pearson	New York Yankees	Beat Chicago Cubs in 4 games
1939	Monte Pearson	New York Yankees	Beat Cincinnati Reds in 4 games
1941	Newt Kimball	Brooklyn Dodgers	Lost to NY Yankees in 5 games
1949	Fred Sanford	New York Yankees	Beat Brooklyn Dodgers in 5 games
1950	Fred Sanford	New York Yankees	Beat Philadelphia Phillies in 4 games
1960	Vernon Law	Pittsburgh Pirates	Beat NY Yankees in 7 games
1961	Ken Hunt	Cincinnati Reds	Lost to NY Yankees in 5 games
1965	Harmon Killebrew	Minnesota Twins	Lost to Los Angeles Dodgers in 7 games
1982	Dane Iorg	St. Louis Cardinals	Beat Milwaukee Brewers in 7 games
1984	Jack Morris	Detroit Tigers	Beat San Diego Padres in 5 games
1985	Dane Iorg	Kansas City Royals	Beat St. Louis Cardinals in 7 games
1986	Bruce Hurst	Boston Red Sox	Lost to NY Mets in 7 games
1988	Dennis Eckersley	Oakland Athletics	Lost to Los Angeles Dodgers in 5 games
1989	Kelly Downs	San Francisco Giants	Lost to Oakland A's in 4 games
1989	Dennis Eckersley	Oakland Athletics	Beat San Francisco Giants in 4 games
1990	Dennis Eckersley	Oakland Athletics	Lost to Cincinnati Reds in 4 games

CMC

A's

Dodgers
36
LA

JOYNER
21

Twins

Sox
Rawlings

SECTION 4

PLAYERS BY TEAM

AND

POSITION

Mormon players have been members of nearly every active team. The Toronto Blue Jays have been a favorite team, hosting a total of seven different Church members between 1977 and 1987 and five players in 1978 alone. The Cleveland Indians hold the team record with nine different LDS players. Check out your favorite teams and see which Church members have played for them.

Which position has been the most popular and which, the least? Which players have played your favorite position? See what your favorite all-Mormon team would be.

TEAM ASSIGNMENTS

Atlanta Braves

1976	Dale Murphy
1977-78	Barry Bonnell, Dale Murphy
1979	Barry Bonnell, Dale Murphy, Jim Wessinger
1980-81	Luis Gomez, Dale Murphy
1982-90	Dale Murphy

Baltimore Orioles

No players

Boston Braves

1929	Red Peery
1945-46	Elmer Singleton

Boston Red Sox

1978-79	Dennis Eckersley
1980-84	Dennis Eckersley, Bruce Hurst
1985-88	Bruce Hurst

Brooklyn Dodgers

1940-43	Newt Kimball

California Angels

1972-73	Doug Howard
1974	Doug Howard, Don Kirkwood
1975-77	Don Kirkwood
1986-88	Wally Joyner
1989-91	Mike Fetters, Wally Joyner

Chicago Cubs

1928	Ray Jacobs
1937-38	Newt Kimball
1957-59	Elmer Singleton
1961-63	Ken Hubbs
1984-86	Dennis Eckersley
1988-89	Vance Law

Chicago White Sox

1968-69	Jerry Nyman
1970	Tommie Sisk
1977	Don Kirkwood
1982-84	Vance Law
1987	Scott Nielsen
1991-	Cory Snyder

Cincinnati Reds

1941	Monte Pearson
1946-47	Bob Usher
1950-51	Bob Usher
1961	Ken Hunt
1969-70	John Noriega

Cleveland Indians

1932-35	Monte Pearson
1951	Doug Hansen
1957	Bob Usher
1969	Gary Kroll
1973-74	Alan Ashby
1975	Alan Ashby, Dennis Eckersley
1976	Alan Ashby, Dennis Eckersley, Doug Howard
1977	Dennis Eckersley
1986-89	Cory Snyder
1990	Cory Snyder, Colby Ward

Detroit Tigers

1977-90	Jack Morris

Houston Astros

1965	Ron Brand
1966	Ron Brand, Gary Kroll
1967-68	Ron Brand
1979-89	Alan Ashby

Kansas City Athletics
No players

Kansas City Royals

1975	Harmon Killebrew
1984-85	Dane Iorg

Los Angeles Dodgers

1990-	Jim Gott

Milwaukee Braves

No players

Milwaukee Brewers

No players

Minnesota Twins

1961-73	Harmon Killebrew
1974	Luis Gomez, Harmon Killebrew
1975--77	Luis Gomez
1991-	Jack Morris

New York Giants

No players

New York Mets

1964-65	Gary Kroll

New York Yankees

1926	Spencer Adams
1936-40	Monte Pearson
1949-51	Fred Sanford
1986	Scott Nielsen
1988	Scott Nielsen

Oakland Athletics

1987-90	Dennis Eckersley
1991-	Dennis Eckersley, Vance Law

Philadelphia Athletics

No players

Philadelphia Phillies

1943	Newt Kimball
1964	Gary Kroll
1972	Dave Kroll
1977	Dane Iorg
1987	Wally Ritchie
1988	Tommy Barrett, Wally Ritchie
1989	Tommy Barrett
1990	Dale Murphy
1991-	Dale Murphy, Wally Ritchie

Pittsburgh Pirates

1923	Spencer Adams
1927	Red Peery
1947-48	Elmer Singleton
1950-51	Vernon Law
1954-61	Vernon Law
1962	Vernon Law, Tommie Sisk
1963	Ron Brand, Vernon Law, Tommie Sisk
1964-67	Vernon Law, Tommie Sisk
1968	Tommie Sisk
1980-81	Vance Law
1987-89	Jim Gott

St. Louis Browns

1927	Spencer Adams
1943	Fred Sanford
1946-48	Fred Sanford
1951	Fred Sanford

St. Louis Cardinals

1940	Newt Kimball
1951	Jay Van Noy
1975	Doug Howard
1978-84	Dane Iorg

San Diego Padres

1969	Tommie Sisk
1970	Jerry Nyman
1986	Dane Iorg
1989-	Bruce Hurst

San Francisco Giants

1985	Jim Gott
1986-87	Kelly Downs, Jim Gott
1988-	Kelly Downs

Seattle Mariners

1984-85	Barry Bonnell

Texas Rangers

No players

Toronto Blue Jays

1977	Alan Ashby, Jerry Garvin
1978	Alan Ashby, Jerry Garvin, Luis Gomez, Garth Iorg, Don Kirkwood
1979	Danny Ainge, Jerry Garvin, Luis Gomez
1980-81	Danny Ainge, Barry Bonnell, Jerry Garvin, Garth Iorg
1982	Barry Bonnell, Jerry Garvin, Jim Gott, Garth Iorg
1983	Barry Bonnell, Jim Gott, Garth Iorg
1984	Jim Gott, Garth Iorg
1985-87	Garth Iorg

Washington Senators

1925	Spencer Adams
1950	Elmer Singleton
1951	Fred Sanford
1954-56	Harmon Killebrew
1957	Bob Usher
1958-60	Harmon Killebrew

POSITIONS

Catcher	First Base	Second Base
Alan Ashby *	Alan Ashby	Spencer Adams*
Ron Brand *	Doug Howard *	Danny Ainge *
Dale Murphy	Dane Iorg	Tommy Barrett *
	Garth Iorg	Ron Brand
	Ray Jacobs	Doug Hansen
	Wally Joyner *	Ken Hubbs*
	Harmon Killebrew *	Garth Iorg*
	Dale Murphy	Harmon Killebrew
	Cory Snyder	Vance Law
		Jim Wessinger

Third Base	Shortstop	Outfield
Spencer Adams	Spencer Adams	Danny Ainge
Danny Ainge	Danny Ainge	Barry Bonnell *
Alan Ashby	Ron Brand	Ron Brand
Barry Bonnell	Luis Gomez *	Doug Howard
Ron Brand	Garth Iorg	Dane Iorg *
Doug Howard	Vance Law	Garth Iorg
Dane Iorg	Cory Snyder	Harmon Killebrew
Garth Iorg *		Dale Murphy *
Harmon Killebrew		Cory Snyder *
Vance Law *		Bob Usher *
Cory Snyder		Jay Van Noy *

LH Pitcher	RH Pitcher
Jerry Garvin	Dave Downs
Bruce Hurst	Kelley Downs
Jerry Nyman	Dennis Eckersley
Red Peery	Jim Gott
Wally Ritchie	Ken Hunt
	Dane Iorg +
	Newt Kimball
	Don Kirkwood
	Gary Kroll
	Vance Law +
	Vernon Law
	Jack Morris
	Scott Nielsen
	John Noriega
	Monte Pearson
	Fred Sanford
	Elmer Singleton
	Tommie Sisk

*Primary Position

+ Secondary Position

Church members regulary receive recognition for their accomplishments in baseball. For example, in the past decade six LDS players made the All-Star team and four players were college All-Americans. In this photo, Harmon Killebrew is receiving one of the many awards he earned in his twenty-two years in the Major Leagues.

SECTION 5

AWARDS

AND

RECOGNITION

Baseball has many awards and nearly every one has been won by at least one Mormon ballplayer. Nine Church members have been Major League All-Stars. Can you name them all?

Dale Murphy was the National League Most Valuable player twice and Harmon Killebrew was an American League Most Valuable Player, and of course, he is in the Hall of Fame! Vernon Law won the Cy Young award when only one was given for the entire Major Leagues instead of each league having one as they do now.

Can you remember back to 1962 when young Ken Hubbs of the Chicago Cubs electrified baseball by taking a record-breaking 418 consecutive errorless chances at second base? He was a shoo-in for National League Rookie-of-the-Year. And how about Wally Joyner taking the American League by storm and becoming the only rookie in baseball history to be voted to the All-Star team.

How has your favorite player been recognized? Who will be next to gain more stardom? Will you or someone you know be listed in this section one day?

AWARDS AND RECOGNITION

All-Star Team

Dennis Eckersley	AL	1977	1982	1988	1990	1991
Bruce Hurst	AL	1987				
Wally Joyner	AL	1986				
Harmon Killebrew	AL	1961	1963	1964	1965	1966
		1967	1968	1969	1970	1971
Vance Law	NL	1988				
Vernon Law	NL	1960				
Jack Morris	AL	1981	1984	1985	1987	1991
Dale Murphy	NL	1980	1982	1983	1984	1985
		1986	1987			
Monte Pearson	AL	1936	1940			

All-Star Team (Sporting News)

Harmon Killebrew	AL	1964	1967	1969	1970
Vernon Law	NL	1960			
Jack Morris	AL	1981			
Dale Murphy	NL	1982	1983	1984	1985

College All-American

Mike Fetters	Pepperdine	1986	
Doug Howard	BYU	1969	1970
Dane Iorg	BYU	1971	
Wally Joyner	BYU	1983	
Scott Nielsen	BYU	1982	1983
Cory Snyder	BYU	1982	1984

Comeback Player of the Year

Vernon Law	NL	1965

Cy Young Pitcher

Vernon Law	NL	1960

Fireman of the Year (Rolaids)

Dennis Eckersley	AL	1988

Gold Glove

Ken Hubbs	2B/NL	1962				
Dale Murphy	OF/NL	1982	1983	1984	1985	1987

Hall of Fame

Harmon Killebrew	AL	1984

Lou Gehrig

Vernon Law	NL	1965

MVP (Baseball Writers)

Harmon Killebrew	AL	1969	
Dale Murphy	NL	1982	1983

Olympic Team

Cory Snyder	USA	1984

Pitcher of the Year (Sporting News)

Vernon Law	NL	1960
Jack Morris	AL	1981

Player of the Year (Sporting News)

Harmon Killebrew	AL	1969	1970
Dale Murphy	NL	1982	1983

Roberto Clemente Humanitarian

Dale Murphy	NL	1988

Rookie All-Star Team (Topps)

Danny Ainge	2B	1979
Dennis Eckersley	P	1975
Jerry Garvin	P	1977
Wally Joyner	1B	1986
Cory Snyder	OF	1986

Rookie Pitcher of the Year (Sporting News)

Dennis Eckersley	AL	1975
Ken Hunt	NL	1961

Rookie of the Year (Baseball Writers)

Ken Hubbs	NL	1962

Rookie of the Year (Sporting News)

Ken Hubbs	NL	1962

Silver Slugger Award

Dale Murphy	NL	1982	1983	1984	1985

Sportsman of the Year (Sports Illustrated)

Dale Murphy		1987

SECTION 6

FIRST MAJOR LEAGUE GAME

ROOKIE CARDS

CURRENT MAJOR LEAGUE PLAYERS

BIRTHDAY LIST

*I*n what year did the first Mormon ballplayer make it to the big leagues? In what year did the most Church members play their first Major League game? How many members are still Major League players? Section 6 contains the answers.

Many collectors like to keep up on rookie cards. If you're one, then this section will tell you the cards to get. Do you know what Bowman cards are? They preceeded Topps cards and you will need a 1951 Bowman, number 203, for Vernon Law's rookie card.

If you want a Harmon Killebrew rookie card, then start saving your dollars--it's over $300 for a mint card and going higher every day. But don't worry about it now; see all the other rookie cards that you can collect!

By knowing the current players you can track their progress in the daily newspapers. Did you ever wonder if any ballplayers were born on your birthday? You can check the birth list. Maybe you will want to send your favorite player a birthday card.

The last page in this section contains advice to would-be Major League players from six former and current players. Their suggestions are appropriate for every worthwhile endeavor.

FIRST MAJOR LEAGUE GAME

YEAR	PLAYER
1923	Spencer Adams
1927	Red Peery
1928	Ray Jacobs
1932	Monte Pearson
1937	Newt Kimball
1943	Fred Sanford
1945	Elmer Singleton
1946	Bob Usher
1950	Vernon Law
1951	Doug Hansen
1951	Jay Van Noy
1954	Harmon Killebrew
1961	Ken Hubbs
1961	Ken Hunt
1962	Tommie Sisk
1963	Ron Brand
1964	Gary Kroll
1968	Jerry Nyman
1969	John Noriega
1972	Dave Downs
1972	Doug Howard
1973	Alan Ashby
1974	Luis Gomez
1974	Don Kirkwood
1975	Dennis Eckersley
1976	Dale Murphy
1977	Barry Bonnell
1977	Jerry Garvin
1977	Dane Iorg
1977	Jack Morris
1978	Garth Iorg
1979	Danny Ainge
1979	Jim Wessinger
1980	Bruce Hurst
1980	Vance Law
1982	Jim Gott
1986	Kelly Downs
1986	Wally Joyner
1986	Scott Nielsen
1986	Cory Snyder
1987	Wally Ritchie
1988	Tommy Barrett
1989	Mike Fetters
1990	Colby Ward

ROOKIE CARDS

Player	Bowman	Donruss	Fleer	Topps
Danny Ainge		1981-569	1981-418	1981-727
Alan Ashby				1976-209
Tommy Barrett				1989-653
Barry Bonnell				1978-242
Ron Brand				1964-326
Kelly Downs		1987-573	1987-272	1987-438
Dennis Eckersley				1976-98
Mike Fetters		1990-35	1990-131	1990-14
Jerry Garvin				1978-419
Luis Gomez				1977-13
Jim Gott		1983-353		1983-506
Doug Howard				1977-112*#
Ken Hubbs				1962-461
Ken Hunt				1961-556
Bruce Hurst				1981-689
Dane Iorg				1980-139
Garth Iorg				1978-704
Wally Joyner		1986-1	1986-59U	1986-51T
Harmon Killebrew				1955-124
Don Kirkwood				1976-108*
Gary Kroll				1965-449
Vance Law				1981-551
Vernon Law	1951-203			
Jack Morris				1978-703
Dale Murphy				1977-476
Scott Nielsen		1987-597		1987-57
Monte Pearson	1939-71*+			
Wally Ritchie			1987-104U	1986-103T
Fred Sanford	1949-236*			
Elmer Singleton	1949-147*			
Tommie Sisk				1963-169
Cory Snyder		1986-29	1986-653	1985-403
Bob Usher	1951-286*			
Colby Ward		1991-330	1991-382	1991-31

*First Card
+Playball #O-Pee-Chee

CURRENT MAJOR LEAGUE PLAYERS

PLAYER	TEAM	L	POS
Kelly Downs	San Francisco Giants	NL	P
Dennis Eckersley	Oakland Athletics	AL	P
Mike Fetters	California Angels	AL	P
Jim Gott	Los Angeles Dodgers	NL	P
Bruce Hurst	San Diego Padres	NL	P
Wally Joyner	California Angels	AL	1
Vance Law	Oakland Athletics	AL	3
Jack Morris	Minnesota Twins	AL	P
Dale Murphy	Philadelphia Phillies	NL	O
Wally Ritchie	Philadelphia Phillies	NL	P
Cory Snyder	Chicago White Sox	AL	O

Former Major League Players Currently in the Minors

Tommy Barrett	Pawtucket Red Sox	IL	2
Garth Iorg	Myrtle Beach (Blue Jays)	S. Atlantic	Manager
Scott Nielsen	Tidewater Mets	IL	P
Jerry Nyman	Welland Pirates	NY-Penn	Coach
Colby Ward	Colorado Springs Indians	PCL	P

BIRTHDAY PARADE

DATE		PLAYER
January	2	Ray Jacobs* and Colby Ward
January	13	Ron Brand
February	6	Doug Howard
March	1	Bob Usher
March	12	Vernon Law and Dale Murphy
March	17	Danny Ainge
March	27	Newt Kimball
April	2	Tommy Barrett
April	12	Tommie Sisk
May	11	Dane Iorg
May	16	Jack Morris
June	16	Wally Joyner
June	21	Spencer Adams* and Dave Downs
June	26	Elmer Singleton
June	29	Harmon Killebrew
July	8	Alan Ashby and Gary Kroll
July	12	Wally Ritchie
August	3	Jim Gott
August	9	Fred Sanford
August	15	Red Peery*
August	19	Luis Gomez
September	2	Monte Pearson*
September	24	Don Kirkwood and Jim Wessinger
October	1	Vance Law
October	3	Dennis Eckersley
October	12	Garth Iorg
October	21	Jerry Garvin
October	25	Kelly Downs
October	27	Barry Bonnell
November	4	Jay Van Noy
November	11	Cory Snyder
November	23	Jerry Nyman
December	14	Ken Hunt
December	16	Doug Hansen
December	18	Scott Nielsen
December	19	Mike Fetters
December	20	John Noriega
December	23	Ken Hubbs*

* deceased

ADVICE TO WOULD-BE MAJOR LEAGUE PLAYERS

"Really want to play and realize there will be obstacles that will test your determination. Stay in tip-top shape and learn to handle the mental pressure of the game, like bases loaded and none out. Keep your nose clean and be ready to take advantage of any breaks that come to you."

Jerry Garvin, Toronto Blue Jays

"Understand the odds. Only the top one percent make it, so give it your all. Use your talent and keep a good mental attitude."

Bruce Hurst, San Diego Padres

"Living the gospel was never a hindrance. Teammates expect you to live up to your standards. You can still be a hard-nosed, tough ball player without sacrificing gospel principles."

Dane Iorg, Kansas City Royals

"A primary reason for playing baseball is to magnify the Church. Everyone knows you are a member. They expect you to live up to high standards. So do it!"

Vance Law, Oakland Athletics

"Keep high standards and work very hard. Don't cheat yourself."

Wally Ritchie, Philadelphia Phillies

"You've got to have the gut drive to play baseball and the determination. Give 100 percent on and off the field. Do your best--nobody can ask more if you do your best."

Cory Snyder, Chicago White Sox

SECTION 7

BASEBALL CARD CHECKLISTS

*D*o you have any idea how many different baseball cards there are of Mormon players? More than you can memorize or keep track on your fingers, that's for sure. There are more than 230 cards just for Dale Murphy, and there are 35 other players with cards. Obviously you need a checklist to track the cards you want and to avoid unwanted doubles.

The checklist is organized by the type of baseball card. Cards are listed by year under Donruss, Fleer, Score, Topps, and Upper Deck. All other cards are listed under Miscellaneous. Minor league cards are not included.

There are no Major League cards for the following players: Spencer Adams, Dave Downs, Doug Hansen, Ray Jacobs, John Noriega, Red Peery, Jay Van Noy, and Jim Wessinger. When these players were in the big leagues, there was only one baseball card company. If they were playing today, there would likely be several cards for each player.

When you obtain a card, you can note it in several ways including circling the card number, putting a check mark next to the number, or putting the date you obtained it next to the card number. The latter method will help you see that your collection is growing.

If you find any missing entries, you can write them in yourself in the available space. So what are you waiting for? It's collecting time!

DANNY AINGE

Donruss

1981	Rookie Card	569
1982		638

Fleer

1981	Rookie Card	418
1982		608

Topps

1981	Traded/Rookie Card	727
1982		125

Miscellaneous

1977	Sportscaster	
1978	Sportscaster	
1979	Sportscaster	

ALAN ASHBY

Donruss

1981		259
1982		317
1983		144
1984		539
1985		283
1986		405
1987		332
1987	Opening Day	17
1988		163
1988	Best '88	8
1989		88

Fleer

1981		64
1982		212
1983		445
1984		220
1985		343
1986		292
1987		50
1988		439
1989		350

Score

1988		73
1989		366

(Continued on next page)

ASHBY (continued)

Topps

1976	Rookie Card	209
1977		564
1977	Cloth Sticker	1
1978		319
1979		36
1980		187
1981		696
1982		433
1983		774
1984		217
1985		564
1986		331
1987		112
1988		48
1989		492
1989	Bowman	327
1989	Doubleheader	

Upper Deck

1989		305

Miscellaneous

1981	Coke	61
1990	Elite Senior Pro	63
1977	Hostess	124
1977	Hostess Twinkie	124
1979	Hostess	142
1986	Lite Beer Astros	14
1984	Mothers Astros	3
1985	Mothers Astros	13
1987	Mothers Astros	11
1988	Mothers Astros	11
1989	Mothers Astros	10
1986	Safety Astros	8
1987	Safety Astros	21
1988	Safety Astros	4
1988	Sportsflics	219
1976	SSPC	514
1988	Starting Lineup	

TOMMY BARRETT

Score

1990		633

Topps

1989	Rookie Card	653
1989	Big	177

BARRY BONNELL

Donruss

1982		432
1983		430
1984		559
1985		191

Fleer

1981		413
1982		611
1983		425
1984		149
1984	Traded	14U
1985		485
1986		460

Topps

1978	Rookie Card	242
1979		496
1980		632
1981		558
1982		99
1983		766
1984		302
1984	Traded	14T
1985		423
1986		119

Miscellaneous

1978	Hostess	142
1984	Mothers Mariners	2
1985	Mothers Mariners	10

RON BRAND

Topps

1964	Rookie Card	326
1965		212
1966		394
1968		317
1969		549
1970		221
1971		304
1972		773

Miscellaneous

1968	Coke
1972	Milton Bradley

KELLY DOWNS

Donruss

1987	Rookie Card	573
1988		145
1988	Best '88	106
1989		367
1990		177
1991		738

Fleer

1987	Rookie Card	272
1988		80
1989		326
1990		55
1991		261

Score

1988		27
1988	Young Superstars	19
1989		124
1990		534
1991		

Topps

1987	Rookie Card	438
1988	Glossy Rookies	19
1988		629
1989		361
1989	Big	112
1989	Bowman	465
1990		17
1991		733
1991	Stadium	193

Upper Deck

1989		476
1990		699
1991		441

Miscellaneous

1988	Classic (red)	194
1987	Mothers Giants	17
1988	Mothers Giants	17
1989	Mothers Giants	4
1990	Mothers Giants	4
1989	Panini	209
1988	Sportsflics	203
1989	Sportsflics	39
1988	Toys R Us Rookies	9

DENNIS ECKERSLEY

Donruss

1981		96
1982		30
1983		487
1984		639
1985		442
1986		239
1987		365
1988		349
1989		67
1989	All-Star	16
1990		210
1990	Best '90	12
1991		270

Fleer

1981		226
1981	Star Sticker	34
1982		292
1982	Stamp	165
1983		182
1983		629
1983	Sticker	63
1984		396
1984	Traded	34U
1985		57
1986		368
1987		563
1987	Traded	30U
1988		279
1989		7
1989	All-Star Team	4
1989	Baseball All-Stars	12
1990		6
1990	League Leaders	11
1991		6
1991	Ultra	245

Score

1988		104
1989		276
1990		315
1991		485
1991	Hottest Players	74
1991	Superstar	73

Topps

1976	Rookie Card	98
1977		525
1978		122
1979		40
1980		320
1981		620
1981	Home Team Photo	
1981	Sticker	48
1982		490
1983		270
1983	Sticker	34
1984		745
1984	Sticker	224
1984	Traded	34T
1985		163
1986		538
1986	Sticker	62
1987		459
1987	Sticker	63
1987	Traded	31T
1988		79
1989		370
1989	Bowman	190
1989	Doubleheader	
1989	Glossy 60 All-Stars	16
1989	Mini	69
1989	United Kingdom	23
1990		670
1990	Big	50
1990	Bowman	451
1990	Glossy 60 All-Stars	53
1990	Mini	27
1991		250

ECKERSLEY (continued)

Upper Deck

1989		289
1989	ALCS	664
1990		513
1991		172

Miscellaneous

1989	Cadaco Disc	16
1989	Classic (light blue)	90
1981	Coca-Cola/Red Sox	2
1982	Coke/Brigham's	5
1986	Gatorade Cubs	43
1989	Hills Team MVP	12
1976	Hostess	137
1977	Hostess	106
1977	Hostess Twinkie	106
1978	Hostess	78
1979	Hostess	145
1990	Kay Bee	9
1976	Kellogg's	19
1977	Kellogg's	9
1990	Leaf Promo	3
1990	Leaf	29
1991	Leaf	285
1988	Mother's A's	10
1989	Mother's A's	10
1990	Mother's A's	7
1989	Panini Sticker	167
1984	7-Up Cubs	43
1985	7-Up Cubs	43
1977	Sportscaster	
1978	Sportscaster	
1979	Sportscaster	
1986	Sportsflics	129
1987	Sportsflics Cubs Team	22
1989	Sportsflics	222
1990	Sportsflics	170
1989	Woolworth Highlights	20

MIKE FETTERS

Donruss

1990	Rookie Card	35
1991		565

Fleer

1990	Rookie Card	131
1991		312

Score

1991		497
1991	Rising Stars	74

Topps

1990	Rookie Card	14
1990	Debut	131
1991		477
1991	Stadium	228

Upper Deck

1991		696

JERRY GARVIN

Donruss

1981		150
1982		430
1983		227

Fleer

1981		429
1982		614
1983		428

Topps

1978	Rookie Card	419
1979		293
1980		611
1981		124
1982		768
1983		258

LUIS GOMEZ

Donruss

1981		88

Fleer

1981		253

Topps

1977	Rookie Card	13
1978		573
1979		254
1980		169
1981		477
1982		372
1990	Senior Baseball	16

Miscellaneous

1990	Pacific Senior League	17
1991	Pacific Senior League	143
1981	Police Braves	9

JIM GOTT

Donruss

1983	Rookie Card	353
1984		268
1985		632
1986		358
1988		606
1988	Best '88	213
1989		362
1990		605
1991		601

Fleer

1984		155
1985		105
1985	Traded	45U
1986		542
1987	Traded	35U
1988	Traded	112
1989		210
1989	Exciting Stars	16
1989	Superstars	18
1990		466
1991		200

Score

1988		320
1989		257
1989	Superstar	98
1990		515
1991		

Topps

1983	Rookie Card	506
1984		9
1985		311
1985	Traded	40T
1986		463
1987	Traded	39T
1988		127
1989		752
1989	Bowman	411
1989	Mini	32
1990		292
1991		606

Upper Deck

1989		539
1990	Error Card	89A
1990		89B
1990		701
1991		690

Miscellaneous

1991	Leaf	229
1985	Mothers Giants	21
1986	Mothers Giants	21
1987	Mothers Giants	19
1989	Panini	163
1990	Safety Dodgers	35
1989	Sportsflics	83
1984	Toronto Fireman	38

DOUG HOWARD

Miscellaneous

1977	O-Pee-Chee	112

KEN HUBBS

Topps

1962	Rookie Card	461
1963		15
1964	In Memoriam	550

Miscellaneous

1989	Cub History Cards	D-7
1963	Jello	174
1963	Post Ceral	174

KEN HUNT

Topps

1961	Rookie Card	556
1962		364

Miscellaneous

1962	Jello	129
1962	Kahn	
1962	Post Ceral	129

BRUCE HURST

Donruss

1983		134
1984		213
1985		493
1986		517
1986	Highlights	47
1987		174
1988	All-Star	14
1988		252
1988	Best '88	233
1989		423
1989	Traded	45
1990		183
1991		83

Fleer

1982	Rookie Card	297
1983		186
1984		400
1985		161
1986		352
1987		37
1987	Limited Edition	22
1987	Star Sticker	65
1988		356
1988	Star Sticker	10
1988	All-Stars	18
1989		91
1989	Traded	124
1990		159
1990	All-Stars	19
1991		533
1991	Ultra	306

(Continued on next page)

HURST (continued)

Score

1988		380
1989		325
1989	Superstar	79
1989	Traded	19
1990		270
1990	Superstar	18
1991		145

Topps

1981	Rookie Card	689
1982	Red Sox Rookies	381
1983		82
1984		213
1985		451
1986		581
1986	Mini	6
1987		705
1987	Baseball Highlights	19
1987	Baseball Highlights	28
1987	Mini	43
1988		125
1988	Superstar Sticker	62
1989		675
1989	Bowman	451
1989	Glossy 60 All-Stars	28
1989	Mini	49
1989	Traded	55
1989	United Kingdom	42
1990		315
1990	Bowman	208
1991		65

Upper Deck

1989		387
1989	Traded	792
1990		433
1991		602

Miscellaneous

1987	Classic (green)	83
1989	Classic (purple)	194
1990	Classic (blue)	102
1989	Coke Padres	7
1990	Leaf	23
1991	Leaf	469
1989	Padres Cards	21
1989	Panini	271
1987	Sportsflic	38
1988	Sportsflic	197
1989	Sportsflic	175
1990	Sportsflic	47

DANE IORG

Donruss

1981		311
1982		166
1983		469
1984		571
1985		252

Fleer

1981		543
1982		116
1983		10
1984		326
1984	Traded	55U
1985		204
1986		9
1986	Traded	54U

Topps

1980	Rookie Card	139
1981		334
1982		86
1983		788
1984		416
1984	Traded	54T
1985		761
1986		269
1986	Traded	49T
1987		690

Miscellaneous

1986	World Series	186

GARTH IORG

Donruss

1982		353
1983		306
1984		561
1985		363
1986		640
1987		394
1988		444

Fleer

1981		423
1982		616
1983		430
1984		157
1985		107
1986		61
1987		229
1988		113

Score

1988		204

Topps

1978	Rookie Card	704
1981		444
1982		518
1983		326
1984		39
1985		168
1986		694
1987		751
1988		273
1990	Senior Baseball	86

Miscellaneous

1986	Ault Foods	16
1990	Elite Senior Pro	36
1990	Pacific Senior League	152
1991	Pacific Senior League	41
1990	T&M Senior League	51
1985	Toronto Fireman	16
1986	Toronto Fireman	16
1987	Toronto Fireman	16
1988	Toronto Fireman	16

WALLY JOYNER

Donruss

1986	Rookie Card	1
1986	Highlights	23
1987	Diamond King	1
1987		135
1987	All Stars	1
1987	Highlights	35
1987	Opening Day	7
1987	Pop Ups	
1987	Super Diamond King	1
1988		110
1988	Bonus Card MVP	BC13
1988	Best '88	115
1989		52
1989	Bonus Card MVP	BC21
1990		94
1991		677

Fleer

1986	Traded/Rookie Card	59U
1986	Sluggers/Pitchers	19
1987		86
1987	Rookie All Stars	628
1987	All Stars	23
1987	Exciting Stars	30
1987	Game Winners	22
1987	Hottest Stars	25
1987	League Leaders	26
1987	Limited Edition	23
1987	Mini	59
1987	Record Setters	17
1987	Sluggers/Pitchers	22
1987	Star Sticker	68
1987	Wax Pack	C7
1988		493
1988	Slugging Sophs	622
1988	All Stars	23
1988	Award Winners	21
1988	Exciting Stars	23
1988	Hottest Stars	21
1988	League Leaders	22
1988	MVP	20
1988	Star Sticker	12
1988	Superstars	18
1989		481
1989	Exciting Stars	28
1989	Superstars	26
1989	Wax Box Card	C16
1990		136
1991		317
1991	Ultra	48

Score

1988		7
1988	Young Superstars	27
1989		65
1989	Superstar	73
1990		120
1990	Superstar	81
1991		873
1991	Superstar	57

Topps

1986	Traded/Rookie Card	51T
1987		80
1987	Glossy Rookies	7
1987	Glossy 22 All Stars	13
1987	Glossy 60 All Stars	39
1987	Mini	45
1988	California Leaders	381
1988		420
1988	Big	52
1988	Glossy 60 All Stars	48
1988	Mini	6
1988	Superstar Stciker	34
1988	United Kingdom	40

(Continued on next page)

JOYNER (continued)

1989		270
1989	Big	201
1989	Bowman	47
1989	United Kingdom	46
1990		525
1990	Big	168
1990	Bowman	299
1991		195
1991	Stadium	2

Upper Deck

1989	Collectors Club	668
1989	'Early Demo Card'	700
1990		693
1991		575

Miscellaneous

1990	Ames All-Stars	30
1988	Bazooka	10
1986	BBC magazine	2
1987	Burger King	
1990	California Sunflower Seeds	19
1987	Classic (green)	6
1987	Classic (yellow)	108
1988	Classic (blue)	206
1989	Classic (light blue)	29
1990	Classic (pink)	42
1987	Drake's	2
1988	Fantastic Sam's	4
1987	Hostess	20
1988	Jiffy Pop	11
1987	Kay Bee	18
1988	Kay Bee Superstars	15
1988	Kay Bee Team Leaders	16
1988	King-B	9
1987	Kraft	9
1990	Leaf	24
1991	Leaf	31
1987	M&M's	1
1989	Masterbread	7
1988	Nestle Dream Team	44
1988	Panini	40
1989	Panini	291
1988	Rite Aid	15
1986	Smokey Angels	22
1987	Smokey Angels	12
1988	Smokey Angels	17
1989	Smokey Angel All-Stars	18
1990	Smokey Angels	9
1986	Sportsflics Rookie Card	7
1987	Sportsflics	26
1987	Sportsflics Tri-Stars	75
1988	Sportsflics	
1989	Sportsflics	2
1990	Sportsflics	49
1986	Star Set	
1988	Starting Lineup	
1987	Stuart Superstars	16
1987	Super Star Discs	10
1987	Toys R Us	14

HARMON KILLEBREW

Topps

1955	Rookie Card	124
1955	Double Header	111
1956		164
1958		288
1959		515
1960		210
1961		80
1962	Home Run Leaders	53
1962		70
1962	In Action	316
1963	Home Run Hitters	4
1963		500
1964	Home Run Hitters	10
1964	RBI Leaders	12
1964	All Star Vets	81
1964		177
1964	Giant Cards	38
1964	Stand Ups	39
1965	Home Run Hitters	3
1965	RBI Leaders	5
1965		400
1965	Embossed	56
1966		120
1967	RBI Leaders	241
1967	Home Run Hitters	243
1967	Twin Terrors	334
1967		460
1968	RBI Leaders	4
1968	Home Run Hitters	6
1968		220
1968	All Star	361
1968	Superstars	490
1968	Game Card Set	5
1969		375
1969	Super Card	19
1970	RBI Leaders	64
1970	Home Run Hitters	66
1970		150
1970	Super Card	4
1971	Home Run Hitters	65
1971		550
1971	Greatest Moments	8
1971	Super Card	60
1972		51
1972	In Action	52
1972	RBI Leaders	88
1973		170
1974		400
1975	'69 MVP	207
1975		640

(Continued on next page)

KILLEBREW (continued)

Miscellaneous

1984	Baseball Immortals	185
1982	Baseball Legends	69
1960	Bazooka	20
1962	Bazooka	44
1963	Bazooka	7
1964	Bazooka	7
1965	Bazooka	7
1966	Bazooka	11
1967	Bazooka	11
1968	Bazooka	31
1971	Bazooka	2
1986	Big League Chew	5
1985	Circle K	5
1968	Coke	
1982	Cracker Jack	5
1962	Jello	85
1963	Jello	5
1989	Kahn's Cooperstown	7
1970	Kelloggs	61
1971	Kelloggs	55
1982	K Mart	15
1987	K Mart	4
1988	Living Legend	86
1989	Living Legend	163
1990	Living Legend	35
1971	Milk Duds	4b
1971	Milk Duds	24b
1969	Milton Bradley	
1970	Milton Bradley	
1972	Milton Bradley	
1987	Nestle Dream Team	22
1960	Nu-Card Hi-Lites	49
1961	Nu Card Scoops	449
1961	Peters Meats Twins	
1960	Post Ceral	
1961	Post Ceral	92a
1961	Post Ceral	92b
1962	Post Ceral	85
1963	Post Ceral	5
1986	Sportsflics Decade	48
1975	SSPC	70
1989	Swell	70
1991	Swell Baseball Greats	49
1969	Transogram	
1970	Transogram	

NEWT KIMBALL

Miscellaneous

1990	Target Dodgers	409

DON KIRKWOOD

Topps

1976		108
1977		519
1978		251
1979		632

GARY KROLL

Topps

1965	Rookie Card	449
1966		548

VANCE LAW

Donruss

1982		582
1983		117
1984		546
1985		122
1986		132
1987		212
1987	Opening Day	94
1988		212
1988	Best '88	60
1989		276
1989	All Star	49
1990		629

Fleer

1982		484
1983		245
1984		68
1985		520
1985	Traded	70U
1986		252
1987		323
1988		187
1988	Traded	79U
1989		430
1989	Baseball All-Stars	27
1990		36

Score

1988		85
1988	Traded	16T
1989		102
1990		73

Topps

1981	Rookie Card	551
1982	Pirates Rookie	291
1983		98
1984		667
1985		413
1985	Fathers & Sons	137
1985	Traded	73T
1986		787
1987		127
1988		346
1988	Traded	60T
1989		501
1989	Big	143
1989	Bowman	292
1990		287

Upper Deck

1989		473
1990		380

Miscellaneous

1988	Cubs Berg Hot Dogs	2
1989	Cubs Marathon Oil	2
1991	Leaf	355
1986	Provigp Expos	23
1988	Sportsflics	41
1989	Sportsflics	162
1983	True Value White Sox	5
1984	True Value White Sox	5

VERNON LAW

Bowman

1951	Rookie Card	203
1952		71
1954		187
1955		199

Fleer

1963		58

Topps

1952	Rookie Card	81
1954		235
1956		252
1957		199
1958		132
1959		12
1959	Buc Hill Aces	428
1960		453
1961	NL Pitching Leaders	47
1961	Buc Hill Aces	250
1961		40
1962		295
1963		184
1964		472
1965		515
1966		15
1966	ERA Leaders	221
1967		351
1985	Father & Sons	137

Miscellaneous

1966	Bazooka	18
1966	East Hills	32
1958	Hires Test	
1962	Jello	179
1958	Kahn's Wieners	
1959	Kahn's Wieners	
1960	Kahn's Wieners	
1961	Kahn's Wieners	
1990	Living Legend	37
1961	Nu Card Scoops	406
1961	Post Cereal	126a
1961	Post Cereal	126b
1962	Post Cereal	179
1991	Swell Baseball Greats	55

JACK MORRIS

Donruss

1981		127
1982		107
1983	Diamond King	5
1983		107
1984		415
1985		415
1986		105
1986	All Star	18
1986	Pop Ups	
1986	Highlights	27
1987		173
1987	Diamond King	13
1987	Opening Day	212
1987	Super Diamond King	13
1988		127
1988	All Star	24
1988	Best '88	181
1989		234
1990		639
1991		492

Fleer

1981		475
1982		274
1983		336
1984		87
1985		18
1985	No-Hitter	643
1985	Limited Edition	21
1986		232
1986	Mini	48
1986	Sluggers/Pitchers	23
1986	Star Sticker	79
1987		158
1987	Baseball Allstars	28
1987	Limited Edition	28
1987	Mini	70
1987	Sluggers/Pitchers	27
1988		64
1988	All Star Righties	626
1988	Award Winners	26
1988	Baseball Allstars	26
1988	Exciting Stars	27
1988	Headliners	3
1988	Hottest Stars	28
1988	League Leaders	28
1988	Mini	22
1988	MVP	24
1988	Record Setters	26
1988	Star Sticker	26
1989		139
1989	MVP	30
1990		90
1990		610
1990	League Leaders	27
1991		343

Score

1988		545
1989		250
1990		203
1990	Scoremaster	8
1991		114

(Continued on next page)

MORRIS (continued)

Topps

1978	Rookie Card	703
1979		251
1980		371
1981		572
1982	Victory Leaders	165
1982		450
1982	All Stars	556
1983		65
1984	Strikeout Leaders	136
1984		195
1984	Tiger Team Leaders	666
1984	Glossy 40 All Stars	10
1985		610
1985	Glossy 40 All Stars	26
1985	Super	43
1985	3 D	28
1986		270
1986	Glossy 22 All Stars	10
1986	Mini Leaders	14
1986	Super	38
1986	3 D	17
1987		778
1987	Glossy 60 All Stars	47
1987	Mini	55
1988		340
1988	Big	170
1988	Glossy 60 All Stars	47
1988	Mini	11
1988	Superstar Sticker	59
1988	United Kingdom	50
1989		645
1989	Big	61
1989	Bowman	93
1989	Mini	1
1989	United Kingdom	54
1990		555
1991		75

Upper Deck

1989		352
1990		573
1991		336

Miscellaneous

1978	Burger King	8
1985	Cain's Potato Chips	14
1986	Cain's Potato Chips	11
1987	Cain's Pototo Chips	14
1988	Chef Boyardee	3
1987	Classic (green)	90
1988	Classic (red)	174
1991	Classic (Series II)	49
1981	Coke	54
1987	Coke Tigers	7
1990	Coke Kroger Tigers	12
1986	Dorman's Cheese	2
1987	Drake Super Pitcher	27
1988	Drake Super Pitcher	32
1987	Jiffy Pop Disc	3
1987	Kay Bee	20
1988	Kay Bee Team Leaders	23
1990	Kay Bee Kings	19
1982	Kellogg's	5
1983	Kellogg's	35
1991	Leaf	294
1987	M & M's	6
1990	Marathon Tigers	47
1989	Panini	334
1981	Perma-Graphics All Stars	5
1988	Rite Aid	27
1988	Safety Tigers	
1989	Safety Tigers	
1987	Smokey	6
1988	Starting Lineup	
1987	Stuart Superstars	19
1985	Thom McAn Discs	
1988	Tigers Pepsi/Kroger	47
1985	Wendy's Tigers	16

DALE MURPHY

Donruss

1981		437
1982		299
1983	Diamond King	12
1983		47
1983	Action All Stars	45
1984		66
1984	Action All Stars	40
1984	Champions	49
1985		66
1985	Action All Stars	25
1985	Highlights	5
1986		66
1986	Action All Stars	4
1986	Highlights	41
1986	Pop Ups	
1987	Diamond King	3
1987		78
1987	Action All Stars	14
1987	Pop Ups	
1987	Opening Day	40
1987	Super Diamond King	3
1987	Wax Pack Box	PC10
1988		78
1988	All Star	46
1988	Best '88	113
1988	Bonus Card MVP	BC14
1989		104
1990		168
1991		484
1991	Mr. Dirt, Mr. Clean	744

Fleer

1981		243
1982		443
1983		142
1984		186
1985		335
1985	Limited Edition	22
1986		522
1986	Braves Dynamic Duo	635
1986	NL West Sluggers	640
1986	Gooden-Murphy Sticker	132
1986	League Leaders	27
1986	Limited Edition	31
1986	Mini	105
1986	Sluggers/Pitchers	24
1986	Star Sticker	80
1986	Wax Pack Box	C4
1987		522
1987	All Stars	29
1987	Award Winner	26
1987	Game Winner	30
1987	Hottest Stars	28
1987	Limited Edition	30
1987	Mini	74
1987	Record Setters	23
1987	Sluggers/Pitchers	28
1987	Star Sticker	83
1987	Wax Pack Box	C8
1988		544
1988	NL All Stars	639
1988	Award Winners	27
1988	Exciting Stars	28
1988	Hottest Stars	29
1988	League Leaders	29
1988	MVP	25
1988	Record Setters	27
1988	Sluggers/Pitchers	28
1988	Star Sticker	77
1988	Superstars	25
1988	Wax Pack Box	C6
1989		596
1989	Exciting Stars	33
1989	League Leaders	28
1990		591
1990	Player of the Decade	623
1990	MVP	28
1990	Traded	46U
1991		409
1991	Ultra	270

(Continued on next page)

MURPHY (continued)

Score

1988		450
1989		30
1989	Superstar	66
1990		66
1990	Scoremaster	15
1990	Superstar	64
1990	Traded	31T
1991		650
1991	Superstar	35

Topps

1977	Rookie Card	476
1978	Rookie Catchers	708
1979		39
1980		274
1981		504
1981	Scratch Off	72
1981	Sticker	146
1982		668
1983	All Star	401
1983	Braves Team Leaders	502
1983	RBI Leaders	703
1983		760
1983	Glossy 40 All Stars	16
1983	Sticker	206
1984	Braves Team Leaders	126
1984	RBI Leaders	133
1984		150
1984	All Star	391
1984	Cereal Set	12
1984	Glossy 22 All Stars	19
1984	Glossy 40 All Stars	31
1984	Sticker	27
1984	Sticker	180
1984	Super 5 X 7	2
1985		320
1985	All Star	716
1985	Glossy 22 All Stars	7
1985	Glossy 60 All Stars	1
1985	Super	11
1985	3 D	3
1986	Braves Team Leaders	456
1986		600
1986	All Star	705
1986	Glossy 22 All Stars	18
1986	Glossy 60 All Stars	37
1986	Mini Leaders	37
1986	Super	39
1986	Superstar	23
1986	Super 3 D	16
1987		490
1987	Glossy 22 All Stars	7
1987	Glossy 60 All Stars	6
1987	Mini	2
1987	Wax Pack Box	M
1988		90
1988	Braves Team Leaders	549
1988	Big	14
1988	Glossy 60 All Stars	26
1988	Mini	41
1988	Superstar Sticker	18
1988	United Kingdom	52
1989		210
1989	Big	172
1989	Bowman	276
1989	Mini	1
1989	United Kingdom	52
1990		750
1990	Big	40
1990	Bowman	19
1991		545
1991	Box Bottom	J
1991	Stadium	243

Upper Deck

1989		357
1990		533
1991		447

(Continued on next page)

MURPHY (continued)

Miscellaneous

1989	Ames 20/20	21
1990	Ames All-Stars	11
1984	Baseball Card Mag	282
1990	Baseball Wit	38
1987	Boardwalk	3
1986	Burger King	11
1988	Chef Boyardee	17
1987	Classic (green)	37
1987	Classic (yellow)	106
1988	Classic (blue)	201
1988	Classic (blue)	215
1988	Classic (red)	156
1989	Classic (orange)	124
1990	Classic (pink)	36
1991	Classic Series I	96
1991	Classic	73
1978	Coca Cola	
1986	Dorman's Cheese	10
1983	Drake	18
1984	Drake	22
1985	Drake	20
1986	Drake	12
1987	Drake	13
1988	Drake	15
1988	Fantastic Sam	13
1989	Hills Team MVP	21
1990	Hills Hit Men	16
1979	Hostess	121
1985	Hostess Braves	16
1987	Hostess Stickers	7
1986	Jiffy Pop Disc	16
1987	Jiffy Pop Disc	2
1987	Kay Bee	21
1988	Kay Bee Superstars	20
1988	Kay Bee Team Leaders	24
1983	Kellogg's	52
1988	King-B	2
1989	King-B	11
1987	K Mart	29
1988	K Mart	18
1987	Kraft	2
1990	Leaf	243

1991	Leaf	412
1987	M & M's	9
1986	Meadow Gold	
1986	Meadow Gold	4
1986	Meadow Gold Milk	
1984	Milton Bradley	
1984	Nestle Dream Team	18
1988	Nestle Dream Team	2
1987	Our Own Ten	15
1982	Perma-Graphics All Stars	14
1983	Perma-Graphics All Stars	12
1983	Perma-Graphics Superstars	9
1981	Police Braves	3
1982	Police Braves	3
1983	Police Braves	3
1984	Police Braves	3
1985	Police Braves	3
1986	Police Braves	3
1990	Post Ceral First Collector	18
1986	Quaker Granola	8
1984	Ralston Purina	12
1988	Rite Aid	1
1988	Slurpee Corn	
1987	Smokey's Braves	14
1988	Smokey's Braves	14
1987	Smokey's NL	2
1986	Sportsflics	5
1986	Sportsflics NL MVPs	62
1986	Sportsflics Decade Great	67
1986	Sportsflics '85 Golden Glv	179
1986	Sportsflics '85 Triple Crwn	183
1987	Sportsflics	3
1987	Sportsflics Tri-Stars	155
1987	Sportsflics Big Six	159
1988	Sportsflics	170
1989	Sportsflics	110
1990	Sportsflics	189
1986	Star 24-card set	
1988	Starting Lineup	
1987	Stuart Superstars	2
1987	Superstar Discs	15
1988	Superstar Discs	14
1988	Talking Baseball	18
1986	True Value	10
1986	Woolworth's	23
1990	Woolworth's Highlights	15

SCOTT NIELSEN

Donruss

1987	Rookie Card	597

Fleer

1989		261

Topps

1987	Rookie Card	57

JERRY NYMAN

Topps

1969	Rookie Card	173
1970		644
1971		656

MONTE PEARSON

Playball

1939		71a
1939		71b
1940		5

Miscellaneous

1937	O-pee-chee	131
1936	World Wide Gum	114

WALLY RITCHIE

Donruss

1988		555

Fleer

1987	Rookie Card/Traded	104U
1988		312

Score

1988		526

Topps

1987	Rookie Card/Traded	103T
1988		494

Miscellaneous

1988	Tastykake Phillies	20

FRED SANFORD

Bowman

1949	236
1950	156
1951	145

Miscellaneous

1951	Berk Ross	D3
1947	Tiptop	

ELMER SINGLETON

Bowman

1949	147

Topps

1957	378
1959	548

Miscellaneous

1949	Sommer	25

TOMMIE SISK

Topps

1963	Rookie Card	169
1964		224
1965		558
1966		441
1967		84
1968		429
1969		152
1970		374

Miscellaneous

1966	East Hills	25
1968	KDKA	25

CORY SNYDER

Donruss

1986	Rated Rookie	29
1986	Rookie Set	15
1987		526
1987	Opening Day	106
1988		350
1988	Best '88	224
1989	Diamond King	9
1989		191
1989	Best '89	168
1989	Super Diamond King	8
1990		272
1991		288

Fleer

1986	Rookie Card	656
1987		260
1987	Exciting Rookies	40
1987	Hottest Stars	39
1987	Mini	103
1987	Star Sticker	113
1988		615
1988	Slugging Sophomores	622
1989		412
1989	Superstars	38
1990		502
1991		378
1991	Ultra	83

Score

1988		92
1988	Young Superstars	40
1989		52
1989	Superstar	6
1990		10
1990	Superstar	28
1991		19
1991	Superstar	74

Topps

1985	Olympic/Rookie Card	403
1987		192
1987	Glossy Rookies	16
1987	Glossy 60 All Stars	9
1987	Sticker with Incaviglia	168
1987	Sticker	213
1988		620
1988	Cleveland Leaders	789
1988	Big	43
1988	Glossy 60 All Stars	23
1988	Sticker	208
1988	Superstar Sticker	53
1988	United Kingdom	74
1989		80
1989	Big	175
1989	Bowman	89
1989	Sticker	210
1989	United Kingdom	73
1990		770
1990	Bowman	336
1990	Sticker	211
1991		323

Upper Deck

1989		170
1989	Collector's Club	679
1990		126
1991		123

(Continued on next page)

SNYDER (continued)

Miscellaneous

1987	Classic (yellow)	110
1988	Classic (red)	184
1989	Classic	19
1987	Gatorade Indians	28
1988	Gatorade Indians	28
1988	Kenner	106
1989	Kenner	83
1988	King-B	10
1987	Kraft	17
1990	Leaf	187
1991	Leaf	506
1988	Panini	80
1989	Panini	329
1990	Panini	56
1986	Sportsflics Rookie Card	3
1987	Sportsflics	24
1988	Sportsflics	29
1989	Sportsflics	196
1990	Sportsflics	3
1988	Star 11-card set	
1988	Starting Lineup	
1989	Talking Lineup	124
1989	Tara Toys	
1987	Toys R Us	25
1988	Toys R Us Rookies	9

BOB USHER

Bowman

1951	286

Topps

1952	157
1958	124

COLBY WARD

Donruss

1991	Rookie Card	330
1991	'90 Debut	79

Fleer

1991	Rookie Card	382

Topps

1991	Rookie Card	31

MEMORABLE QUOTES

"The basepath is mine. If you're in the way, I'll kill you." *Ty Cobb to Spencer Adams*

"I'm a competitive ballplayer and baseball is very important to me, but nothing is more important than my family and my relationship with Jesus Christ." *Alan Ashby*

"I'll be playing in pain, but I want to prove I can still play." *Tommy Barrett*

"The secret is good conditioning, concentration, and staying ahead of the hitters." *Dave Downs*

"The earthquake was a reminder that we are not really in control as much as we think we are." *Kelly Downs*

"The Lord had prepared my heart." *Luis Gomez about his conversion*

"The recovery from my injury made me realize how fortunate I am to be a Major League player. I developed a real desire to win, to go all out." *Jim Gott*

"One thing the Yakima club will have is fight and hustle; we're not going to be licked until the last putout." *Ray Jacobs*

"I was never in a game long enough to get thrown out." *Newt Kimball*

"The first day I was in the Angels' locker room as a starry-eyed kid only knowing four fellows, Nolan walked all the way across the room, stuck out his hand and said, 'Nice to have you on the team.' " *Don Kirkwood on meeting Nolan Ryan*

"You can't know what it feels like to have already given up four home runs and nearly the entire game is still ahead of you." *Jack Morris*

"After you've been around, rookie, you help someone else." *Pete Rose to John Noriega*

"I threw really hard, but I was so wild the hitters would swing to get out of the batter's box as fast as they could." *Jerry Nyman*

"Fred is one of the cleanest-living boys I have ever seen in the big leagues." *Zack Taylor speaking of Fred Sanford*

"I cherished every time I went to the mound." *Elmer Singleton*

SECTION 8

TRIVIA QUESTIONS

How many times has someone said, "I bet you don't know this?" Well now you can say, "Sure I do, but I bet you don't know who won the Golden Tomahawk award or who was picked the Best All-Around Athlete in Southern California!" But hey don't be too tough! Remember they're your friends.

Before you test your friends, perhaps you should test yourself. The questions start off rather easy but as you would expect, they get harder as you progress. So score one point for each correct answer from the first ten questions; two points for correct answers to questions 11-60; and three points for correct answers to the last ten questions.

If you got 112 or more points you really know your stuff. If you earned between 72 and 112 points you can hold your own. Anything less than 72 points and you should be studying this book night and day--just kidding.

If you like Trivia then create your own Trivia Championship for your friends or family.

TRIVIA CHAMPIONSHIP

Select answers from the listed players. You may wish to write your answers on a blank sheet of paper. Some players may appear as answers more than once. See page 262 for the answers--after you've given it a "big league" try yourself.

ADAMS	FETTERS	IORG, D.	LAW, VA.	RITCHIE
AINGE	GARVIN	IORG, G.	LAW, VE.	SANFORD
ASHBY	GOMEZ	JACOBS	MORRIS	SINGLETON
BARRETT	GOTT	JOYNER	MURPHY	SISK
BONNELL	HANSEN	KILLEBREW	NIELSEN	SNYDER
BRAND	HOWARD	KIMBALL	NORIEGA	USHER
DOWNS, D.	HUBBS	KIRKWOOD	NYMAN	VAN NOY
DOWNS, K.	HUNT	KROLL	PEARSON	WARD
ECKERSLEY	HURST		PEERY	WESSINGER

<u>One-Point Questions</u>

1. I was a college All-American in basketball at BYU. ______________
2. I played on the 1984 U.S. Olympic baseball team. ______________
3. I have more than 200 wins and 2,000 strikeouts. ______________
4. I am the only Mormon to be a two-time MVP. ______________
5. I am the only Mormon to win the Cy Young award. ______________
6. I played in three straight World Series with the Oakland A's. ______________.
7. I won two games in the 1986 World Series for the Boston Red Sox. ______________
8. I played baseball in Japan in 1990. ______________
9. I hit 25 or more homers in 13 different years. ______________
10. I caught Nolan Ryan's record-breaking fifth no-hitter. ______________.

<u>Two-Point Questions</u>

11. I picked off 22 runners in my rookie year. ______________
12. I struck out 309 batters in one minor league season. ______________
13. I was drafted by the Los Angeles Rams as their # 1 pick. ______________
14. I baptized Dale Murphy. ______________
15. I won the Rookie of the Year award in 1962. ______________
16. I went on a mission to Argentina. ______________
17. I set the "Save" record in Pittsburgh in 1988. ______________
18. I won the sixth game of the 1985 World Series with a pinch hit. ______________
19. I was noted as the best golfer in baseball during my playing days. ______________
20. I had seven LDS teammates while playing in the Majors. ______________
21. I didn't become a catcher until I was in the minor leagues. ______________
22. As a pitcher, I hit two home runs in the same game. ______________
23. I was in the same pitching rotation with Nolan Ryan. ______________
24. I signed a pro baseball contract when I was 16. ______________
25. I led the Pacific Coast League in strikeouts in 1989. ______________
26. I was involved in an argument with Ty Cobb. ______________

27. I out-pitched Carl Hubbell in the 1936 World Series. ______________
28. I pitched against Bob Feller on Opening Day in Cleveland. ______________
29. Casey Stengel was my manager on the New York Yankees. ______________
30. Casey Stengel was my manager on the New York Mets. ______________
31. I was a Topps rookie all-star pitcher in 1977. ______________
32. I led the Pirates in complete games and shutouts in 1967. ______________
33. I was a roommate of Pete Rose. ______________
34. I was in baseball 20 years but played in only two Major League games. ______________
35. I played in the World Series my rookie season. ______________
36. I played in two straight World Series for different teams. ______________
37. I have two World Series rings from different teams. ______________
38. I have two World Series rings from the same team. ______________
39. I was on the cover of *Sports Illustrated* in October 1989. ______________
40. I pitched in 671 pro games. ______________
41. Parade magazine picked me as a high school All-American in 3 sports. ______________
42. I played in the play-offs for both the Chicago Cubs and White Sox. ______________
43. I equalled or exceeded many of Babe Ruth's pitching records. ______________
44. I set an NCAA record for pitching 26 consecutive wins. ______________
45. I am featured in the book, *Men at Work,* written by George Will. ______________
46. I became BYU's winningest pitcher in 1986. ______________
47. I held Mickey Mantle to one hit and beat the Yankees in my first game. ______________
48. Dale Murphy and Barry Bonnell were my teammates in 1979. ______________
49. I struck out Dave Parker and Buddy Bell in my first Major League game. ______________
50. I was selected to play in the All-Star game in three different positions. ______________
51. I have been a 20-game winner twice in the Major Leagues. ______________
52. I played in the first official NL game held outside the USA. ______________
53. I was on the Pirates when they won the NL pennant in 1927. ______________
54. I was the Georgia Baseball Player of the Year in high school. ______________
55. I won a Gold Glove my rookie season. ______________

56./57. We are both members of the Utah Baseball Hall of Fame. ______________
____

58./59. We both are the youngest of 3 brothers to sign pro contracts. ______________
____

60. I became a pilot after playing baseball. ______________

Three-Point Questions

61. My high school football jersey was retired in 1971. ______________
62. I went to the American Legion Nat'l Championship two years in a row. ______________
63. I won my first Major League game 1-0 against the Atlanta Braves. ______________
64. My first Major League home run was a grand slam. ______________
65. I was drafted by the Chicago Bulls. ______________
66. In my first two years of college ball, I had a 24-4 record. ______________
67. I pitched three consecutive no-hitters in a college summer league. ______________
68. I pitched in the Triple A all-star game in 1988. ______________
69. In my first pro game, I pitched a no-hitter. ______________
70. Five of my Cleveland Indian teammates became Hall of Famers. ______________

TRIVIA ANSWERS

One-Point Answers.

1. Danny Ainge
2. Cory Snyder
3. Jack Morris
4. Dale Murphy
5. Vernon Law
6. Dennis Eckersley
7. Bruce Hurst
8. Vance Law
9. Harmon Killebrew
10. Alan Ashby

Two-Point Answers

11. Jerry Garvin
12. Gary Kroll
13. Jay Van Noy
14. Barry Bonnell
15. Ken Hubbs
16. Scott Nielsen
17. Jim Gott
18. Dane Iorg
19. Newt Kimball
20. Garth Iorg
21. Ron Brand
22. Jim Gott
23. Don Kirkwood
24. Jay Van Noy
25. Mike Fetters
26. Spencer Adams
27. Monte Pearson
28. Fred Sanford
29. Fred Sanford
30. Gary Kroll
31. Jerry Garvin
32. Tommie Sisk
33. John Noriega
34. Ray Jacobs
35. Ken Hunt
36. Spencer Adams
37. Dane Iorg
38. Fred Sanford
39. Kelly Downs
40. Elmer Singleton
41. Danny Ainge
42. Vance Law
43. Bruce Hurst
44. Scott Nielsen
45. Jim Gott
46. Colby Ward
47. Jerry Nyman
48. Jim Wessinger
49. Wally Ritchie
50. Harmon Killebrew
51. Jack Morris
52. Ron Brand
53. Red Peery
54. Wally Joyner
55. Ken Hubbs

56./57. Fred Sanford & Elmer Singleton

58./59. Tommie Barrett & Garth Iorg

60. Barry Bonnell

Three-Point Answers

61. Luis Gomez
62. Bob Usher
63. Dave Downs
64. Barry Bonnell
65. Doug Howard
66. Wally Ritchie
67. Don Kirkwood
68. Scott Nielsen
69. Newt Kimball
70. Doug Hansen

Count Your Points

Correct 1-pointers _____ X 1 = _____pts
Correct 2-pointers _____ X 2 = _____pts
Correct 3-pointers _____ X 3 = _____pts
Total points _____

112-140 pts ==You Know Your Baseball
72-111 pts ==You Can Hold Your Own
0--71 pts ==A Little More Practice

SECTION 9

READING REFERENCES

When it comes to baseball, some of us just can't get enough. So if you are still hungry for "more data" then this section can be your menu. Over 200 articles are listed covering most players.

If there is a double asterisk (**) at the end of the reference, then you know that the article identifies the player as a member of the Church. This is not as common as it used to be, as more Mormons are in the big leagues so it is not as noteworthy as it once was.

TSN means *The Sporting News* and SI means *Sports Illustrated.* In a few articles it was not apparent which paper or magazine printed the article. If the source was a guess, a '??' is used to inform you. A non-standard reference format is used with the periodical or book title listed first.

If you are school age, your parents may get a shock when you ask them to take you to the library so you can check out some reading material! Your larger libraries will have older copies of *The Sporting News* in binders and some libraries will have microfilm copies back to the 1890s.

Spencer Adams

TSN "Griffith May Have Something On Fire" by Paul Eaton, January 21, 1926.

Danny Ainge

The Oregonian "Cage Star Ainge Adapts to Pro Baseball" by Augie Borgi, June 1978.

The Oregonian "Ainge Holds Off Deciding Sports Career" by Borgi, June 1978.

The Virginia--Pilot "Sky's the Limit for the Member of Blue Jay Family" by George McClelland, June 11, 1978, p. E-2.

SI "A Double Danny Dandy" January 29, 1979, p. 34-35. **

The Virginia --Pilot "Ainge Believes Life Will Be Sweeter in I.L." by McClelland, May 1979.

SI "Meet Danny Two-Sport" by William Nack, June 11, 1979, p. 44-45. **

TSN "Ainge Rules Out Career in NBA" by Neil MacCarl, October 11, 1980.

Los Angeles Times "Two Talents" by Richard Hoffer, April 1, 1981.

TSN "Cage Star Ainge Says Jays Offer Him a Longer Career" by MacCarl, April 18, 1981. **

SI "Thank Heaven for Danny" by Jack McCallun, April 20, 1981, p. 50-56. **

SI "The Courting of Danny Ainge" October 12, 1981, p. 70-72. **

The Providence Journal "Danny Ainge Will Be a Celtic, in Time" by Art Turgeon, October 28, 1981, p. B-13.

The Detroit Free Press "A Man for Both Seasons Has Chosen the Right One" by Mike Downey, December 4, 1984.

SI "At Last, The Kid Is a Big Hit" by Alexander Wolff, June 3, 1985, p. 36-43.

Alan Ashby

TSN "Woman Fan Passes Hat to Support Fines Ashby" by Pete Swenson, July 21,1973.

TSN "Ashby Comes on Indians Like Calvary Charge" by Russell Schneider, August 4, 1975.

TSN "Ashby Eases Tribes Catching Woes" by Schneider, September 27, 1975.

TSN "Ashby Swings Indians' Tomahawk" by Schneider, May 8, 1976.

TSN "Ashby Remains with Jays Despite Trade Talk" by Neil MacCarl, December 31, 1977.

The Cincinnati Post "Catching Fire" by Greg Hoard, 1979.

TSN "Ashby Set to Test Astros New Policy" by Neil Hohlfeld, November 29, 1982.

Ashby (continued)

TSN "Once Again, Ashby Is Astros' Man" by Hohlfeld, August 25, 1986.

TSN "Ashby Is a Regular Guy" by Hohlfeld, June 8, 1987.

Barry Bonnell

TSN "Braves' Bonnell--A Budding Star" by John Brockman, November 1, 1975.

TSN "Braves Unveil New Weapon: Bonnell's Bat" by Wayne Minshew, June 18, 1977. **

TSN "Braves' Bonnell Bases Goals on Book" by Pat Harmon, March 1978. **

TSN "Bonnell, Jays Argue over Flying" by Neil MacCarl, December 6, 1982.

TSN "Bonnell: True Blue Blue Jay" by Alison Gordon, August 2, 1982. **

TSN "No One Kicks Sand in Bonnell's Face" by Bill Plaschke, March 18, 1985.

Ron Brand

TSN "Last of Hungry Ball Players" by John Wilson, January 29, 1966. **

Dave Downs

TSN "Eastern League Report" September 2, 1972, p. 38.

TSN "Eastern League Report" September 16, 1972, p. 44.

Kelly Downs

TSN "Downs Season Turns Upward Toward End" by Nick Peters, October 6, 1986, p.16.

TSN "Downs Has 'Nasty Stuff' But Only So-So Record" July 18, 1988, p. 22.

SI "The Day the World Series Stopped" October 30, 1989, cover photo.

Dennis Eckersley

San Antonio Light "Eckersley Bottling Up Brewers' Foes with Strikeouts, Eyes 200" by Galen Wellnicki, July 27, 1974.

San Antonio Light "Eckersley Hopeful of Good Finish Despite Injury" by Wellnicki, August 1974, p. 1-C.

TSN "Indian Love Call Rings Out for Kid Eckersley" by Russell Schneider, June 21, 1975, p. 7.

Eckersley (continued)

TSN "Tribe's Eckersley Guns for Rookie Hill Laurels" by Schneider, October 4, 1975.

TSN " 'E' Is for Eckersley and Easy No-Hit Effort" by Schneider, June 18, 1977, p. 5.

TSN "Eckersley Rivals Hill Greats" by Schneider, June 25, 1977.

TSN "Traveling Man Eckersley Plans to Reduce Routes" by Joe Giuliotti, February 23, 1980.

TSN "Eckersley Sharp, Though in Pain" by Giuliotti, July 12, 1980.

TSN "Eckersley Feels 'Heavenly' after 'Other-Place' Season" by Giuliotti, November 1, 1980.

TSN "Eckersley a Boost to Ailing Staff" by Dave van Dyck, June 4, 1984.

TSN "Eckersley Decides to Remain a Cub" by Joe Goddard, December 10, 1984.

TSN "Eckersley Success Product of Therapy" by Goddard, May 6, 1985.

TSN "A Homecoming, Sort Of" by Kit Stier, April 20, 1987.

TSN "New Role for Eckersley" by Stier, June 1, 1987.

TSN "Finding Relief from 'Ba-Boombas'" by Stier, May 9, 1988.

TSN "A's, Eckersley Brought Quickly Back to Earth" by Stier, May 23, 1988.

TSN "Was It Scuffing, or Storytelling?" by Stier, July 4, 1988.

SI "One Eck of a Guy" by Peter Gammons, December 12, 1988, p. 50-59.

TSN "Eckersley's Back, Too" by Stier, July 31, 1989.

TSN "Fall and Rise of Eckersley, Shows Life Can Be Uplifting" by Stier, May 28, 1990.

Jerry Garvin

TSN "Jays Discover a Jewel--Rookie Southpaw Garvin" by Neil MacCarl, May 7, 1977, p. 10.

Toronto Star "Jerry Garvin, Pitching Ace Takes Life Seriously" by Arlie Keller, June 1977. **

TSN "A Treat for Jays' Garvin: Bat Support" by MacCarl, September 10, 1977.

TSN "Gutsy Garvin Wins Blue Jay Praise Despite Lean Rations" by MacCarl, October 8, 1977.

Toronto Star "Trip Back Up Mountain No Picnic for Jerry" by Alison Gordon, June 21, 1980, p. D-3.

TSN "Garvin Bolsters Jays' Bullpen" by MacCarl, June 28, 1980.

Luis Gomez

TSN "Unsigned Gomez Doubts Twins Are in His Future" by Bob Fowler, July 30, 1977.

TSN "Braves Bench Gomez, Promote Ramirez" by Ken Picking, August 23, 1980.

Jim Gott

TSN "Scouting Network Pinpointed Gott" by Neil MacCarl, December 13, 1982.

TSN "Gott Experiment in Relief a Failure" by MacCarl, October 1, 1984.

TSN "Hurlers Carry Batting Load" by Nick Peters, May 27, 1985.

TSN "Giants Angry that Shoving Match Between Gott and Leonard Becomes Public Knowledge" June 16, 1986, p. 28.

TSN "Pirates Acquire Jim Gott" August 17, 1987, p. 17.

TSN "Pirates Finally Able to Spell Relief" May 16, 1988, p. 14.

TSN "Finding Relief in Pittsburgh" August 22, 1988,

TSN "Jim Gott Set Club Record for Saves" October 3, 1988, p. 21.

Men at Work by George Will, Harper Prentice, 1991, p. 136-142.

Doug Hansen

Cleveland Plain Dealer (??) "Tribe Rookie, Hansen, Seeks 'Silver' Lining" by Lebovitz, February 1953.

Cleveland Plain Dealer (??) "Indians Hope Slick Rookie Excels on Double Play Pivot" by Harry Jones, February 1953.

Cleveland Plain Dealer (??) "Tribe Keystone Kid Clicks on the Keys" by Doug Hansen, March 1953.

Cleveland Plain Dealer "Praise for Hansen's Spirit Confirms Impression Ex-G.I. Has Made on Tribe Staff at Second Base" by Gordon Cobbledick, March 1953.

Doug Howard

Salt Lake Tribune "Salt Lake City's Doug Howard--Hometown Boy Making Good" by Ray Herbat, July 2, 1972.

Ken Hubbs

Chicago's American "Meet the New Cubs" by James Enright, January 11, 1962.

Chicago Sun Times "Cubs Won't Have to Worry about Hubbs in the Clutch" March 1962.

Hubbs (continued)

Chicago's American "Cubs Hubbs Right on Time" by Enright, June 3, 1962.

TSN "Cubs Glove Whiz Hubbs Sets NL Fielding Records" by Jerry Holtzman, August 22, 1962.

Chicago's American "How Hubbs Rose to Glove Records" by Enright, September 15, 1962.

TSN "Midway Marvel Hubbs Passes Doerr in 74th Errorless Game" by Holtzman, September 15, 1962, p.33.

Chicago Daily News "Hubbs Hopes to 'Keep Job'" by Bob Smith, March 4, 1963, p. 17.

Chicago Sun Times "Hubbs Wants Pennant--Not a Record" March 12, 1963.

TSN "Cubs' Ken Hubbs Dies in Crash of Own Plane" by Edger Munzel, February 29, 1964, p. 35. **

Chicago Daily News "Hubbs 'Man' on Diamond, '21-Year-Old' Off It" by Smith, February 1964. **

Chicago Sun Times "Proud Dad's Dream Ends in Tragedy" by Dick Hackenberg, February 17, 1964. **

TSN "Musial Mementos Pride of Hubbs' Trophies" by Enright, April 18, 1964, p. 9.

Los Angeles Times "The Pride of Colton" by Jim Murray, April 28, 1964. **

Look "Tragic Rebirth of the Chicago Cubs" by T. Cohane, June 16, 1964, p. 60.

Ken Hunt

Columbia Record (??) "Ken Hunt Is Writing His Comeback Story" by Ron Wenzen, June 1, 1960.

Columbia Record (??) "Ken Hunt" by Jake Penland, Spring 1960.

Cincinnati Enquirer "Rookie Hunt Beats Giants" April 20, 1961.

Cincinnati Enquirer "Reds Get Back on Beam As Hunt, Brosnan Cool Pirates" by Lou Smith, May 15, 1961.

Cincinnati Enquirer "Hunt Wins 7th" by Bill Ford, June 17, 1961.

Cincinnati Post "Blisters Cost Hunt Chance for Big Year" by Earl Lawson, March 1962.

Bruce Hurst

TSN "PaxSox Hurst Back from Retirement" by Steven Krasner, May 1981.

TSN "Hurst Shifts into High Gear" by Joe Giuliotti.

TSN "Elbow Surgery for Lefty Hurst" by Giuliotti, December 6, 1982.

TSN "Houk Is Counting on Healthy Hurst" by Giuliotti, April 18, 1983.

TSN "Hurst Defies Hex at Fenway" by Giuliotti, July 30, 1984.

Hurst (continued)

TSN "Hurst Declared AL Pitcher of the Week" May 26, 1986, p. 5.

TSN "Someday Is Here for BoSox Hurst" by Giuliotti, October 13, 1986.

TSN "Hurst in Red Sox Driver's Seat" October 27, 1986, p. 5.

Flood Street to Fenway by Lyman Hafen, Publisher's Place, 1987. **

This People "Bruce Hurst: Life in the Strike Zone" by Judd Turner, Winter 1987.**

SI "And Here We Go Again" by Peter Gammons, December 19, 1988, p. 50.

TSN "Padres Lock Up Hurst with Lockout Exception" by Bill Plaschke, December 19, 1988, p. 51.

TSN "Padres: Bruce Hurst Treated as Savior" by Plaschke, January 9, 1989, p. 38.

Dane Iorg

TSN "Toledo Rookie Iorg Makes 'Great Dane' Move at First" by John Gugger, June 8, 1974. **

TSN "Long-Shot Iorg Lands Phil Job with Sizzling Bat" by Ray Kelly, April 30, 1977. **

TSN "Iorg Adjusts to Part-Time Role" by Rick Hummel, July 5, 1980.

TSN "Royals Call Iorg's Bluff" by Mike Fish, December 31. 1984.

TSN "AL's Sibling Rivalry" by Joe Gerger, October 21, 1985.

TSN "Iorg, Royals Part Amicably" by Fish, December 2, 1985.

TSN "It's Iorg in a Pinch" by Phil Collier, February 17, 1986.

Garth Iorg

SI "Mullinorg: Birds of a Feather" by Hank Hersch, July 22, 1985, p. 54

TSN "AL's Sibling Rivalry" by Joe Gerger, October 21, 1985.

SI "Babes of Summer" by Steve Wulf, June 23, 1990, p.53-57.

Ray Jacobs

Illustrated Daily News "Jacobs' Bat Gives Seraphs Win" April 25, 1925, p. F-19.

Los Angeles Examiner "Jacobs' Home Run Brings Angels 9-8 Victory" by Martin Burke, ??? 1927, p. I-17.

Los Angeles Record "Jacobs' Broken Leg May Halt Brooklyn Deal" by Stub Nelson, July 1927.

Los Angeles Record Jacobs Traded to Cubs" by Stub Nelson, April 1928.

Wally Joyner

Baseball America "Big Shoes to Fill" by Peter Schmuck, March 1986.

SI "The Wonderful World of Wally" by Craig Neff, May 26, 1986, p. 26. **

TSN "Joy over Joyner in Angels Camp" by Tom Singer, April 7, 1986.

TSN "Wally World Catch Joyner Fever" by Singer, May 26, 1986.

Time "Reggie and the Rookie" by Tom Callahan, June 2, 1986, p. 84.

TSN "Joyner Grazed by Knife in Yankee Stadium" September 8, 1986.

TSN "Staph Stopped Joyner" by Singer, November 3, 1986.

TSN "Young Sluggers" by Dave Nightingale, Spring 1987. **

TSN "Wally Has His Priorities" by Singer, August 17, 1987.

TSN "Joyner's Numbers Rising As Angels Sink in the West" by Singer, September 21, 1987.

TSN "Joyner in Camp" March 7, 1988, p. 30.

TSN "Joyner Does A Number" January 23, 1989, p. 41.

TSN "Fractured Kneecap Puts Joyner on Disabled List" July 30, 1990, p. 13.

Harmon Killebrew

Time "Killer" May 25, 1959, p. 41.

TSN "Killebrew King-Size Biffer as 12-Year Old Legion Star" by Herb Heoft, August 26, 1959.

Saturday Evening Post "Strong Boy of the Twins" by Shirley Povich, September 15, 1962, p. 54

SI "Out of the Park on a Half Swing" by B. Heilman, April 8, 1963, p. 85.

Time "Nuclear Bomber" August 14, 1966, p. 44.

TSN "Killer and Boog--Top Guns in Shootout for RBI Prize" by Mike Lamey, August, 30, 1969.

SI "Ideal Team in Harm's Way" by William Leggett, October 6, 1969, p. 20.

TSN "MVP Title Alters Killebrew Home Life" by Lowell Reidenbaugh, April 4, 1970, p. 3. **

SI "Head First for a Triple Crown" by P. Carry, August 3, 1970, p. 14.

SI "Twin Mortar Gets the Range" by R. Blount, August 14, 1972, p. 55.

TSN "Twins Planning a Big Day for Their Gentleman Killer" by Bob Fowler, June 29, 1974.

Mormon Athletes Book 2 by William Black, Deseret Book, 1982, p 74-79. **

Killebrew (continued)

TSN "Shrine Trio: Aparicio, Killer, Drysdale" by Jack Lang, January 23, 1984.

Sports Collectors Digest "Killebrew Discusses his Career" by Fluffy Saccucci, June 9, 1989, p.83

Sports Collectors Digest "Hall of Famer Harmon Killebrew Interviewed" October 19, 1990, p. 200-201.

Newt Kimball

Los Angeles Daily News "Newell Kimball" by Ned Cronin, June 28, 1945.

Don Kirkwood

TSN "Reliever Kirkwood Breaks Up Angel's Arson Squad" by Dick Miller, May 17, 1975, p. 29.

Salinas Californian " 'Redwood' Fells AL Batters" by Mel Bowen, July 9, 1975, p. 22.

Gary Kroll

TSN "Hats Off to Gary Kroll" by Barney Kremenko, May 1, 1965.

Vance Law

The Oregonian "Son of Pittsburgh Baseball Ace Shows Major League Promise" by Norm Mayes, May 6, 1979.

TSN "A Backup Job for Law" by Charley Feeney, March 6, 1980.

TSN " 'New' Law Gaining Respect of Pirates" by Feeney, April 5, 1980.

TSN "Bucs' Berra, Law Making Names for Selves" by Feeney, June 21, 1980.

TSN "Stability Aids Laws Concentration" by Ian MacDonald, April 14, 1986.

TSN "Infielder Law Makes Appearance as Relief Pitcher" June 16, 1986.

TSN "Vance Law's Daughter to Undergo Chemotherapy Treatments" December 15, 1986.

SI "Fathers and Sons" April 6, 1987, p. 68.

TSN "Law Upset at Expos" November 2, 1987, p. 28.

TSN "Something Besides a Utility Player" by Dave Van Dyck, January 4, 1988, p. 59.

TSN "Law Hits Safely in 1st 13 Games" May 2, 1988, p. 16.

TSN "Law Is a Good Bet to Replace Lansford" January 14, 1991, p. 37.

TSN "Law Knows His Role Is Defense, Not HRs" January 21, 1991, p. 35.

Vernon Law

TSN "Bing Helped Pirates Sign Prize Rookie Vernon Law" by Les Biedeman, June 21, 1950. **

St. Louis Post Dispatch "The Double Life of Vernon Law" by John Keasler, August 16, 1954, p. 31. **

TSN "Bucs' Law Climbing Lofty 20-Win Ladder" by Biedeman, June 22, 1960, p. 3. **

TSN "Bucs Heave Sign of Relief--Vern's Sore Ankle Okay" by Biedeman, December 21, 1960.

TSN "A Long Road Back--But Law Made It" by Biedeman, September 4, 1965, p. 3. **

Mormon Athletes Book 2 by William Black, Deseret Book, 1982, p. 90-98. **

SI "Fathers and Sons" April 6, 1987, p. 68.

Jack Morris

TSN "Tiger Ace? Try Morris" by Tom Gage, February 9, 1980.

TSN "Bullpen Therapy Cools Down Morris" by Lynn Manning, September 13, 1980.

TSN "Morris Masterpiece Silences White Sox" by Gage, April 16, 1984.

People Weekly "Morris Cools Down to Become King of the Hill for Detroit" by J. Greenwalt, July 16, 1984, p. 129-131.

TSN "Sour Morris Buttons Lip" by Gage, August 6, 1984.

TSN "Morris Finally Unbuttons Lip" by Gage, September 17, 1984.

SI "Armed to Win the Big Ones" by Ron Fimrite, October 29, 1984, p. 42. **

TSN "Annoying Gopher Pitches Now Frustrating Morris" by Gage, June 23, 1986.

TSN "Tigers' Morris Turns Season Around" by Gage, July 28, 1986.

TSN "Morris' Recovery: Slow, Steady" by Gage, September 6, 1986, p. 15.

TSN "Morris' 5th Shutout Brings No Satisfaction" by Gage, September 29, 1986.

TSN "Twins, Morris Far Apart" by Patrick Ruesse, January 5, 1987.

TSN "Twins Killing: Failure to Let Morris Go Home" by Moss Klein, January 5, 1987.

TSN "Morris Boosted Nearly a Million" by Murray Chass, February 23, 1987.

TSN "Winner Morris, Loser Tigers: No Hard Feelings" by Gage, March 2, 1987.

Minneapolis Star "Above All Else, Driven Morris Is a Competitor" by Dennis Brackin, May 24, 1987.

TSN "From Rock Bottom to Win Column" July 11, 1988, p. 16.

Morris (continued)

TSN "Morris Is Determined to Have Last Laugh" May 28, 1990, p. 10.

TSN " 'Too Many Reasons' for Morris To Leave" February 18, 1991, p. 28.

TSN "Morris Takes Gamble, Goes Home to Twins" February 18, 1991, p. 29.

TSN "Morris Says He Won't 'Get Cutesy' at 36" February 25, 1991, p. 29.

Dale Murphy

Atlanta Journal "But There's a Catch..." by Gary Caruso, February 13, 1977, p. D-1. **

TSN "Throwing Flaws Block Path to Majors for Murphy" by Vic Fulp, May 7, 1977. **

Atlanta Constitution "Erratic Arm Threatens Murphy's Future" by Vic Dorr, June 4, 1977. **

TSN "Braves Flash Old Grin Over Murphy's New Arm" by Wayne Minshew, October 15, 1977.

TSN "MVP Murphy Stays Humble" by T. Tucker, March 7, 1983.

Atlanta Weekly "Nice Guys Finish First" by Paul Lieberman, April 10, 1983. **

SI "Murphy's Law Is Nice Guys Finish First" by Steve Wulf, July 4, 1983, p. 24. **

Sport Magazine "Too Good for His Own Good" by J. Dalton, June 1984, p. 34.

TSN "Dale Murphy: After a Peaceful Spring, This Braves' Star Is Slugging His Way to a Productive Peak" by Gerry Fraley, April 29, 1985.

SI "So Good, He's Scary" by Rick Reilly, June 3, 1985, p. 74. **

People Weekly "Dale Murphy's Plate Runneth Over with Fan Adoration and Home Run Pitches" by G. Cameron, June 10, 1985, p. 141.

Murph by Dale Murphy with Brad Rock and Lee Warnick, Bookcraft, 1986.**

Atlanta Journal "Brother Murphy" by Bud Snow, February 2, 1986, p. B-10. **

Sport Magazine "Who Will Make the Hall of Fame?" by Bill James, July 26, 1986, p. 26.

TSN "Murphy Discouraged over Streaky Season" by Fraley, August 18, 1986.

Saturday Evening Post "Dale Murphy: Baseball's Mr. Nice Guy" by Jack Hayes, October 1986, p. 48. **

Boy's Life "Dale Murphy on the Path to Fame" September 1987, p. 40.

SI "A Man Who Can't Say No" by Peter Gammons, December 21, 1987, p. 16.**

TSN "The Struggle Continues for Murphy" July 18, 1988, p. 22.

TSN "Dale Murphy Says He's Willing to Be Traded" November 28, 1988, p. 52.

Murphy (continued)

TSN "Phillies Like Murphy Big-Time" August 13, 1990, p. 15.

Baseball America "Murphy Works Hard to Reinvigorate his Career" by Paul Hagen, April 10, 1991, p. 3.

Philadelphia Inquirer "Phillies Outfielder Murphy Is Most Welcome in Atlanta" by Dick Polman, June 5, 1991, p. 4C **

Scott Nielsen

Deseret News "Patience Pays Off for Nielsen" by Nate Hyde, August 8, 1986.**

Columbus Dispatch "Nielsen Posts No-Hit Victory" by Mike Sullivan, June 9, 1988.

Columbus Dispatch "Infield Hit Costs Nielsen No-Hitter" by Makr Znidar, May 12, 1989.

John Noriega

Cincinnati Enquirer "Noriega to the Rescue" May 30, 1969.

Los Angeles Journal Herald (??) "Noriega Has Just One Eye on the Game" by Bucky Albers, August 6, 1970. **

Jerry Nyman

TSN "Just Too Good to Be True, White Sox Rookie Muses" by Edgar Munzel, September 1968. **

TSN "Chisox Desperate--Till Nyman Solved Their Hill Woes" by Munzel, June 14, 1969, p. 10. **

Monte Pearson

TSN "Pearson, Near 30-Mark, Improves with Age" by Frederick Lieb, July 1, 1939.

Dayton Journal "Reminiscing with Monte Pearson" by Jack Frong, March 27, 1941.

The Fresno Bee "Pearson Gives Up Hope of Rejoining Majors" by Ed Schoefeld, August 9, 1942.

The Fresno Bee "Pearson, World Series Star, Dies in Fowler" January 28, 1978.

The Fresno Bee "Yanks' Pearson Saved Best for October" by Bruce Farris, September 22, 1985, p.5.

Wally Ritchie

TSN "Ritchie Could Be the Lefty Phillies Have Been Seeking" by Rich Westcott, June 9, 1987.

Fred Sanford

TSN "Big Fred's Blanks Make Brownie Fans Blink" by Frederick Lieb, October 2, 1946. **

New York Sunday Mirror "DiMaggio Recommended Sanford to Yankees" by Dan Parker, March 6, 1949.

TSN "Stengel Counting on Sanford" by Will Wedge, March 9, 1949. **

TSN "Sanford Foes Hungry to Feast on Wins" by Dan Daniel, March 16, 1949.**

TSN "Sanford 'Mystery' Solved by Fred" by Daniel, March 7, 1951

Elmer Singleton

TSN "Singleton's Hurling in Last Three Games Is Impressive" by Ernest Mehl, May 1944.

TSN "Singleton, Bonham, Singleton, Bonham--Who Was the Winner?" by Les Biederman, July 23, 1947, p. 36.

TSN "Elmer Singleton Beaten, 1-0, Just Short of Record" by Bob Stevens, April 24, 1952.

TSN "Singleton's Solution for Victory--Club that Gets You Some Runs" by Lenny Andersen, July 6, 1955. **

The Seattle Times "A Soggy Solution? Elmer Acts Innocent" by Hy Zimmerman, December 24, 1961.

Tommie Sisk

TSN "Sisk Lived and Learned in Year of Hard Knocks" by Paul Cour, October 11, 1969.

TSN "Sisk Sheds Suet in Pitch for Padre Job as Starter" by Cour, February 14, 1970, p. 43.

Cory Snyder

TSN "Snyder Could Get Shot at Second" by Sheldon Ocker, November 5, 1984.

TSN "Snyder Experiment Is No. 1 Priority" by Ocker, March 4, 1985.

TSN "Indians Slugger Snyder Has Position Problem" by Dave Nightingale, July 28, 1986.

TSN "Going for the Major League Gold" July 28, 1986, p. 4.

Baseball America "Snyder Leads Indian Uprising in Cleveland" by Jim Ingraham, September 10-24, 1986.

TSN "Cory Puts Together 17-Game Hitting Streak" October 13, 1986, p. 29.

TSN "Young Sluggers" by Nightingale, Spring 1987.

SI "Pow! Wow!" by Ron Fimrite, April 6, 1987, p. 74.

Sport Magazine "The Erie Sensation" by G. Macnow, May 1987, p. 37.

Snyder (continued)

TSN "All the Wrong Weaknesses" May 9, 1988, p. 22.

Sport Collectors Digest "Cory Snyder Has All the Tools for Success" by Brent Kelley, June 29, 1990, p. 200.

Baseball America "Snyder Should Bust Out with White Sox" by Steve Buckley, January 10, 1991, p. 7.

Bob Usher

Cincinnati Enquirer "Watch for Bob When Southpaw Works" April 14, 1950.

Jay Van Noy

TSN(??) "In this Corner" by George Beahon, May 1951.**

TSN "Van Noy Runningest, 'Sharpest' of Birds" by Paul Walker, July 1952.